BASEBALL'S GREATEST PLAYERS

BY

TOM MEANY

WITH A FOREWORD BY

FORD C. FRICK

The Big League Baseball Library

GROSSET & DUNLAP *Publishers*

NEW YORK

CONTENTS

CONTENTS

FOREWORD

IT IS NATURAL that I should be enthusiastic about any books on baseball, since I was a baseball writer long before I became a baseball administrator. I am particularly attracted, however, to documented books on baseball, books which record the history of the game, backed by its statistics.

When Tom Meany first began writing baseball some thirty years ago, I knew him, traveled with him, played golf and bridge with him. I'm not going out on a limb when I say his writing was better than either his golf or his bridge. It almost had to be if he were to keep his job, because he certainly never could have made a living playing golf or bridge.

Baseball's Greatest Players is a fairly ambitious title. I'm not going to say that I am in complete agreement with Tom in all of the players he has selected, because I naturally have my own choices, too, although in my present office as Commissioner of Baseball, I am not at liberty to express them. I will say, however, that all of the 25 players listed in this book certainly are, or were, players of exceptional ability. With some—Babe Ruth and Ty Cobb, Lou Gehrig and George Sisler, Matty, Alexander and Walter Johnson—there can be no disputes. Of the so-called moderns, certainly Stan Musial, Ted Williams and Joe DiMaggio belong.

I appreciate the problems of any author in attempting to make up a "greatest" list—whether of baseball players or football players, statesmen or actors. The list, no matter what the profession, has to stop somewhere.

A book such as this is a boon to the sports writing profession. Some of the most able men writing baseball in America today are young men, men who never saw Ruth hit a homer, Cobb run the bases or Johnson blaze his fast one. Those great stars are merely names in the record book. In Meany's book, I honestly believe they come alive again, not only as players, with the conditions under which they played made plain, but also as flesh-and-blood human beings.

If this book assists the modern-day sports writer to get a better perspective on the stars of bygone days, it certainly does the same for the baseball fan of today. He can learn intimate details of players he only heard about, players who to him are merely names on the honor roll of the Hall of Fame at Cooperstown, New York.

Although *Baseball's Greatest Players* goes back into baseball's past, as well as listing the stars of today, it isn't a dry book, for ball players were never dull or dry to Meany's point of view.

FORD C. FRICK
Commissioner of Baseball

PREFACE

IT PROBABLY WILL save a lot of arguments if I explain right off the bat that the players in *Baseball's Greatest Players* are listed in alphabetical order. Just making the decisions about which players to include in the book was difficult enough without making the attempt to rate them after I had them between covers.

There are twenty-five players listed in this book, less than half as many as are inscribed on the rolls of the Hall of Fame at Cooperstown, New York. Since there are annual clamorings as to the exclusion of this player or that from the Cooperstown shrine, it is obvious that many people will be displeased at the omissions —some, perhaps, even at the inclusions.

All I can say by way of apology is that it can't be helped. You couldn't carry a book with the names of all the players who deserve to be listed in the category of *Baseball's Greatest Players*— and I couldn't write it.

It is my sincere belief, however, that the players included here represent an accurate cross-section of baseball's stars since the turn of the century. There are sluggers and hitters, outfielders and infielders, pitchers and catchers. There are players of the dead-ball era, players of the lively-ball era and players who bridged those gaps. There are players who never played under arc lights during their entire careers and players who grew up with the phenomenon of night ball and there are Negro players, who have been in the major league only since Branch Rickey broke the color line by bringing Jackie Robinson to the Dodgers in 1947.

The material from which this book was compiled has been drawn from many sources, from old, almost forgotten, baseball books and from ones which were published only a few months before this one; from magazines and from newspaper files.

The principal material source, however, was conversation, conversation with men like Edward Grant Barrow, the builder of the Yankee empire; with Branch Rickey, the inventor of the farm system and developer of countless stars at St. Louis, Brooklyn and, in the near future, Pittsburgh, with managers, past and present, scouts, players, writers.

While all of these talks were helpful, I must confess that the final selections were made by me. I'll take the rap.

TOM MEANY

BABE RUTH breaking the record at the Stadium against the
Washington Senators, September 30, 1927.

GROVER CLEVELAND ALEXANDER

CHRISTY MATHEWSON

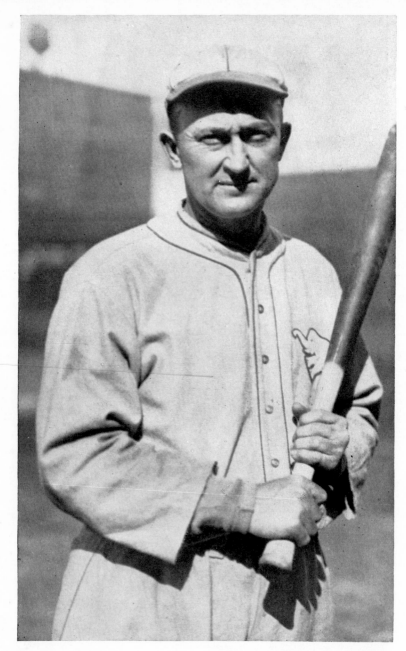

TY COBB

CHAPTER I

EASY DOES IT

Grover Cleveland Alexander

JOSEPH VINCENT MCCARTHY was a most meticulous man and never more so than in the spring of 1926, when he was handling his first major league assignment, managing the Chicago Cubs. The Cubs, opening an Eastern swing, were quartered at New York's Hotel Commodore and Joe was holding a meeting in one of the hotel's smaller banquet rooms.

McCarthy knew that, despite his great success with Louisville in the American Association, he was still an unproven "busher" to the majority of his players, excepting those who knew him from the Association. The Cubs had finished a rousing last the season before and took tactful handling.

The preliminary phases of the meeting were over when the door opened and Grover Alexander, the team's veteran right-hander, entered. Alex walked slowly and somewhat unsteadily to the rear, seated himself and promptly proceeded to doze off. There was a titter from some of the players which McCarthy ignored.

McCarthy got around to the subject of "signs," as baseball signals are called. "Maranville is with Brooklyn now," said Joe, referring to the merry elf who had laughed his way out of the Cub stewardship the season before. "No matter what you think about him. Rabbit is a smart baseball operator. He knows all the Chicago signs from last season and we'll have to change those signs today. Otherwise, the first time Maranville gets to second base, he'll have every one of our signs."

It was at this point the drowsing Alexander roused himself. "I wouldn't worry about Rabbit, Joe," advised the red-eyed Alex. "He won't even reach second base."

I

That broke up the meeting and it also finished Alexander's chances of remaining under McCarthy. A month or so later, he was waived on to the St. Louis Cardinals, to achieve his greatest glory that fall in fanning Tony Lazzeri in the seventh game of the World Series with the Yankees.

The meeting was a minor incident in the career of Alexander but it was a revealing one. The man who became a legend in his own lifetime was his own worst enemy. He won more games than any other pitcher in National League history—indeed, only two pitchers, Cy Young and Walter Johnson, ever won more major league games than Alex—but he never could win over himself.

It is easy to moralize about Alexander, who died in semi-poverty in his native St. Paul, Nebraska, November 4, 1950; but Old Pete himself never was one for moralizing. He never blamed his fondness for the bottle on anybody but himself.

Christy Mathewson, whose star was fading as Alex's was rising, was credited with 372 victories in his National League career. The mark stood for a long time but finally Alexander, pitching for the Cardinals, surpassed it in a game in Philadelphia in July of 1929. It wasn't one of his best games. The Phils gave him a pretty good pounding, but equally heavy hitting by the Cards, plus deeds of derring-do on defense, enabled Alex to escape with the victory. He celebrated in elegant style, and Bill McKechnie, his current manager, had reason to suspect that the old master has been celebrating number 373 beforehand as well as after.

McKechnie made up his mind to suspend Alexander and send him back to St. Louis. Because of Alex's great record, it was to be a "cover up." It would be announced that his arm, rather than his thirst, was the trouble and that he was being sent home for treatment and not in disgrace.

The plan leaked, however. A young reporter on a New York paper got wind of it and printed the story, brashly asserting that Alexander's record-breaking victory would turn out to be his last. McKechnie denied there was any disciplinary action contemplated, and to prove it announced he was starting the veteran against the Giants in the Polo Grounds. Old Pete never got by the fourth inning, being well clouted.

Eventually McKechnie could protect Alex no longer and had to send him home. That winter he was traded back to the Phillies, the team with which he had first gained stardom. In 1930, he could do nothing with the Phils, losing three decisions, and eventually was shipped that same year to Dallas where he concluded his professional career.

It was ironic, but somehow symbolic of Alexander's fading days, that he was unable to carry with him to his grave the distinction of having won more games than any other National League pitcher. In the late 1940's a statistician discovered that Christy Mathewson had beaten the Pirates by a score of 4 to 2 on May 21, 1902, but that inexplicably the game had been entered on the records as a defeat. Thus, Matty, like Alex, achieved a lifetime total of 373 victories in the National League.

When the Phillies released him in 1930, Alexander packed his grip in his room at the Majestic Hotel with Manly Jackson, who had been a young sports writer in Syracuse when Old Pete broke in.

"Well, Jackson," said Alex, "you were here in 1911 when I came up from Syracuse. I'm leaving the same way I came—with nothing."

It is doubtful if there ever was a smoother pitcher than Alexander. He worked without exertion while warming up and when he went to the mound he pitched with the same easy motion. Alex threw three-quarters, scarcely seeming to stride and with no waste motion. There were no three-hour ball games when Alexander was pitching.

Tom Sheehan, now a Giant scout, recalls the first time he saw Alexander pitch in the tiny National League Park in Philadelphia, which later came to be known as Baker Bowl. Sheehan was a rookie with the Athletics and Joe Bush, another A's pitcher, took Tom to see the Phils perform on an off-day.

"I knew who Alex was and all about him," explained Sheehan, "because he had been a winning pitcher for the Phils for a couple of seasons, but this was the first time I had ever seen him. He certainly didn't look like much. He warmed up like a guy playing catch and then he went out and pitched the same way. He was six feet but he kinda scrunched down so he didn't look tall. And he had a funny cap that didn't look like it fit him.

"I took one look at Baker Bowl and I was glad I didn't have

to pitch there. It looked like the right fielder was breathing down the second baseman's neck and the stands were so close to the infield that there was no chance of catching a pop foul.

"Well, Alex goes to work on these guys and he murders 'em. He breaks curve balls on their fists and he sneaks fast balls that don't look like fast balls right by 'em. I never saw such pitching in my life—and I haven't seen anything to beat it since.

"When it's all over, I turns to Bush and I says, 'Joe, how the hell do they ever beat this guy?'

"And Joe says, 'They don't—very often!' "

It is no wonder that his first look at Alexander left Sheehan bug-eyed in admiration at the artistry of his effort, for Alex was that type of pitcher. His pitching was founded on sheer skill, not brawn.

Another admirer of Alexander was Casey Stengel, who recently guided the Yankees to four straight World's Championships. Stengel broke into the National League shortly after Alex and, although in 1916 Stengel hit a home run against him which was one of the deciding factors in Brooklyn's beating out the Phils for the pennant, he always considered Alexander the smoothest pitching machine he ever had seen.

"I remember in 1914 or thereabouts when I thought I had a way figured out to fool Alex," recalls Stengel. "He used to break his curve in on me—as he did on all the other hitters—and I figured that if I moved up four or five inches just as he was about to pitch, I'd be able to meet the curve ball before it broke.

"You had to move quick with Alex because he took hardly any windup, but I did it and I managed to pull the ball against the right field fence for two bases. As I rounded first, I saw the guys in our bull pen standing up amazed-like. Pulling Alexander! Why, it just wasn't being done.

"When I came back to our bench Uncle Robbie and all the boys are asking, 'What happened, Case?' and, 'How'd you do it, Case?' but ole' Case ain't saying a thing but just giving 'em the big wink. Tell my secrets? Not me! Why, I'm the guy who's got Alexander the Great solved.

"At least that's what I thought until the next time I go to bat. Again I inch forward as Alex winds up. In comes the curve and smack!—right against my knuckles where I'm gripping the bat.

Boy, it stung! I dropped the bat and commenced shaking my hands, just like a kid who's been rapped across the knuckles by teacher's ruler. And out on the mound, old Alex is grinning and shaking his finger at me as if to say, 'Naughty boy! Teacher spank.' Believe me, I never tried to get smart with that guy again."

Although in one three-year span, the seasons of 1915, 1916 and 1917, Alexander won a grand total of 94 games for the Phillies and gave up the amazingly low total of 170 bases on balls in 1,153 innings—an average of lower than three every two full ball games —he is best remembered for his strikeout of Lazzeri in the 1926 World Series, which occurred after McCarthy had exiled him from the Cubs.

When McCarthy found rebuilding the Cubs would be impossible with Alexander on the club, he asked waivers on the veteran, and the Cards claimed him on June 22 for $6,000. Alex, who had a mediocre 3–3 record with the Cubs, won nine and lost seven for St. Louis as the Cards won their first pennant in history. It was a close fit with the Reds and Pirates for Rogers Hornsby's club, and the nine victories the 39-year old Alexander had picked up were important.

After Herb Pennock had beaten Willie Sherdel 2 to 1 in the opener in New York, Hornsby called on Alex. The Yanks got two runs off him in the second but after Earle Combs had opened the third with a single, Alexander shut up shop, retiring the last 21 Yankees in a row to win by 6 to 2.

When the Series moved to St. Louis, the Yanks won two out of three and came back to the Stadium faced with the pleasant prospect of merely splitting even to win the title. They might have made it, too, if it hadn't been for Alexander. In the course of his career, the old master had picked up a lot of nicknames, Alex, Alec and Aleck being interchangeable. By now most of the Cardinals knew him as "Old Pete." By whatever name, he was no rose to the Yankees as he beat them 10 to 2 in the sixth game to even the Series at three-all.

It was here that legend began taking over the story of Alexander. Jesse Haines started the seventh game for the Cardinals on a chilly, misty, murky Sunday against Waite Hoyt. Babe Ruth got the Yanks off in front with his fourth home run of the Series in the third but the American Leaguers fell apart behind Hoyt in the fourth and the Cardinals got three runs. The Yanks nudged Haines for one in the sixth and really began to go to work on him in the seventh.

Haines had a blister on the index finger of his pitching hand from the rigor with which he had been bearing down on every pitch. Combs walked to open the inning and Mark Koenig sacrificed. Ruth was intentionally passed and forced by Bob Meusel, Combs reaching third. Hornsby took no chances with Lou Gehrig and ordered another intentional pass, filling the bases, bringing up Lazzeri and setting the stage for Alexander and myth.

Here is Alex's version of what happened, told at the 1950 World Series in his final visit to New York, less than a month before he died:

"I was cold sober the night before I relieved Haines in the seventh game," flatly declared Alexander. "After Saturday's game, Hornsby came over to me in the clubhouse and asked me not to celebrate, telling me he might need me in the seventh game. So I stayed in my hotel room all night.

"There were a couple of other fellows in the bull pen with me—Art Reinhart and Herman Bell—when the phone from our bench rang. Hornsby said he wanted me, even though the others had been loosening up and I hadn't."

As far as Hornsby giving out any epigrams or instructions, Alex says there was none of that. "He was standing out by second base and when I reached the mound he just threw me the ball," said Pete. "That's all there was to it."

Actually, there was a little more to it than that—the matter of Alexander striking out Lazzeri to silence the last Yankee threat and then to hold them back in the eighth and ninth to preserve the 3 to 2 margin which gave St. Louis its first World's Championship.

Alexander struck out Poosh-'Em-Up Tony on four pitches, and the second strike against Lazzeri was a ringing drive down the third-base line, foul by a few feet, which would have cleared the bases. Tony went down swinging.

Everything that Alex had done before that in baseball, all of his escapades since, have been forgotten. The strikeout of Lazzeri is the high-water mark of the old master's career, few caring to note that Alex fanned 2,227 major league hitters in his lifetime. Just as other feats of Alexander's have been ignored, so have other deeds by Lazzeri, including the foul drive to left field which might have made a bum out of Alex. Everybody knows Tony as the man Alexander fanned in the 1926 World Series, few remember that Tony is one of three players in World Series history to hit a home run with the bases filled.

As glamorous as Alexander's record on the field was, his record off it was as sorry. After serving overseas in World War I, the great pitcher suddenly became subject to epileptic seizures. Whether he had any beforehand is not known, but George (Potsy) Clark, director of athletics at the University of Nebraska, recalls that Alex did have one overseas in 1918 when both were in the AEF.

Aimee Amanto, whom Alexander married before he sailed for France in 1918, was the one person who could influence the pitcher but even her influence didn't work always. They were divorced, remarried and divorced again, and when Alex was found dead in his rented room in St. Paul, Nebraska, an unfinished letter to Aimee was found in his typewriter.

After being cast adrift by Dallas, Alex pitched for the House of David, various semi-pro clubs, and worked with Hubert's Museum on West 42nd Street, New York, sharing the bill with performing fleas. Interviewed by sports writers, Alexander told his story with a pathetically quiet dignity.

Until his very last year in baseball, Alexander never had a losing season as a pitcher. In 1909, he won fifteen games and lost eight for Galesburg, Illinois, in the Illinois-Missouri League; and in 1929, he was 9–8 with the Cardinals. The following year he won none and lost three with the Phils and won one and lost two for Dallas in the Texas League.

Alexander, with the background of a farmboy, played town ball in the Corn Belt whenever the opportunity offered, and finally was signed by Galesburg. He was drafted by Indianapolis of the American Association but then sold to Syracuse in the old New York State League. The story is that Indianapolis was fearful of an injury Alex had sustained when he was hit with a thrown ball playing for Galesburg, an injury which left him with double vision for some months.

The Phils were interested in George (Dut) Chalmers's pitching for the Scranton team in the same Class B organization, but Patsy O'Rourke, managing Albany in that league, tipped off Horace Fogel, the Philly owner, that Alex was the better pitcher. The Phils purchased Chalmers and drafted Alexander for $750.

From the very beginning, Alexander was a star. He won 28 games in 1911 with the Phils, a total no freshman pitcher has ever reached since in the major leagues. In that first year one of Alexander's victories was a 1–0, twelve-inning triumph over the Boston Braves, a historic win if ever there was one, for Alex's opponent that day was Cy Young, who bowed out of the majors with that game as his swan song, after winning 511 games.

Control, as well as economy of pitching, was the secret of Alexander's success. He pitched ninety shutouts in his career, a National League record, and holds the major league record for shutouts in a season, sixteen in 1916. Twice Alexander pitched and won both ends of a double-header. He once pitched a game in 58 minutes and, although he never pitched a no-hitter, he did pitch four one-hitters in one season, 1915, something no other pitcher has ever done.

Although the dead ball employed before World War I undoubtedly was of great assistance to Alexander in the years when he was winning thirty and upward, it is revealing that he won 27 games for the Cubs in 1920 and 21 games for the Cardinals when he was over forty years old.

While Alexander won the great majority of his games in the dead-ball era, it is worth while noting that he continued to be a winning pitcher for a decade after the introduction of the jack-rabbit ball and a decade, it might be remarked, in which Alex didn't take the best of care of himself, to put it mildly.

It was ironical that Alex complained of a sore arm only once in his career, in 1915 when he was in his first World Series with the Phillies. He beat the Red Sox 3 to 1 in the opener in Philadelphia, went back with three days' rest and was beaten 2 to 1 in Boston. When the Sox won three in a row after the opener, it was believed that Alexander would pitch the final game, even though there was only a one-day interval, but he complained that he had wrenched his back in the third game. It was unfortunate for the Phils that he couldn't pitch, for it was the only game in the Series in which they did any substantial hitting against the pitchers of Bill Carrigan.

In winning his first World Series game, Alexander made an involuntary contribution to baseball history, because in the ninth inning of that game he faced a young Boston pinch hitter, George Herman Ruth. It was the Babe's first appearance in a World Series—he was to play in nine more, an all-time record—and Alec retired him on a grounder to Fred Luderus at first base, a ball the Babe pulled and hit sharply.

It was eleven years before Ruth and Alex again faced each other in a World Series and the master pitcher horse-collared the great slugger four times as he pitched a four-hitter in Yankee Stadium, to even the 1926 Series for the Cardinals at one-all. In the sixth game of that Series, Alexander blanked Ruth three times as he won again to even the Series, making a total of eight straight times Ruth had failed to hit him.

After Alex had struck out Lazzeri with the bases filled in the final game, he had to face Ruth only once and he walked him, Babe ending the Series a few seconds later when he was thrown out stealing by Bob O'Farrell.

It wasn't caution that caused Alex to walk Ruth, even though the Babe already had hit four home runs in the Series. He walked Babe on a three-two pitch which many, including Alexander, thought was close enough to be called a strike. In fact, Alex grumbled over the decision of plate umpire George Hildebrand.

Ruth made his first World Series hit against Alexander, a single, in the second game in 1928, in which the Yanks knocked Old Pete out of the box, scoring eight runs in three innings. In that same Series, Babe finally bagged a home run off Alexander in the final game.

When Alexander visited New York for the 1950 Series, he was quoted as saying that he had faced Ruth fifteen times in World Series play and held him to one single. Alex apparently forgot all about the 1928 home run. Actually, Pete had a remarkable record against Ruth—one single, one homer and three bases on balls in thirteen trips. The big fellow's average against Alexander was a puny .200.

Alexander had such natural talent that he would have been a stick-out under any conditions, yet oddly enough he wasn't figured as a regular when he first went South with the Phillies in 1911. Manager Charley Dooin was unimpressed, even though Alex came to the club with a record of 29 victories with Syracuse in the Class B New York State League. The ease with which Alex pitched, the nonchalance which was to be his trademark, struck Dooin as being nothing but indolence.

It was Pat Moran, Dooin's coach, who pleaded Alex's case at the Wilmington, North Carolina, training camp. "Let the kid come North with me on the second squad, Red," importuned Moran, "and I'll have a pitcher for you when we get back home."

When the two Philly squads reassembled in Philadelphia for the city series with the Athletics which preceded the regular season, Moran told Dooin he'd make no mistake counting on Alexander as a regular. "He's a pitcher if ever I saw one," declared Pat.

Dooin, still wanting to be shown, pitched Alexander in one of the exhibition games against the A's, who were then World's Champions. The kid from Nebraska turned in seven scoreless innings and Dooin was convinced. For the next twenty years nobody at all had to be convinced that Old Pete was truly Alexander the Great.

GROVER CLEVELAND ALEXANDER

Born February 26, 1887, St. Paul, Neb.
Height, 6' 1". Weight, 185. Threw and batted right-handed.
Elected to Hall of Fame in 1938.

YEAR	CLUB	LEAGUE	G	IP	W	L	PCT	SO	BB	H	ERA
1909	Galesburg	Ill.-Mo.	24	219	15	8	.652	198	42	124	...
1910	Syracuse	N. Y.									
		State	43	245	29	14	.674	204	67	215	...
1911	Philadelphia	Nat.	48	367	28	13	.683	227	129	285	...
1912	Philadelphia	Nat.	46	310	19	17	.543	195	105	289	2.81
1913	Philadelphia	Nat.	47	306	22	8	.733	159	75	288	2.79
1914	Philadelphia	Nat.	46	355	27	15	.642	214	76	327	2.38
1915	Philadelphia	Nat.	49	376	31	10	.756	241	64	253	1.22
1916	Philadelphia	Nat.	48	389	33	12	.733	167	50	323	1.55
1917	Philadelphia *	Nat.	45	388	30	13	.698	200	56	336	1.83
1918	Chicago	Nat.	3	26	2	1	.667	15	3	19	1.73
1919	Chicago	Nat.	30	235	16	11	.593	121	38	180	1.72
1920	Chicago	Nat.	46	363	27	14	.659	173	69	335	1.91
1921	Chicago	Nat.	31	252	15	13	.536	77	33	286	3.39
1922	Chicago	Nat.	33	246	16	13	.552	48	34	283	3.62
1923	Chicago	Nat.	39	305	22	12	.647	72	30	308	3.19
1924	Chicago	Nat.	21	169	12	5	.706	33	25	183	3.04
1925	Chicago	Nat.	32	236	15	11	.577	63	29	270	3.39
1926	Chicago †-St. Louis	Nat.	30	200	12	10	.545	47	31	191	3.06
1927	St. Louis	Nat.	37	268	21	10	.677	48	38	261	2.52
1928	St. Louis	Nat.	34	244	16	9	.640	59	37	262	3.36
1929	St. Louis ‡	Nat.	22	132	9	8	.529	33	23	149	3.89
1930	Philadelphia	Nat.	9	22	0	3	.000	6	6	40	9.00
1930	Dallas	Texas	5	24	1	2	.333	4	11	35	8.28
	Major League Totals		696	5189	373	208	.642	2198	951	4868	...

WORLD SERIES RECORD

YEAR	CLUB	LEAGUE	G	IP	W	L	PCT	SO	BB	H	ERA
1915	Philadelphia	Nat.	2	17⅔	1	1	.500	10	4	14	1.53
1926	St. Louis	Nat.	3	20⅓	2	0	1.000	17	4	12	0.89
1928	St. Louis	Nat.	2	5	0	1	.000	2	4	10	19.80
	World Series Totals		7	43	3	2	.600	29	12	36	3.35

* Traded with William Killefer to Chicago N. L. for Mike Prendergast, Pickles Dilhoefer and $60,000, December 11, 1917.

† Waived to St. Louis N. L., June 22, 1926.

‡ Traded to Philadelphia N. L. with Harry McCurdy for Homer Peel and Bob McGraw, December 11, 1929.

CHAPTER II

THE CAT

Roy Campanella

THERE IS NO QUESTION that the home run Bobby Thomson streaked into the lower right field stands of the Polo Grounds in the ninth inning of the third play-off game against Ralph Branca will be told and re-told as long as baseball is played. It gave the Giants, who had been 13 games behind in mid-August, the 1951 pennant over a bewildered Dodger team.

Historically, Thomson's blow will rank with Babe Ruth's "called-shot" home run against Charley Root and the Cubs in the 1932 World Series; with the failure of Fred Merkle to touch second in 1908, which resulted in the Giants and Cubs being tied for the pennant and the Cubs winning the replay; with Fred Snodgrass' muff of a seemingly simple fly which prevented the Giants from winning the 1912 Series from the Red Sox.

There was anguish on the Brooklyn bench when the ball sailed into the stands to transform a 4–2 Dodger lead into a 5–4 Giant victory—anguish and utter disbelief. There was one man who watched the ball with even more anguish and more disbelief than any of his teammates.

"Sink, you devil, sink," he prayed under his breath. But the ball didn't sink.

The man was Roy Campanella, the Dodger catcher, riding the bench with an injured thigh that day. To all of the Brooks, Thomson's three-run homer seemed like a bad dream but to Campy it was worse—it was a bad dream, an incredible nightmare repeating itself.

His mind went back to his second season in organized baseball, to 1947 when he played with Montreal, Brooklyn's farm team in the International League. The Royals had a 14-game lead at one stage but Jersey City, then the Giant's International farm team, started to eat it away.

It came down to the final game of the season, with the Jerseys now only percentage points behind. Montreal was at home for a pair with Toronto and Jersey City was playing a single game with Baltimore. Since the Royals had lost a game through rain, they needed both for the pennant.

Montreal led Toronto 5 to 3 going into the ninth, but Jack Van Cuyk ran into trouble. The Leafs got two on with one out and Manager Clay Hopper lifted Van Cuyk and called on Chet Kehn. Chet retired the first man and needed only to get by Len Kensecke to sew up the victory. Kensecke belted the ball over the right field fence for a home run and Toronto won, 6 to 5, and the pennant was gone.

That winter, in a letter to a teammate, Campanella confessed that in his dreams he still saw Kensecke's ball go flying over the screen. "I still don't believe we lost that pennant after being so far in front," he wrote. "There'll never be anything like that game again."

He was to recall that letter on October 3, 1951. History had repeated with a bang and the bang was supplied by Bobby Thomson.

Until he dons his armor and crouches down behind home plate, Campanella doesn't look like what he is—the best catcher in baseball today. He's a roly-poly sort of guy, a real butter-ball. He reminds old-timers a little bit of Bob O'Farrell, who caught in the National League for two decades, quitting in the mid-30's. He's chunky like O'Farrell but even more catlike behind the plate. And faster afoot, too.

More than one observer has likened Campanella's quickness behind the plate to that of a cat. He can pounce on bunts placed far out in front of the plate and he gets his throws away with no waste motion. He has not only a rifle arm but an accurate one.

Campanella's record against would-be base stealers is phenomenal. It is only since 1950 that the National League has been keeping records of the success of catchers against base stealers and the over-all record of the league has held at a steady one-for-two ratio. In other words, the other National League catchers (Campy excepted) are something like the Ancient Mariner "who stoppeth one of three."

This is in direct contrast to Roy's record. He nails two out of three. Allen Roth, the Dodger statistician, has been keeping records of this phase of catching for some time. Through 1952, during which period Campanella caught over 600 games, the squatty catcher has nailed 138 base stealers out of 209. And he has kept to this average closely, too, getting 30 out of 45 in 1951 and 31 out of 46 in 1952. In the 1952 World Series against the Yankees, Campy improved his average, nailing three out of four.

Perhaps the greatest boost for Campanella is his record in the All-Star games. He was selected for the National League team for the first time in 1949, when the game was played at Ebbets Field. In the fourth inning, Campanella was sent behind the plate by Billy Southworth to relieve Andy Seminick of the Phillies and he caught every inning of every All-Star game after that—14 innings in Chicago's Comiskey Park in 1950, nine in Detroit's Briggs Stadium in 1951 and five in Shibe Park, Philadelphia in 1952 when the game was halted by rain—a total of 34 consecutive innings of All-Star play.

You won't endear yourself to Campanella by talking of his All-Star record, though. When the 1952 game ended in the rain in Philly, he was still looking for his first All-Star base hit!

Another of Campanella's catching assets is his willingness to throw. He is one of the very best of the pick-off artists because he has utter confidence in his ability to get the ball where he wants it. No less a judge than Mickey Cochrane raved about the play Roy made to pick Phil Rizzuto off third in the fourth game of the 1949 World Series.

In that same game against the Yankees, Campy averted disaster in the very first inning when he had Rizzuto trapped between third and home in a run-down play and not only tagged Phil but alertly threw the ball to Jackie Robinson at second to nab Tommy Henrich who had rounded the bag on the play. It takes a heads-up catcher to nail skilled veterans like Rizzuto and Henrich on the one play.

Since Campanella came to the Dodgers he has been a real home run threat. In four full seasons he batted a total of 111 round-trippers, an average of better than 27 a season which is unusually high for a catcher.

Campanella's home runs, like bananas, seem to come in bunches. Roy, in 1950, hit six in six games, just one short of the record. The next year he hit seven homers in eight games. Roy will go a week or ten days without a homer and then suddenly he'll lower the boom. Incidentally, the majority of Roy's homers come with men on base and account for a great many of his runs-batted-in.

Since he came into baseball from the Negro leagues, Campanella has improved as a hitter. When Branch Rickey, at that time president of the Dodgers, first heard of Campy he personally scouted him, although Roy didn't know he was in the stands.

"In those days," declared Rickey, "Campanella had a blind swing. He would turn his head at the last second, taking his eyes off the ball. In that way he would strike out a lot and it wasn't easy to see his potentialities as a hitter."

Somewhere between Walter Alston, who managed Campanella at Nashua, New Hampshire, in the now defunct New England League, and Clay Hopper who had him at Montreal the next year, Roy found the home run range. He hit thirteen at Nashua in 1946 and the same number at Montreal, but when he was optioned to St. Paul in 1948, he broke loose with 13 homers in 35 games before he was recalled to Brooklyn.

One of the toughest pitchers for the Dodgers was Ken Raffensberger, the veteran southpaw of the Reds. The Brooks beat him fairly frequently, which is only natural considering the disparity between the clubs, but Ken always made it rough for them. Oddly enough, Campanella hit him as though he owned him.

In a night game in Cincinnati in 1950, Campanella tore into Raffensberger for three home runs. All cleared the left field fence at Crosley Field, the first landing on the roof of a laundry behind the barrier, the second hitting the second story window and the third just disappearing from sight, clearing the laundry, the sign atop its roof and all. Tom Swope, veteran baseball writer of the Cincinnati *Post,* couldn't recall any longer drives, although he cautiously admitted that perhaps Ernie Lombardi and Walker Cooper, both catchers, by the way, might have hit drives as far.

"That Raffensberger," grinned Campy after the game, "I'd get up at six-thirty in the morning to hit against that guy!"

No Dodger is any more popular with his teammates than Campanella. Despite his fine competitive fire, Roy is affable and easy going, no more complex than any one of his five young children. His disputes with umpires are infrequent—the Frank Dascoli incident in Boston in the waning days of the 1951 season was exceptional—and he never tries to show up an umpire as some catchers will. There is nothing of the show-boat in Campanella.

In the winter of 1952 an umpire wrote anonymously, and bitterly, in *Sport Magazine* about the rough times the boys in blue were having. The umpire related how Umpire Jocko Conlan was smacked by two foul tips in an early season game at Ebbets Field and declared "Among ourselves we also wondered if the accident to Conlan was no accident at all, and if it were anybody else but Roy Campanella behind the bat for Brooklyn that day some of us could have jumped to harsh conclusions. Roy is a sweet man, but not all catchers are."

Because Campanella began playing in the Negro leagues when he was only 16, he developed a religious streak unusual in ball players. Ball players, as a group, are no more irreligious than bankers or grocers or cops or sports writers, but Campanella has probably read the Bible more often than any ball player I know since Pepper Martin of the Cardinal Gas House Gang.

Roy's mother, Mrs. Ida Campanella, gave him a Bible for his first trip away from home because he was to be away from parental guidance so young and counselled him to read it. It has been Roy's constant travelling companion ever since, no matter where he has gone.

Campanella has great faith in the efficacy of prayer. Three times during that feverish final playoff game with the Giants in 1951, Roy sneaked off to the closet at the end of the visitors' dugout in the Polo Grounds to pray for the cause of the Dodgers. That his prayers were in vain in that particular instance didn't weaken his faith.

"God has been good to me more often than not," he says simply.

On a cold night in October, 1945, Campanella was catching at Ruppert Stadium in Newark, New Jersey, for the Negro All-Stars against the Major League All-Stars, the latter team organized by Charley Dressen, then the Dodger coach.

The major leaguers had a pretty good club, Eddie Stanky, Whitey Kurowski, Buddy Kerr, Tommy Holmes among others. On this particular night, Ralph Branca was breezing his fast one by Campy and his mates and the score was 11 to 0.

As Dressen walked past Campanella to coach at third, he asked Roy to meet him after the game.

"Where?" asked the catcher.

"Outside the park," said Chuck.

And as simply as that, Campanella's major league career was launched, although neither Roy nor Chuck dreamed that those few words were to prove so momentous to the two of them. This was 1945, you see, and there were no Negroes in organized baseball at any level at all.

When Campanella and Dressen met outside the park after the game, Charley told him simply that Branch Rickey, the Dodger president, wished to see him in the Brooklyn offices at ten the following morning. That was all Dressen had to tell him because that was all Dressen knew—he wasn't privy to the Mahatma's plans.

"Take an 'A' train of the Independent and get off at Borough Hall. Anybody'll tell you where Montague Street is. The number is 215," instructed Dressen.

About all that could be said about Campanella's meeting with Rickey is that the catcher was flattered and bewildered. It meant a lot that his reputation in the Negro League should have reached the ears of a man placed as highly in baseball as the Mahatma, but on the other hand, Roy couldn't see it leading to any advancement.

Campanella was neither the first nor the last to listen to Rickey and leave, hours later, in a state of pleasant befuddlement. He was amazed at how much the Dodger president knew of his background, how much he knew about other players in the Negro League. Roy had read that a new Negro league was to be formed, the United States League, which was to be more or less subsidized by major league clubs. Brooklyn was to back an entry in this league, the Brown Dodgers, who were to play at Ebbets Field.

It was easy for Roy to assume that this was the purpose of the meeting with Rickey. There were two Negro leagues at the time, the National, to which Campanella's Baltimore Elite Giants belonged and the American, which operated in the Middle West. There had been a lot of talk among Negro players about the United States League. It opened up new fields of employment and therefore the possibilities of more money.

When Campanella left Rickey that October afternoon in 1945, he felt that an offer for the Brown Dodgers would be forthcoming, but he wasn't particularly excited about it. With Baltimore, he was making about $3000 a season and in the winter months he played with other Negro stars in the Latin-American circuit. The United States League was a new thing and it might blow up entirely, as so many new organizations did.

A week or so later, Campanella was in Harlem's Hotel Woodside where Negro ball players from all over the country were gathering for an invasion of Venezuela. They would play against local teams in the South American capital, Caracas. As Dick Young reported the story in his fine biography of Campanella (A. S. Barnes & Co., New York), it was Jackie Robinson who first tipped off Roy to the importance of his meeting with Rickey.

"I hear you were over to Brooklyn to see Mr. Rickey," said Robbie casually as they dealt a hand of gin rummy.

"How did you ever find that out?" asked the surprised Campanella.

"Because I was over to see him myself," was Robinson's answer.

Campanella then launched into a discussion with Jackie, in which he pointed out that whereas it would be all right for him, a newcomer to Negro baseball, to take a chance with the United States League, he, Campanella, couldn't afford to.

"Did you sign?" asked Robbie.

"I didn't sign to play ball for him, no," answered Roy, "but I did sign an agreement that I wouldn't sign with any other team for next season without letting him know. But I don't want to play with the Brown Dodgers."

"Did Mr. Rickey mention the Brown Dodgers?" persisted Robinson.

"Come to think of it, Jackie, he didn't mention any team," said Roy. "He just talked and talked but I couldn't really pin him down on anything he said."

"Well, I signed with him," declared Robinson.

Campanella promptly congratulated the young Negro, who had been the shortstop of the Kansas City Monarchs, and told him he was certain Jackie would make good with the Brown Dodgers.

"But I didn't sign with the Brown Dodgers," said Robbie. "I signed with Montreal."

Then the words tumbled forth as Campy listened first in bewilderment and then excitedly. "I'm going to be the first Negro in organized baseball," said Jackie with rising excitement. "I'm to be signed at a public ceremony in Montreal tomorrow. It means the end of the Jim Crow law in baseball."

It was only then that Campanella realized the full import of Robinson's statement and realized the full import of his meeting with Rickey. He knew then that the Mahatma had tapped him for organized baseball, too.

The first step up was a long one for Campanella. He wrote Rickey from Caracas and eventually, months later, received a telegram telling him to report at the Dodger office on March 10. Roy flew back and was a little upset to find that Branch was in Sanford, Florida, and that his destiny was in the hands of Rickey's assistant, Bob Finch.

Finch tried to place Campanella with the Danville, Illinois, farm of the Dodgers in the Three-Eye League but there was no room there. He finally made arrangements for Roy to join Nashua, New Hampshire, in the New England League, like the Three-Eye, a Class B organization.

It turned out to be the best break Campanella possibly could have gotten. The general manager at Nashua was Emil (Buzzy) Bavasi, an intelligent, understanding young man. Like Campanella, Buzzy was to go right up the ladder of the Brooklyn organization and in December, 1950, after Rickey moved to Pittsburgh, Walter F. O'Malley, who succeeded Branch as president, promoted Bavasi to the vice-presidency of the parent club.

Class B salary limitations are rigid. Campanella would have to play for $185 a month, a third of what he was receiving in the

Negro National League. However, the Dodgers offered him a post-season job at twice his Nashua salary, so he was getting the $3000 he had made with Baltimore. The post-season job turned out to be a detail of scouting the Negro leagues and Campanella is particularly proud of his scouting record. Among the players he recommended to Rickey were Lary Doby, later a Cleveland star, and Monte Irvin, the Giant slugger.

On the Nashua team was another Negro, Don Newcombe, the fire-balling pitcher, and he and Campanella got through their first season in organized ball with a minimum of trouble. Roy had one run-in with Sal Yvars, catching for Manchester. Sal flung a handful of dust into Campy's face.

Campanella ripped off his mask and roared at Yvars, "If you ever try that again, I'll beat you to pulp."

There was no further trouble.

It is not generally known but one of the reasons which cost Leo Durocher his job as Dodger manager in 1948 was his refusal to see eye-to-eye with Rickey on the subject of Campanella's serv-ices. The Lip wanted to use Campy with Brooklyn. The Ma-hatma, taking the long view, wanted to use Roy at the Dodgers' St. Paul farm and thus break the color line which still existed in the American Association.

Rickey, of course, gained his point. Campanella obediently went to St. Paul, where he broke out in one of his famous home run rashes. He was recalled by the Dodgers, again at the insistence of Durocher, but Leo lasted only a couple of more weeks with the club. He went to the Giants when that club released Mel Ott as manager, and Burt Shotton took over the Brooklyn stewardship for the balance of the season.

The Dodgers finished third that year, although they were in first place in September, but Campanella proved he was a major league catcher, maybe the best catcher in the major leagues. He set what probably was some sort of a record in the closing weeks by throwing out a dozen would-be base stealers in succession.

Campanella came into a World Series in 1949 and it was here for the first time that his true worth became generally recognized. His pickoff of Phil Rizzuto—the first time in his life the Yankee infielder had ever been picked off third base—and his amazing agility behind the plate drew raves from those who saw the Series, not merely raves from the press box but raves from baseball people, particularly American Leaguers who never had seen Campy before.

Although he didn't make the World Series in 1950—Dick Sisler's last game home run for the Phils took care of that—nor in 1951, when Bobby Thomson's homer took care of *THAT*— Campanella was steadily climbing. He had his reward in 1951 when he was named the Most Valuable Player in the National

ROY CAMPANELLA

Born November 19, 1921, Philadelphia, Pa.
Bats right. Throws right. Height 5'9". Weight 206.

YEAR	CLUB	LEAGUE	POS	G	AB	R	H	2B	3B	HR	RBI	PCT
1946	Nashua	N. Eng.	C	113	396	75	115	19	8	13	96	.290
1947	Montreal	Int.	C	135	440	64	120	25	3	13	75	.273
1948	St. Paul	A. A.	OF–C	35	123	31	40	5	2	13	39	.325
1948	Brooklyn	Nat.	C	83	279	32	72	11	3	9	45	.258
1949	Brooklyn	Nat.	C	130	436	65	125	22	2	22	82	.287
1950	Brooklyn	Nat.	C	126	437	70	123	19	3	31	89	.281
1951	Brooklyn (a)	Nat.	C	143	505	90	164	33	1	33	108	.325
1952	Brooklyn	Nat.	C	128	468	73	126	18	1	22	97	.269
	Major League Totals			610	2125	330	630	103	10	117	421	.287

WORLD SERIES RECORD

YEAR	CLUB	LEAGUE	POS	G	AB	R	H	2B	3B	HR	RBI	PCT
1949	Brooklyn	Nat.	C	5	15	2	4	1	0	1	2	.267
1952	Brooklyn	Nat.	C	7	28	0	6	0	0	0	1	.214
	World Series Totals			12	43	2	10	1	0	1	3	.233

ALL-STAR GAME RECORD

YEAR	LEAGUE	POS	AB	R	H	2B	3B	HR	RBI	PCT
1949	National	C	2	0	0	0	0	0	0	.000
1950	National	C	6	0	0	0	0	0	0	.000
1951	National	C	4	0	0	0	0	0	0	.000
1952	National	C	1	0	0	0	0	0	0	.000
	All-Star Totals		13	0	0	0	0	0	0	.000

(a) Voted Most Valuable Player in National League for 1951.

League, getting all of 24 first place votes and finishing with a score of 243 against 191 for Stan Musial, the Cardinal slugger who was the runner-up. He was the first National League catcher to be named the MVP since Ernie Lombardi of the Reds in 1938.

Campanella had come a long way since he took the "A" train to Brooklyn that October morning in 1945.

CHAPTER III

THE GEORGIA PEACH

Tyrus Raymond Cobb

IF YOU like that sort of thing, you can't beat Sherman Billingsley's Stork Club. The threesome chatting animatedly at a table looked as though they liked it. The charming lady, the chunky round-faced chap with the heavy-rimmed glasses and the husky balding gentleman with the pin-striped suit fit into the general picture of soft music, soft lights and soft laughter. There was something familiar about the big man, a look of command to him. Maybe one of the big brass out of uniform?

You couldn't be blamed if you didn't recognize the man right off. It was years since you had seen him and the Stork Club wasn't where you had last seen him, either. He was Tyrus Raymond Cobb, possibly the best ball player who ever lived, certainly the most dynamic.

While his bride of a few weeks looked on, Cobb was explaining to an old crony of his, Ward Morehouse, that he really wasn't the ferocious, hell-for-leather ball player everybody said he had been. Morehouse, Georgia-born like Cobb, a dramatist, author and columnist, listened attentively.

"I didn't come in high with my spikes as everybody says," explained Ty, "because I used a fallaway or a hook slide and couldn't come in high. I can honestly say I never tried to spike but two fellows in my life—and I don't mind saying who they were. They were Lou Criger and Dutch Leonard."

The Dutch Leonard to whom Cobb referred was not the Dutch Leonard who wound up the 1951 season with the Chicago Cubs but an earlier namesake, who had been a left-handed pitcher with the Red Sox back in the days when Babe Ruth first joined that club. Lou Criger was a long since gone catcher who publicly declared he didn't think much of Ty as a base runner.

Perhaps the most outstanding characteristic of Cobb as he enters his sixties is his suavity and his generally apologetic air for the fire he breathed through his youth and middle age. His California golfing partners often have been shown Cobb's legs, nicked with hundreds of scars from spike wounds and asked by Ty, "Do these look as if the spiking was all one-sided?"

This doesn't square away with the Ty Cobb who savagely attacked his roommate, the mild-mannered Nap Rucker, one afternoon in Augusta in 1905, or the snarling Cobb who needed police protection in nearly every city in the American League, nor yet the Cobb who went into the stands after a fan with his fists swinging one day in New York in 1912 or the Cobb who flung his bat at Carl Mays in Boston in 1915.

Cobb has become a complex man but this deals with Cobb the ballplayer, the ballplayer who, to paraphrase General Forrest, was called "the bestest by the mostest." John McGraw called Honus Wagner the best, many called Babe Ruth the best but the most called Ty Cobb the best. Cobb came into baseball with a chip on his shoulder and went out of it with a bag of gold over his back.

For all of his brawling reputation as a ballplayer, Cobb came into the game with a better family background than most of his contemporaries. His father, who bitterly opposed Ty's entrance into baseball, was a State Senator in Georgia and later county superintendent of schools. Cobb was born in Narrows, Bank County, but the family later made their home at Royston. It is there today that a hospital has been built to which Ty contributed $100,000 in memory of his parents.

Ty was eighteen when he broke in with Augusta in the South Atlantic (Sally) League in 1904. He was farmed to Anniston to finish out the season but was recalled to Augusta for the next year largely at the insistence of a young sports writer who has been one of Cobb's few friends ever since, fellow named Rice, Grantland Rice.

Cobb told Morehouse that he was inclined to be nonchalant and lackadaisical about baseball in his second year with Augusta until straightened out by George Leidy. That Leidy was a great help to young Ty there is no doubt but it is almost impossible to imagine Cobb being lackadaisical about baseball—or about anything else for that matter.

On the Augusta team with Cobb in 1905 was a young left-handed pitcher named Nap Rucker, another pitcher named Eddie Cicotte and an outfielder named Ducky Holmes. Rucker was destined to be one of the National League's great southpaws, saddled with a Brooklyn team which couldn't do him any good; Cicotte became one of the game's greatest exponents of trick deliveries until he became too tricky in the 1919 World Series and was banished with other members of the Black Sox. Holmes tried outfielding and umpiring although, unlike Cobb, not at the same time. Ducky later became a minor league magnate whose greatest claim to fame was that he pulled the switch in a night game at Dayton, Ohio, plunging the ball park into darkness at the precise moment the sheriff arrived to impound the receipts. All these and Cobb, too, and Augusta finished last in the Sally League, although Ty had gone on to Detroit before the season ended.

Rucker was as mild a mannered man as ever came into baseball and the luck of the draw gave him Cobb as a roommate. They got along well, principally because it was impossible for anybody, even the fiery Cobb, not to get along with George Napoleon Rucker.

Clubhouse showers were a refinement which had not yet reached the Sally League and it was the custom of Cobb and Rucker to tub themselves in their room after the game. There never was any difficulty about it because Cobb was always first home and first into the tub. It never bothered the slow going Nap but one day he got home ahead of Ty, having been knocked out of the box.

Cobb paced the room like a caged lion while Rucker bathed and as Nap stepped from the tub, Ty rushed at him. Despite the unexpectedness of the onslaught, Nap managed to hold off his enraged roomie.

"Have you gone crazy?" demanded Rucker, "a-fussin' and a-fightin' like this? Just because I happened to be in the bath first today! And for the first time, too!"

"You don't understand, Nap," pleaded Cobb, "I've got to be first—all the time."

That was the credo of Tyrus Raymond Cobb. And he was first, too. And nearly all of the time. Before another year was out, the American League was to learn that. And the lesson was to stick in that league for nearly a quarter of a century.

Figures, unless you and they are in the front row at a Broadway musical, are apt to be on the boring side. Yet there is no way to illustrate the greatness which was Cobb's unless you call on the statistics, particularly for those who never saw the Georgia Peach. Those who saw him when he was making a shambles of the American League need have no recourse to the records—they know without having to look it up.

Cobb went to bat more times, scored more runs, stole more bases and made more hits than any other major leaguer in history. He has the highest lifetime average of any long-service player, .367. He batted better than .300, and usually much better, for twenty-three consecutive seasons. He led the American League in batting from 1907 through 1915, tailed off in 1916 with a mere .371, and came back again to lead it for the next three seasons. Fourteen times he made five hits in one game and when he was thirty-nine years old, he hit six-for-six, including three home runs. He also played more games than any other ballplayer, 3033. Are there any questions?

Just as putting it baldly in figures doesn't do justice to Cobb's batting, neither will mere statistics give you an appreciation of his base stealing, yet he stole 96 bases in one season (1915) for the modern record and in the four seasons of 1909 through 1912, he stole an aggregate of 285 bases, an average of better than 70 steals per season!

For all his rashness on the baselines, all of his feuding with teammates and rivals, Cobb was a coldly scientific ballplayer, a ballplayer who made himself with his brain as much as with his great physical skills. His talent was predicated on the dead ball employed when he broke in, in 1905, and on the basis of low score games, yet Ty bridged the gap between the dead ball and the lively one. He batted .400, not .300, with the dead ball and a decade later he batted .400 with the jack-rabbit ball.

No better illustration of Cobb's craftiness may be offered than his approach to the blazing speed of Walter Johnson. The great

Washington pitcher is generally conceded to have thrown a baseball over the sixty feet, six-inch route between the mound and the plate faster than any man who ever lived. Some have held out for Bobby Feller, Dizzy Dean or Dazzy Vance but nobody who saw Johnson will concede the palm to any but Sir Walter.

It is axiomatic in boxing that nobody can out-think a solid belt on the chin. The same is supposed to hold true in baseball for a fast ball. Yet Cobb was able to hit Johnson because he could outwit him!

Ty based his strategy against Johnson on the fact that Big Barney, as they called him, was a kindly, gentle soul. Aware that God had gifted him with overpowering speed, Johnson exercised his great control so as not to hit a batsman. Cobb took advantage of this by crowding the plate while facing Johnson. The result was that Walter pitched wide and thus got in the hole against Cobb. Then Ty took his normal stance, knowing that Walter would have to come in with the pitch or else walk him.

This was checked with a contemporary of Cobb and Johnson and found to be so. The fellow couldn't help adding, "I wonder what would have happened had the situation been reversed and Johnson the batter and Cobb the pitcher. Imagine depending on Ty's mercy!"

One of the oddities of Cobb's baseball uniform was its long sleeves. This was not an affectation, as was popularly supposed, even by those who played with Ty, but an example of his attention to detail. The long sleeves were for the purpose of protecting Cobb's elbows when he slid—and Cobb slid more than anybody else.

To improve his speed on the bases, Ty wore weighted shoes in spring training, gradually lessening the weight as the season approached. By the time Cobb had removed the last of the weights, he felt as though he were flying on the basepaths. It often seemed that way to others, too.

Back in the spring of 1913, Casey Stengel was a young squirt with the Dodgers and the club was training at Macon, Georgia. Cobb, already an American League star of the first magnitude was holding out because he didn't think Detroit was prepared to reward him in the way a man who had hit .400 for two consecutive seasons should be rewarded. Baseball being somewhat more lax in those days, Cobb decided to work out with the Dodgers pending the settlement of his financial problems with the Tigers.

Simply because he was a rookie, Stengel wasn't bashful, then or ever. Knowing of Cobb's great reputation as a base runner, particularly at stretching outfield singles into doubles, Casey braced him for the formula, if there was one.

"I knew I couldn't run like Cobb," explained Stengel, "but I knew it wasn't his speed alone which enabled him to stretch hits. So, if there was any racket to it, I wanted to find out what it was.

"What Cobb told me was very revealing. Ty said that on any ball hit to the outfield, he always rounded first at full speed. And if the ball was hit to the outfielder's gloved hand side, he never broke stride but kept going because that meant that the outfielder would have to turn around to throw.

"Well, that sounded pretty good to me, but now here's what made Cobb great—if the ball was hit to the outfielder's 'meat' hand, that's his bare hand, Ty made the turn at full speed anyway and watched the second baseman and the shortstop. If he saw either one of them move out toward the outfield to take the throw, that meant that the throw was short and he kept going to second.

"I tried it and it worked sometimes for me. I didn't have Ty's gift of speed but I caught a couple of guys napping with his tricks."

Cobb has since revealed in interviews that when he slid into a base, it was the fielder's eyes he watched, not the ball. That tipped him off on which side to slide on and which way the tag was likely to be attempted.

Leidy, the Sally League mentor whom Ty credits with arousing him to the seriousness of baseball, also is the man who taught Cobb how to bunt. He placed a sweater down the third baseline at just the precise spot where a bunted ball was tough for either third baseman or pitcher to handle—too far in for the third baseman, too far out for the catcher and near enough to the foul line so the pitcher couldn't come over and throw him out. Cobb, working by the hour under George's eye, reached the point where he could drop the ball on the sweater on almost every try. Modern ballplayers, who consider bunting practice onerous, might give a thought to Cobb.

Today's ballplayers will have difficulty in believing that a man who batted .367 over a twenty-four year span in the majors ever knew what a slump was but, incredible as it may seem, Cobb had his slumps. And the remedy for them, too.

"The way I used to come out of a slump was to simply stroke the ball back at the pitcher," Cobb has explained in countless interviews. "Not try to kill the ball, or pull it, but just meet it with an even swing and try to hit it directly back at the pitcher. It always worked for me and got my timing and stride readjusted."

Cobb's method for breaking a slump was backed by logic, as were most of his moves. The pitcher's box is the least defended spot on the diamond and Ty, in one of his rare slumps, usually faked a bunt before attempting to hit back at the pitcher. This alerted the first and third basemen and weakened the defense at those spots, too.

Ty batted with his feet close together in the batter's box and employed a shifting grip, his right hand about three inches from the knob of the bat, his left hand about three inches above his right. This sliding grip enabled him to swing from the end of the bat; choke up and hit to the opposite field or bunt. All of these things Cobb could do superlatively well and his grip served to keep the defense in a constant state of flux. The fielders had to guess what was coming next.

There haven't been many hitters in baseball who employed the sliding grip of Cobb, practically none at all since Babe Ruth's home runs caused the place-hitter to all but disappear from the scene. Yet when Cobb and another great hitter, Hans Wagner, met to pose for photographers before the opening game of the 1909 World Series between Detroit and Pittsburgh, each noted with amazement that the other gripped the bat the same way. Incidentally, Cobb was the leading batter of the American League that season and Wagner led the National and it has been only once in the forty years since that the two leading batsmen of the rival leagues met in a World Series, when Al Simmons and Chick Hafey appeared in the Mackmen-Cardinal set-to in 1931.

Probably the greatest tribute Cobb ever received from the press, and he received many, was in 1911 when he was unanimously voted the most valuable player in the American League. The most valuable player voting was not conducted as loosely then as now. Only one man in each city voted and votes were cast for only eight players. A first place vote counted eight points and Cobb received exactly 64 votes—first place on every ballot! It was duplicated only once while that form of voting was in vogue, in 1923 when Babe Ruth received a 64-vote total.

Every time there is talk of Cobb and his brawls on the diamond the subject of his fight with Charley (Buck) Herzog, Giant infielder, is brought up. His series of fights with Charley Schmidt, the burly catcher who was Ty's teammate, isn't mentioned nearly as often as the Herzog tussle, yet Cobb conducted a running feud with Charley the like of which baseball, nor any other sport, has ever seen. They fought countless times, with Schmidt always winning, yet it finally was Schmidt who called off the feud by going to Ty's rescue when Cobb became embroiled with an opposing player.

The Tigers came North with the Giants on a barnstorming series in the spring of 1917. The series opened in Dallas on a Saturday and Cobb was late arriving at the park. The Giants, led by Art Fletcher, rode him unmercifully when he came in, accusing him of delaying his entrance to take bows and other charges, more bitter and less printable. When the game started, the Giant bench, led by John McGraw, kept up a running fire of abuse.

On Cobb's first time at bat, Jeff Tesreau nicked him on the shoulder with an inside pitch. It wasn't a "dust-off" but a ball which got away from big Jeff but Ty, in view of the heckling, took it as deliberate. He went down to first base, vowing vengeance at the Giants in general and Tesreau in particular. The rhubarb was really stewing.

From second base, Herzog dared Cobb to steal. And Ty came roaring down on the first pitch. Lew McCarty, the catcher, had expected this and called for a pitch-out. But his throw to second well ahead of Cobb didn't stop Ty. He came in high, his spikes gleaming, ripped Herzog's uniform and cut him in two places.

Buck was bowled to the ground with the crash but came up swinging.

Other players joined in and umpires and the police had their hands full not merely stopping a fight but preventing a riot. Each time the fighters were separated they redoubled their struggles to get at each other. Both were banished, of course, but Cobb declared that if he were put out of the game he would not play in another game in the exhibition series. And Ty was the No. 1 box office attraction in baseball at the time. Hughey Jennings, the Tiger manager, knowing he couldn't control Cobb's actions, tried to cop a plea for Ty but out he went, along with Herzog.

That night in the lobby of the Oriental Hotel, McGraw's path crossed that of Cobb and the Giant manager lit into the Georgian with all the vituperation and invective at his command, which was plenty. Ty, realizing the two decades in age which separated them, kept his temper, coldly insulting Mac in return and driving him to the verge of apoplexy.

Later, through pre-arrangement, Herzog went to Cobb's room, accompanied by Heinie Zimmerman, the Giant third baseman. Buck had specified that Ty have one second in the room, the Tiger trainer, but there were several Detroit players in the room. Herzog and Cobb stripped to the waist and went to it. Buck sent Ty down with the first punch but it also was Herzog's last. From there Cobb beat him savagely before spectators stopped the fight. In later years, Buck always maintained that both fought to the point of exhaustion and that he might have taken Cobb had he been able to muster the strength to throw one more punch but the witnesses said it was Ty all the way after the first punch.

Still playing in Dallas the next day, which was a Sunday, the park was jammed with fans hoping for a renewal of hostilities. Cobb however refused to play, just as he had threatened, and Herzog was unable to play, so severe was the beating he had absorbed the night before.

Cobb, as may be gathered, was not the most popular man in baseball, with his teammates any more than with his opponents. Yet there is one record of the Tigers rallying around Ty as few clubs ever have rallied around a ballplayer. To protect Cobb against what they considered an unjust ban by Ban Johnson,

American League President, the Tigers went on a general strike, the only one ever carried through in the history of baseball. The Red Sox and Cubs threatened one during the 1918 World Series in Boston because they thought their shares weren't large enough and the Dodgers threatened one in 1943 against Manager Leo Durocher because of an interview the Lip had given out in which the players felt he had been unfair to Bobo Newsom, of all people. The Tiger strike, however, was the only one which ever materialized.

The trouble started in New York when Cobb went into the stands after a spectator and gave him a lathering. He was banished from the game by the umpire and President Ban Johnson, who was present that day, suspended Cobb. That the spectator was abusing Cobb there seems no doubt but Johnson apparently felt that the Yankees of that day (1912) had so few customers that they couldn't spare any for the purposes of assault.

May 16, 1912, in Philadelphia the Tigers struck when told they would have to play the Athletics without Cobb. Manager Jennings frantically rallied what semipros he could gather and put a team on the field to play the A's. Apparently, the Philadelphia players, too, felt a surge of sympathy for Cobb for they went out and really plastered Jennings' misfits, winning by a score of 24 to 2. That was laying it on thick.

Cobb now showed where he stood with the players, who had sent a corporate telegram to Johnson protesting his suspension. He urged them to return to the lineup and they consented, which is more than anybody in authority with the Tigers could have got them to do. The upshot of it was his suspension was lifted and he was fined $50. The players who supported him, ironically enough, were each fined $100.

Despite this evidence of support from both his own team and the Athletics, Cobb was so generally hated by the opposition that in 1910, the Browns, or some members of them, acted in collusion in an attempt to deprive Cobb of the batting championship and decide it in favor of Larry Lajoie, who was with Cleveland. That year a Chalmers automobile was to be presented to the American League's leading hitter.

Cobb and Lajoie came down the wire neck and neck and it was touch and go on the last day of the season. Cleveland was playing in St. Louis and the Browns, managed by John O'Connor, were a cool eighth. Cleveland was in fifth place and there was nothing at stake save the batting championship in which the Browns were supposed to have only an academic interest.

Playing third for the Brownies that day was a young infielder just up from Omaha, John (Red) Corriden, the Lollypop Kid. Red, who years later was to make himself an enviable reputation as a coach with the Cubs, Dodgers and Yankees, was a young man of twenty-three. When Lajoie came to bat the first time, Red, respecting the right-handed power of the great Frenchman, was playing him fairly deep. Nap laid down a bunt and beat it out with ease. Corriden came in on the grass the next time and was waved back to a deep position by Manager O'Connor. Again Lajoie bunted and again Lajoie beat it out.

Between innings, Corriden asked O'Connor if it wouldn't be a good idea to play shallow on Lajoie, since Nap seemed determined to bunt all day.

"I'm the manager here," roared O'Connor, "and you'll play where I place you or I'll get somebody who will."

There was nothing Johnny could do for the rest of the afternoon but retrieve the ball after Lajoie had beaten out another bunt. The case was so flagrant that it couldn't be kept a secret, even though it was the last day of the season in old League Park in St. Louis.

Corriden was summoned to Chicago by Ban Johnson at the end of the season and asked for details. Truthfully, as always, Johnny supplied them. No official action was taken but it may be significant that the Brownie manager never appeared in organized ball again.

P.S.: Cobb got the automobile. Final averages, Cobb .385; Lajoie .384.

One thing even Cobb's worst enemies never could accuse him of was a lack of courage. Ty's courage was as high as his skill. He may have started most of the fights which marked his stormy career but he finished all of them. Rival managers used to caution their players not to heckle Cobb.

"It only makes him worse," they explained.

It did, too. The raging of a hostile crowd was music to his

ears. The louder the crowd booed, the better Cobb played. When Cobb threatened to steal a base, he did steal it. More than one catcher learned to his sorrow that to heckle Cobb while Ty was batting only meant to be bowled over at home plate, armor or no armor, the next time Cobb got the chance to come in from third base.

On August 16, 1916, Ray Chapman, shortstop of Cleveland, was struck with a pitched ball by Carl Mays of the Yankees at the Polo Grounds and died the next day, the only fatality in the history of major league baseball. The results of the incident may well be imagined.

Cobb was in Boston with the Tigers and was asked for a statement on the death of Chapman. The gist of what he said was: "If Mays deliberately threw at Chapman he should be suspended from baseball for life."

In transmission, the statement was garbled as statements so often are. New Yorkers never heard the first part, "If Mays deliberately . . ." All they did hear was that part about ". . . suspended from baseball for life." They raged at Cobb giving so pontifical an opinion some 230 miles distant from the event.

By the time the Tigers reached New York to play the Yankees the town was seething with resentment at Cobb. The press whooped it up to such an extent that there were extra police on hand to protect Cobb.

The Polo Grounds was packed with howling fans long before game time. Just before the Tigers came out on the field for practice, Cobb approached Manager Hughey Jennings.

"I'm not taking batting practice," Ty told the manager. "I'm going out on the field just five minutes before game time. If they want to boo me, let 'em get a good blast at me when every seat is filled."

And every seat was filled, too, when Cobb took the long walk from the clubhouse in center field to the Detroit bench. The fans screamed at him in impotent rage as he made his lonely way the entire length of the Polo Grounds.

When Cobb came out of the dugout to await his turn to bat, he turned his attention to the New York writers, the press coop then being on the lower level just behind home plate. He told them what he thought of their skill at garbling his statements.

TYRUS RAYMOND (TY) COBB

Born Dec. 18, 1886, Narrows, Banks County, Ga.
Height 6′ ¾″. Weight 175. Batted left, threw right.

YEAR	CLUB	LEAGUE	G	AB	R	H	HR	SB	RBI	BA
1904	Augusta	So. Atl.	37	135	14	32	1	4	—	.237
1904	Anniston	S. E.	22	—	—	—	0	6	—	.370
1905	Augusta	So. Atl.	104	411	60	134	0	40	—	.326
1905	Detroit	Amer.	41	150	19	36	1	2	—	.240
1906	Detroit	Amer.	97	350	44	112	1	23	—	.320
1907	Detroit	Amer.	150	605	97	*212	5	*49	*116	*.350
1908	Detroit	Amer.	150	581	88	*188	4	39	*101	*.324
1909	Detroit	Amer.	156	573	*116	*216	*9	*76	*115	*.377
1910	Detroit	Amer.	140	509	*106	196	8	65	88	*.385
1911	Detroit	Amer.	146	591	x147	*248	8	*83	x144	*.420
1912	Detroit	Amer.	140	553	119	x227	7	61	90	*.410
1913	Detroit	Amer.	122	428	70	167	4	52	65	*.390
1914	Detroit	Amer.	97	345	69	127	2	35	57	*.368
1915	Detroit	Amer.	156	563	*144	*208	3	*96	95	*.369
1916	Detroit	Amer.	145	542	113	201	5	*68	67	.371
1917	Detroit	Amer.	152	588	107	*225	7	*55	108	*.383
1918	Detroit	Amer.	111	421	83	161	3	34	64	*.382
1919	Detroit	Amer.	124	497	92	x191	1	28	69	*.384
1920	Detroit	Amer.	112	428	86	143	2	14	63	.334
1921	Detroit	Amer.	128	507	124	197	12	22	101	.389
1922	Detroit	Amer.	137	526	99	211	4	9	99	.401
1923	Detroit	Amer.	145	556	103	189	6	9	88	.340
1924	Detroit	Amer.	155	625	115	211	4	23	74	.338
1925	Detroit	Amer.	121	415	97	157	12	13	102	.378
1926	Detroit	Amer.	79	233	48	79	4	9	62	.339
1927	Philadelphia	Amer.	134	490	104	175	5	22	93	.357
1928	Philadelphia	Amer.	95	353	54	144	1	5	40	.323
	Major League Totals		3033	11429	2244	4191	118	892	1901	.367

WORLD SERIES RECORD

YEAR	CLUB	LEAGUE	G	AB	R	H	HR	SB	RBI	BA
1907	Detroit	Amer.	5	20	1	4	0	0	0	.200
1908	Detroit	Amer.	5	19	3	7	0	2	3	.368
1909	Detroit	Amer.	7	26	3	6	0	2	5	.231
	World Series Totals		17	65	7	17	0	4	8	.262

* Led league
x Tied for lead
Managed Detroit Tigers, December 1920 to November 1926
Elected to Hall of Fame, 1936

And then he went up to bat. All Ty did was hit four for four that afternoon and when he left the field he had the fans cheering him as vociferously as they had booed him two hours earlier.

Somehow that afternoon was symbolic of Cobb. As a ballplayer, he stood alone. And he walked alone, too.

CHAPTER IV

BRAINS DON'T HURT

Edward Trowbridge Collins

ONE OF THE most interesting phases of baseball, and one written about rarely, is the "giveaway." It has nothing to do with quiz programs but with the mannerisms of a pitcher which inform the batter in advance whether the next pitch is going to be a fast ball or a curve. Ballplayers are among the most observant of all professional athletes and always are on the lookout for the telltale signs that will give them an edge over the opposition.

Sometimes the signs are fairly obvious. Sometimes a second baseman, with a right-handed hitter at the plate, will move a step toward first base on a fast ball, a step toward second base on a curve ball. Sometimes the art of detection may be carried to a high degree by the keen observation of the most minute mannerism. Art Fletcher, when managing the Phillies, found out he could call Burleigh Grimes' spitfall in advance because Burleigh's cap was too tight! The Dodger spitballer faked a spitball on every pitch, of course, but the keen-eyed Fletcher noticed that when Burleigh actually expectorated in his glove the muscles of his jaw moved and caused the peak of his cap to jiggle up and down.

There are other methods, too, such as the actual stealing of the catcher's signals. Billy Herman, when he reached second as a base runner, was amazingly adept at this. When signs are stolen this way, they usually are relayed verbally to the batter. An exhortation with the word "kid" in it, such as "Be ready, kid," may be the tip-off for the curve and can be given either by the coach or the base runner.

Information picked up about a pitcher usually doesn't remain a secret very long. And if the pitcher doesn't correct the "giveaway," he doesn't remain around very long. Players on opposing clubs will trade secrets with one another, much after the manner of housewives swapping cooking recipes. Or a player will be traded to the victim's club and promptly inform him of the mistake which enabled the batters to "read" his pitches.

All of which lengthy preamble brings us to the king of all "give-away" detectives—Edward Trowbridge Collins. Eddie broke into baseball with an accomplished gang of signal thieves, the Athletics of the early 1900's. Yet, among these masters at the art, Collins was a lone wolf. He refused to take signals from the bench or from the coach but studied the pitcher on his own. He preferred to pit his own powers of observation against the pitcher and wanted no help. This policy of Collins doesn't stamp him as anti-social. Many good hitters prefer to duel with the pitcher on their own, rather than be crossed up, and maybe beaned, by a wrong call. Joe DiMaggio once requested a Yankee coach not to give him any tip-offs, explaining he wanted to pick out his own ball to hit.

Collins' refusal to take signals from his teammates on the A's eventually led to an unpleasant situation and not because of Eddie's independence, either. After Philadelphia had won the American League pennants of 1910 and 1911, Eddie accepted $2,000 from *The American Magazine* to do a series of ten articles and one of them explained that the A's did not have foreknowledge of what was coming by stealing the signals from the catcher but by watching the pitcher himself for "giveaways."

All of the skill of Collins in studying the pitchers would have gotten him nowhere had he not abetted it by commensurate skill with the bat. Eddie was one of the most skillful bat-handlers the game has ever seen, who could place hits to either field and was an adroit hit-and-run man. A left-handed batter, Collins hit as frequently to left field as he did to right. His great speed—he stole 81 bases one season—enabled him to beat out many hits.

Collins qualified with his special skills as the ideal batter to hit in the No. 2 spot in the batting order, the man who could hit behind the runner, who could bunt if need be and whose speed made him a good risk to avoid the double play. Yet he hit so consistently that he always batted in the third spot until near the tail-end of his career when he was playing with the White Sox. He holds the American League record for sacrifice hits with 514.

One of the few players ever to make more than 3000 base hits— Cap Anson, Ty Cobb, Nap Lajoie, Tris Speaker, Hans Wagner and Paul Waner are the others—Collins is the only one in this select group who made 200 base hits in a single season only once. Yet only three players in baseball history made more base hits than Collins—Cobb, Speaker and Wagner. Eddie's grand total was 3313. He made the first in 1906 playing with the Athletics and the last in 1930, again in the uniform of the club with which he had broken in.

As might be expected from the description of Collins' style, he was not a slugger. Indeed, the most home runs he ever hit in any one season was a half-dozen and there were several seasons when he was blanked altogether. He had a grand home run total of 47 for a quarter of a century of service in the American League.

While Collins never was considered a colorful ball player, he had one of the most delightful idiosyncrasies to be found in a profession in which the abnormal is often normal. Eddie was a gum chewer in an era when most ballplayers preferred to masticate on something more pungent. Whenever he approached the plate, his wad of chewing gum was affixed to the button atop his baseball cap. When the pitcher got two strikes on him, Eddie stepped out of the batter's box, removed the gum from the top of his cap, put it in his mouth and chewed vigorously.

For all of his calculating shrewdness on the field and at the plate, Collins was notably superstitious in a field where most performers cheerfully admitted trying to propitiate the gods. At one stage while he was managing the White Sox in the mid-twenties, the club rolled off a string of eleven straight victories. This was remarkable in view of the fact that the Sox were a second division club and it cheered Manager Collins no end.

When the Sox reached Cleveland, Collins made the horrible discovery at old League Park that the clubhouse attendant, through laudable sanitary reasons, had committed the *faux pas* of washing the inner stockings of the Chicago players. Eddie's rage was by no means abated when the winning streak ended that afternoon. The stockings had not been laundered throughout the streak.

The superstition of Collins is all the more remarkable in view of the fact that he was a college product at a time when the old school tie was conspicuously absent from the street attire of ballplayers. Eddie had come to Connie Mack direct from the campus of Columbia University, in fact somewhat more directly than the faculty at Morningside Heights desired.

Collins was a standout shortstop at Columbia, although his build at the time was so slight as to make major league scouts wary of him. Eddie had played summer ball, a common enough practice then and now, between terms. He played under a former professional, Billy Lush, who recommended him to Mack. Connie sent a scout to look him over and decided to sign him.

The summer baseball season for collegians ended about Labor Day, since most of the teams were sponsored by resorts and the vacation period ended on that date. Mack invited Collins to make the final Western swing with the Athletics in 1906, since his courses at Columbia didn't begin until October.

It was Mack's thought that the trip would give Collins some experience but Eddie didn't realize how much until he suddenly found himself batting against Big Ed Walsh one day in Chicago. It wasn't any soft touch, either, for the White Sox were fighting for the pennant and Walsh hooked up in an extra-inning battle with Rube Waddell. Walsh won, 5 to 4, in eleven innings to keep alive a Chicago winning streak which eventually reached nineteen, unmatched in the American League until forty-one years later when the 1947 Yankees tied it.

Collins, playing under the nom de diamond of Eddie Sullivan, was able to hit Walsh's spitball for a single, to steal a base and to play errorless ball at short. He played in a few more games with the A's, also under the name of Sullivan, before he returned to Columbia to begin his senior year. There was a lifting of eyebrows and a clamping down of suspensions when it was discovered that Collins, the captain-elect of Columbia's 1907 baseball team, had been playing major league baseball. He was advised to sit that one out and he did, although he remained at Columbia for his bachelor of arts degree.

Eddie looked like a ballplayer to Connie but not like a short-stop. Mack tried Collins in the outfield but found he was a poor insurance risk out there. After experimenting with Eddie as a shortstop, third baseman, second baseman and outfielder for most of the 1908 season, Connie finally settled on second base for Collins in 1909 and Eddie stayed there for the rest of his days, which were long and full of base hits.

Collins never looked flashy in the infield. As one of his contemporaries put it, "Eddie looked like your aunt out there but he seemed to be in front of every ball that hit anywhere near him." Whether he looked flashy or not, there was no questioning the confidence of the young collegian. It wasn't very long until the American League hung the nickname of Cocky Collins on Eddie because of his self-assurance.

Black Jack Barry from Holy Cross also broke into the Athletic lineup in 1908 and so did Franklin (Home Run) Baker. Barry played short alongside of Collins, while Baker was at third. A year later the trio of youngsters were joined by a nineteen-year-old infielder, one John (Stuffy) McInnis who thought he was a short-stop. By 1911, Stuffy was the regular first baseman of the famous $100,000 infield, a unit which, offensively or defensively, will stand comparison with any which has been assembled by one ball club since.

Collins broke in with the best and was one of the best of the best. He played on a ball club which might have won five straight pennants, something no major league team ever has accomplished. The A's won in 1910 and 1911, missed out in 1912, and won again in 1913 and 1914, after which Mack broke up his great machine and sold his players in all directions, getting $50,000 from the White Sox for Eddie.

Collins was in his first World Series when he was twenty-three and was in three more by the time he was twenty-seven. His reputation as a money player is justified by any examination of his Series records. Eddie is the only player ever to hit better than .400 in three World Series and he never played in a Series without stealing at least one base, holding the record for total World Series thefts with fourteen.

Collins demonstrated his extraordinary skill by functioning

smoothly with two great baseball machines—the Athletics of
1910–1914 and the White Sox of 1917–1919. How far the latter
team might have gone had it not been for the larceny in the souls
of some of its key-members there is no telling.

The two clubs were as different "as night and day," to quote
Eddie himself. The Athletics, under the smooth handling of
Mack, were as united as a happy family. With the White Sox,
it was like having the in-laws over every night. The Sox were
riven by personal jealousies and bickering, often close to breaking out in open fist fighting in the clubhouse. Some of the key
players weren't on speaking terms. Collins, himself, never spoke
to Chick Gandil, the first baseman, off the field for two years.

In the heat of the battle between Chicago and Boston for the
1917 pennant race, Gandil proposed that the White Sox take up a
collection for the Detroit players as a "reward" for beating the
Red Sox in a series. The Tigers were to get $1,000 for "bearing
down" against Boston. This was a common practice of the period
until Judge Kenesaw Mountain Landis became commissioner of
baseball and put a stern stop to the euphemism known as "pres-
ents." It was the Judge's quaint idea that ball clubs were paid by
their employers to "bear down" for all of the 154 games they
played.

When Gandil, the self-appointed collector, turned over the pool
to the Tigers it was $150 short. Collins, assessed at $45 for his
share, refused to pay until the 1917 World Series actually was in
progress. The collecting done by Gandil did nothing to improve
relations between the first baseman and Eddie.

Despite his personal dislike for many of the members of the
White Sox teams, a dislike which was present before their perfidy
in the 1919 World Series with Cincinnati, Collins more than once
called it the greatest baseball team ever assembled, rating it
over even his own Athletic teams which romped through the
American League a few years earlier.

In many respects the 1917 World Series was even daffier than
the 1919 one, except that it was played on its merits. The White
Sox met the Giants and in every one of the six games, McGraw
started a left-hander against the American Leaguers. Clarence
(Pants) Rowland, since president of the Pacific Coast League, but

then an obscure busher out of Peoria, managed the Sox to the pennant and although he used five pitchers in the Series, all but two innings were pitched by two men. Big Ed Faber, master of the spitball, pitched 27 innings and Eddie Cicotte, of shine-ball fame, pitched 23 innings. Williams and Danforth each pitched one inning and Russell pitched no innings at all, even though he was the starting pitcher in the fifth game in which he failed to retire a batter.

The Sox won the first two games in Chicago but the Giants returned to New York and evened it up with two shutout victories in the Polo Grounds. In Chicago, the Sox took the fifth game and the clubs returned to the banks of the Harlem for the sixth game.

McGraw started a southpaw for the sixth time, opening with Rube Benton against Red Faber. The first three innings were scoreless and Collins opened the fourth with a sharp grounder to Heinie Zimmerman at third, which Der Zim fielded but threw wildly, Eddie sprinting to second. Davey Robertson muffed Joe Jackson's fly and Collins took third.

Hap Felsch hit back at Benton and Rube threw to Zim, hanging up Collins between third and home. Eddie hop-scotched toward the plate, hoping to become involved in a prolonged rundown, which would give the other base runners a chance to advance. Bill Rariden, the Giant catcher, came down the line to meet him. Suddenly Collins saw a chance and he made a dash past Rariden and on to the uncovered plate with Der Zim in mad, but futile, pursuit.

Zimmerman chasing Collins home has gone down in baseball history as one of the bonehead classics of all time and regrettably so, for Heinie had no choice but to chase Collins. McGraw always blamed Walter Holke, his first baseman, for not coming down to cover the plate and even held that Benton was not without censure for not coming in to protect the dish.

Actually the play was the result of the opportunism of Collins. When Eddie saw that Rariden was close enough for him to get past with a dash he did so. There was nobody between Collins and the plate, nobody between Zimmerman and Collins but Rariden, weighed down by his catching impedimenta.

Zimmerman was understandably bitter about the reputation he

received from this play. As Heinie said of his critics, "Who the hell did they expect me to throw the ball to—Klem?" Bill Klem was the plate umpire.

The passage of time has dimmed the facts and, in recent years, there actually was a story in print that Collins deliberately started his run for the plate at a slow pace to lure Zimmerman into

EDWARD TROWBRIDGE (EDDIE) COLLINS

Born May 2, 1887, Millerton, N. Y.
Height 5′ 9″. Weight 175. Batted left, threw right.

YEAR	CLUB	LEAGUE	POS	G	AB	R	H	2B	3B	HR	RBI	BA
1906	Philadelphia (A)	Amer.	3B-SS	6	15	1	3	0	0	0	—	.200
1907	Philadelphia	Amer.	SS	14	25	0	8	0	0	0	3	.320
1907	Newark	East.	SS	4	16	6	7	0	0	0	—	.43⁘
1908	Philadelphia	Amer.	OF-IF	102	330	39	90	18	7	1	37	.27⁘
1909	Philadelphia	Amer.	2B	153	572	104	198	30	10	3	80	.34⁘
1910	Philadelphia	Amer.	2B	153	583	81	188	16	15	3	80	.32⁘
1911	Philadelphia	Amer.	2B	132	493	92	180	22	13	3	71	.36⁘
1912	Philadelphia	Amer.	2B	153	543	137	189	25	11	0	66	.34⁘
1913	Philadelphia	Amer.	2B	148	534	125	184	23	13	3	75	.34⁘
1914	Philadelphia †	Amer.	2B	152	526	122	181	23	14	2	81	.34⁘
1915	Chicago	Amer.	2B	155	521	118	173	22	10	4	78	.33⁘
1916	Chicago	Amer.	2B	155	545	87	168	14	17	0	56	.30⁘
1917	Chicago	Amer.	2B	156	564	91	163	18	12	0	67	.28⁘
1918	Chicago	Amer.	2B	97	330	51	91	8	2	2	32	.27⁘
1919	Chicago	Amer.	2B	140	518	87	165	19	7	4	73	.31⁘
1920	Chicago	Amer.	2B	153	601	115	222	37	13	3	75	.36⁘
1921	Chicago	Amer.	2B	139	526	79	177	20	10	2	58	.33⁘
1922	Chicago	Amer.	2B	154	598	92	194	20	12	1	69	.32⁘
1923	Chicago	Amer.	2B	145	505	89	182	22	5	5	67	.36⁘
1924	Chicago	Amer.	2B	152	556	108	194	27	7	6	86	.34⁘
1925	Chicago	Amer.	2B	118	425	80	147	26	3	3	80	.34⁘
1926	Chicago ‡	Amer.	2B	106	375	66	129	32	4	1	62	.34⁘
1927	Philadelphia	Amer.	2B	95	225	50	76	12	1	1	15	.33⁘
1928	Philadelphia	Amer.	SS-PH	36	33	3	10	3	0	0	7	.30⁘
1929	Philadelphia	Amer.	PH	9	7	0	0	0	0	0	0	.000
1930	Philadelphia	Amer.	PH	3	2	1	1	0	0	0	0	.500
	Major League Totals			2826	9952	1818	3313	437	186	47	1318	.333

(A) Played under name of Sullivan
† Sold to Chicago White Sox for $50,000
‡ Released as manager by Chicago White Sox, November 11, 1926; signed with Philadelphia Athletics, December 23, 1926

WORLD SERIES RECORD

YEAR	CLUB	LEAGUE	POS	G	AB	R	H	2B	3B	HR	RBI	BA
1910	Philadelphia	Amer.	2B	5	21	5	9	4	0	0	1	.429
1911	Philadelphia	Amer.	2B	6	21	4	6	1	0	0	2	.286
1913	Philadelphia	Amer.	2B	5	19	5	8	0	2	0	3	.421
1914	Philadelphia	Amer.	2B	4	14	0	3	0	0	0	1	.214
1917	Chicago	Amer.	2B	6	22	4	9	1	0	0	2	.409
1919	Chicago	Amer.	2B	8	31	2	7	1	0	0	0	.226
	World Series Totals			34	128	20	42	7	2	0	9	.328

Manager, Chicago White Sox, 1925–26
Coach, Philadelphia Athletics, June 1931–32
Vice-president, Boston Red Sox, 1933–
Elected to Hall of Fame, 1938

chasing him. Nothing could be more ridiculous. Once Eddie had dashed by Rariden, there was nothing to stop him from scoring unless Zim could overtake him. It didn't matter to Collins whether Heinie chased him or not, as long as he didn't catch him.

Collins played three times in a World Series against McGraw's Giants and was on the winning side each time, with the Athletics in 1911 and 1913 and with the White Sox in 1917. In the first meeting of Eddie and Mac in a Series, Collins failed to hit .300 but McGraw was quick to recognize the ability of the ex-collegian.

"Collins," said John J. after the Series, "was the greatest player on the field for either team."

It was indeed high praise, for McGraw was not extravagant with his compliments, particularly to American League players.

During the second decade of this century, the American League was dominated by three clubs—the Athletics, the Red Sox and the White Sox. No other team won a pennant between 1910 and 1919. The A's won in 1910, 1911, 1913 and 1914; the Red Sox in 1912, 1915, 1916 and 1918, Chicago in 1917 and 1919. Collins played in six World Series, a better than fair percentage.

The last eight years of Collins' career as a regular were spent with teams which were not in the thick of pennant contention, although the White Sox in 1920 might have won if the facts of the fixed World Series had not come out in the final days of the pennant race. Yet, first division or second division, Eddie went right on collecting his base hits. Collins spent nineteen seasons in the American League as a regular and in sixteen of those seasons hit over .300, both in the era of the dead ball and the jackrabbit.

A teammate once was asked why a fellow as smart as Collins stooped to the superstition of removing the wad of gum from the top of his cap and placing it in his mouth when the count went to two strikes against him.

"Eddie ain't superstitious," explained the ball player. "He just thinks it's unlucky not to get base hits."

CHAPTER V

DIZZY LIKE A FOX

Jay Hanna Dean

IT WAS A perfect indian-summer Saturday afternoon at Sportsman's Park in St. Louis but not many of the crowd of 37,492 showed much interest in the weather. The fact that the Gas House Gang seemed about to rally against Detroit in the fourth inning was more important.

Mickey Cochrane's Tigers, losers to Dizzy Dean in the first game and Paul Dean in the third, were battling to even the 1934 World Series. And doing a good job of it, too. Detroit had knocked Tex Carleton out in the third and picked up another run against Dazzy Vance in the top of the fourth to lead 4 to 2. Pinch hitter Virgil Davis singled home a run for the Cards and sent the tying run to third.

Things were looking up and a roar went from the crowd as Dizzy Dean dashed to first base as a pinch runner for Davis. Dean, a thirty-game winner that season, was the idol of the city, indeed, of the entire league.

Pepper Martin slapped a grounder to Charley Gehringer at second, who deftly ferried the ball to Billy Rogell for a forceout of Dean. As Rogell cocked his arm to throw to first in an effort to double up Martin, Diz leaped high in the air and took the throw squarely in the center of his forehead. The ball caromed off to right field, Dean dropped as if he had been pole-axed and Leo Durocher came home from third with the run that tied the game at 4 to 4.

There was a hush over the crowd as Dean stretched inert on the diamond. Doc Weaver, the Cardinal trainer, Coaches Mike Gonzales and Buzzy Wares and Brother Paul formed a foursome to lug the stricken athlete from the premises. He was rushed to the hospital and it was assumed he would be out of the remainder of the Series.

Paul set newspapermen right about that that evening. "Diz'll probably pitch tomorrow," he laconically informed Joe Williams of the Scripps-Howard chain. "Warn't hurt much. Just hit on the haid."

"Was he unconscious when you helped carry him from the field?" asked Williams.

"Oh, no," said Paul. "Diz warn't unconscious at all. Was talking all the time, in fact."

"What was he saying?" persisted Joe.

"Nuthin'," said Paul. "Jest talkin'."

When Dean first burst on the baseball scene, he was interviewed at every stop. And he invariably told different stories. His birthplace has been listed as Lucas, Arkansas, and also as Holdenville, Oklahoma. His birthday has been recorded as being in January and August and the year has been set anywhere from 1909 to 1912. As far as that goes, he has told some people his proper name was Jay Hanna and others that it was Jerome Herman. The result has been a grand confusion, with historians finally settling for January 16, 1911, for his natal date, Lucas, Arkansas, as the place of his birth and Jay Hanna Dean as his baptismal name.

Dean always has an explanation for the discrepancies in autobiographical material he supplies. "Like to give all the boys scoops," he says with a wink. He explained the name switch from Jay Hanna to Jerome Herman with a human interest story. When he was six or seven a playmate of his, named Jerome Herman, died and, in an effort to console the boy's father, Diz told him he would take the dead boy's name for his own.

It could be true, too, for the line between fact and fancy is hard to find when the narrator is Dizzy Dean. He made a policy of telling sports writers what they wanted to hear, or what he thought they wanted to hear.

Leo Durocher can be an entertaining speaker, although you won't find any umpires who will agree. The Lip's fund of stories about Dizzy are limitless, humorous and possibly mostly apocryphal. In his trips to North Africa, Italy and the Pacific as a USO-

Camp Shows performer, Durocher was a big hit with his stories to the armed forces about Dean. Most of Durocher's stories concerned Dean and his altercations with Frankie Frisch. Frank was inclined to take a dim view of Leo's fame as a raconteur.

"Those stories are awfully funny when Durocher tells them," granted Frisch, "but, then, he was only playing with Diz—he didn't have to manage him." There were surely times when Frisch must have wondered whether it was worth while to have the best pitcher in baseball on your side when the best pitcher in baseball happened to be as much of an individualist as Dizzy Dean.

Dean was as prankish, if that's not too mild a word, as were the rest of the Gas Housers whom Frisch managed, but Diz also was insubordinate. There was the time in 1934 when he refused to go with the Cardinals to an exhibition game in Detroit and persuaded Brother Paul to stay home with him.

Another day at the Polo Grounds, Frisch called on Dean to warm up to start the game and discovered the great man was in the clubhouse. Frank scooted pell-mell to center field and up the steps to find out what the trouble was. There was Dizzy seated in front of his locker nonchalantly staring into space.

"What's up?" demanded Frisch.

"I tell ya, Flash," answered Dizzy, "I've decided to quit. I'm thinking of buying a farm and raising peanuts."

Instead of exploding, as Dean had expected and which was the reason behind almost of all of Diz's gags, Frisch quietly sat down beside him.

"I envy you," said Frank. "I wish I had enough money to quit. It must be nice and quiet on a peanut farm. No more dashing around the country with dopey ballplayers, no more yelling crowds, no more World Series worries. That's the life."

And, pausing to sigh with just the proper tone of regret, Frisch stood up and started for the door. "Within five minutes that Dizzy was on the field and in uniform, begging to pitch," relates the Fordham Flash. "He must have dressed like a fireman."

Not all of Frisch's troubles with Dean ended as pleasantly as that. In 1937, Carl Hubbell and the Giants were beating Diz at Sportsman's Park and Dean didn't like it. He began to take his own sweet time about pitching and forced Umpire George Barr to invoke a rarely enforced rule about the pitcher delaying the game by holding the ball too long.

Dean blew his top—and almost blew the top off Jimmy Ripple, who happened to be the Giant batter at the time. One close pitch dropped Jimmy and he then bunted the next one toward first. Ripple's intentions were plain. It was the traditional retaliatory move of a batter who thinks the pitcher is trying to bean him. Jimmy wanted to bunt so as to force Dean to cover first base, where he would be a target for spikes. Dean took the challenge and in no time he and Ripple were locked in combat.

Neither Ripple nor Dean was injured but the resulting melee involved both squads on a grand scale riot. And its repercussions spread even farther. Speaking across the Mississippi at Belleville, Illinois, a few days later, Dean remarked that in his opinion President Ford Frick of the National League and Umpire Barr were "a couple of crooks."

Dean was promptly suspended until he apologized. President Sam Breadon of the Cards, who didn't want his drawing card sidelined, pleaded with Frick. There were some hasty meetings, one in Philadelphia and another in New York, as the Cards were moving East. Dean refused to retract, apologize or repudiate his Belleville statements. When a watered-down statement was prepared for his signature, he stonily declared, "I ain't signin' nuthin'."

It was an impasse—and it was costing Frisch the services of his best pitcher and Breadon his box-office value. It was Frick who took a realistic view and restored Dean to active duty. Diz's first start was against the Giants and he won handily.

However much of a headache Dean may have been to Frisch it is safe to say that the headaches he distributed among opposing players balanced it off. His performance, and that of his brother Paul, was truly magnificent in 1934. Dean won thirty games that year, something no major leaguer has done since, while Paul won nineteen as a freshman, and each won two games in the World Series against Detroit, Diz pitching a shutout in the seventh game with only one day between starts.

After being beaned in the fourth game as already described, Dean came back the next day and lost to Tommy Bridges by 3 to 1. The victory of the little curve-baller over the great Diz put the Tigers in front, three games to two, and they returned to Navin Field needing only an even break for the pot of gold. They might have had it, too, had it not been for the Deans. Young Paul beat Schoolboy Rowe to even up the Series and left it up to Diz for the pay-off game.

As Durocher tells the story, Frisch had some doubts about starting Dizzy, who had been conked by Rogell's throw on Saturday, pitched eight innings in a losing cause Sunday and had only Monday to rest.

"How do you feel, Diz?" asked the solicitous Frisch.

"Wotta ya mean, how do I feel?" asked the indignant Dean. "Ya wanna *win,* don't ya?"

Dean was late appearing for his warm-up chores, having spent some time in front of the Detroit bench observing the warm-up motions of Eldon Auker, the under-handed right-hander upon whom Manager Cochrane was staking all. Mickey noticed Dean stalking Auker and advised him to get over where he belonged.

"Hey, Mike," yelled Dean in mock concern, "is *he* gonna pitch? Is *he* the best ya got?"

This brought forth only roars from the outraged Cochrane, and Dean plodded toward the Cardinal bench, shaking his head sadly and muttering, "Won't do. Won't do."

The game itself turned out to be a travesty when the Cardinals scored seven times in the third inning, which Dean himself started with a double to left. Dean, as a matter of fact, got another single in this inning, thus equaling a World Series batting record held by only seven other players. The pay-off blow was contributed by Frisch himself, a double which emptied the bases. As Dean dashed across the plate and into the Cardinal dugout he shouted, "That's all, boys! I said one run was all I needed and I brought it in myself. The others don't matter."

Dean was as good as his word. He blanked the Tigers all the way and the Gas House Gang won 11 to 0.

It was that 1934 World Series which brought Pappy Dean back into the fold. Albert Monroe Dean joined the Series when it reached St. Louis, after the first two games had been played in Detroit. According to Diz, he and Paul sent their dad the money to fly up from Houston, Texas, but the father decided to come by bus. He was intercepted at Sullivan, Missouri, by a St. Louis reporter who drove him in the rest of the way.

Dean, senior, talked with tongue in cheek, too. He talked of the early poverty of the family, surely no exaggeration, but then went on to tell tall tales of the marksmanship of his two sons in bagging squirrels by flinging stones. Diz, he claimed, could bag 'em with either arm and preferred to do it left-handed so as not to bruise them.

This astonishing statement brought a dry remark from a writer to the effect that the feud between the Dean family and the squirrels seemed to be going on still.

"Could be," happily agreed Pappy with an outrageous wink.

Dean was one of five children. He never saw his oldest sister, Sara May, who died in infancy. Diz's oldest brother, Charlie, died at the age of nine and Dean was only three when his mother died. His brother Elmer was then five and Paul was two.

It was tough going to keep the family intact. The Deans were migratory workers, facing all the hardships of John Steinbeck's Joad family. They picked cotton wherever it was to be found and there was little time for schooling, nor any time for taking cognizance of child labor laws. Diz swears that Brother Elmer became separated from the family because the car in which Dad, Paul and Diz were riding crossed a railroad just ahead of a long freight train. The jalopy bearing Elmer was held up and it was some four years before the Deans were united again.

Branch Rickey was the first person to hear of Dean. Diz joined the army at sixteen—he says—and served over three years with the 12th Field Artillery in Texas, and when he came out landed a job with the San Antonio Public Service Co. He read meters and pitched for the company ball team. It was then that a passenger conductor wrote a letter to Rickey about him.

Then or now, the Mahatma was never one to pass up a prospect. He knew that far, far more pitchers are born than are made and he sent one of his scouts, Don Curtis, over to look at the kid.

Dean must have been a sight for a scout's eyes. He was, according to his own statistics, nineteen—tall, rangy, strong and loose, a nonchalant athlete who could be great and knew it. The report sent in by Curtis was good enough to have Rickey order the boy to a Cardinal tryout camp at Shawnee, Oklahoma. Just watching Dean in action was enough for the Mahatma.

Dean was signed to a contract to pitch for St. Joseph, Missouri, in the Western League and he promptly tore it apart. He won seventeen games, losing eight, and then was moved to the Cardinal farm at Houston in the Texas League. The Texas was two notches higher than the Western but it looked just the same to Diz, who had an 8–2 record with the Buffs before being called up to finish out the 1930 season with the Cardinals.

Dean immediately began badgering Manager Gabby Street for a chance to pitch, although the Cardinals were in a red-hot pennant fight with the Dodgers, Cubs and Giants. The Ole Sarge finally gave in on the last day of the season and Dean whipped the Pirates with a three-hitter, giving them exactly one run.

Dean should have remained with the Cardinals right then for he was a major league pitcher from the very moment he threw a ball in the tryout camp in Oklahoma. The Cards were riding high and Rickey figured the pennant was coming up the next year again and that another year in the minors might take some of the brashness out of Dean. He was right about the pennant but wrong about Diz.

There was trouble at the training camp in Bradenton, Florida, with Dean. He took his time reporting, he talked big and he was in hock. Ballplayers now get a $25 weekly allowance in the training camp for tips and sundries but that wasn't so in 1931. Dean, who hadn't been making any money from which to save any, tried desperately to live on the buck-a-day Secretary Clarence Lloyd advanced him but the lure of the slot machines and the poker games was too much.

Shipped back to Houston, Dean just romped through the Texas League. He won 26 games, which is only half the story. Diz fanned 303 batters in 304 innings and had an earned run average of 1.53. More important than his pitching was the fact that during the summer he wooed and won Miss Patricia Nash, who was to be as great an asset to the pitcher as his fast ball and to last considerably longer. She still is at Dean's side wherever he goes and deserves no small amount of credit for the fact that Diz became a successful television reporter and, even more important, a successful businessman.

When Dean came up to the Cardinals as a regular in 1932, he joined a World's Championship club but one which had fallen apart. His record was an ordinary 18–15, but he led the National League in strikeouts, as he did for the next three seasons, and he worked nearly 300 innings.

The aura of greatness was about Dean in 1932, even though the Cards finished in an inglorious tie for sixth place. Diz, working for $3,000 a year—there was no $5,000 minimum in the majors then—ran into the usual monetary difficulties. He spent so much money in long distance calls to his wife when the team was on the road that Pat decided it would be cheaper to make the trips with him.

It was in his first season in the majors that Dean "bunted a home run," as the story is told. Actually, Diz bunted a double but, to all intents and purposes, it was as good as a home run. He was pitching against the Giants one Sunday in St. Louis and came to bat with men on first and second and a bunt in order.

Dean bunted a pop fly toward third which sailed over the head of Johnny Vergez, who was playing in. It was retrieved by the left fielder—Len Koenecke, if memory serves—who threw wildly to second base to head off the flying Dean. The ball eventually was run down in the right field bull pen by, of all people, Shanty Hogan, the Giant catcher, Diz was home free by then.

For the next four years after the 1932 season, Dean was one of the greatest pitchers baseball ever has seen. He won a total of 102 games while losing fifty and seemed unbeatable when the mood seized him. Relaxed and easygoing, Dean only bore down when he had to. His earned-run averages during the seasons from 1933 to 1936 were good but not startling. His thirty victories in 1934 was, of course, the high mark, making him the first National League pitcher to win thirty since Grover Alexander in 1917. And the only one since then.

On September 21, 1934, the Cardinals played a double-header against Casey Stengel's Dodgers at Ebbets Field. These were two games which had previously been rained out and were squeezed in on what had been an open date. Had it been impossible to play them, the Cards could have lost the pennant. Also, it might be mentioned, had the Cards not won them, they would have lost the pennant. These were indeed "money games."

Diz pitched the opening game and won easily, 13 to 0. He was in front 7 to 0 as early as the third and he gave up just three hits. Brother Paul stepped to the rubber in the nightcap and flung a classic into the teeth of the Dodgers. He got the first two batters, Buzz Boyle and Lonnie Frey, and then walked Len Koenecke. The ill-fated Koenecke, who was to die in a plane crash a year later, was the last Dodger to reach first base, Paul retiring the next 25 batters in succession. The pass to Koenecke was all that kept him from a perfect game, something the majors haven't seen since Charley Robertson hurled one for the White Sox against Detroit in 1922.

After Paul's feat, Diz paid him the usual compliments and then said, "Shucks, Paul, if I'da knowed you wuz gonna pitch a no-hitter, I'da throwed one myself."

The chances are he could have, too, for it was before that game that Dean wandered into the Brooklyn clubhouse and told the astonished Dodgers precisely how he intended to pitch to each of them. On another occasion Diz walked by the Boston Braves bench and announced, "I'm throwin' nuthin' but curve balls today, fellas. No fast balls." He kept his word and won easily.

It was a batter who eventually brought Dean to earth, though, and a batter he rarely pitched against. Earl Averill, the Cleveland outfielder, accomplished this in the All-Star game of 1937 at Washington.

Joe McCarthy loaded the American League lineup with Yankees against the Nationals. He had Red Rolfe, Lou Gehrig, Joe DiMaggio, Bill Dickey and Lefty Gomez of the Yanks in the starting nine against Dean. The game was scoreless until the third when DiMaggio singled with two out. Gehrig, who had been fanned by a fast ball in the first inning, hit one practically out of sight.

Averill followed Gehrig and he lashed a drive through the box which struck Diz on the toe, bounded off to second base, where Billy Herman retrieved it and threw Earl out at first. It was the last out of the inning and it ended Dean's prescribed three-inning stint. As a consequence, the full extent of Averill's smash wasn't learned until the Cards moved into New York the next day.

It developed that Dean had a fractured toe, a diagnosis which made Diz snort, "Fractured, hell! It's broke!" Dean tried to pitch too soon and altered his stride and his graceful sweep. The awkward motion strained unused muscles in his arm and Diz came up with his first—and his last—sore arm.

Even though Dean was through, he still had market value. Informed in advance of the condition of Diz's arm, Phil Wrigley, owner of the Cubs, gave up $185,000 and two players for Dean. One of the players, Curt Davis, later became a twenty-game winner for the Cards. The deal was made just before the opening of the 1938 season.

Dean had nothing with the Cubs, nothing but his native pitching sense and great control. It was enough to give him a 7–1 record and, with Chicago nosing out the Pirates for the pennant, Dean's record was of vast importance. He couldn't pitch any longer but he was worth the $185,000 Wrigley had paid for him.

After Red Ruffing had scored an easy 12–6 win for the Yanks in the World Series opener at Wrigley Field, Lefty Gomez, who never lost a Series game, faced Dizzy Dean in the second game at Chicago. Pitching with nothing but his head and his heart, the great Diz stood off the Yankees for eight innings.

Dean had a 3–2 lead going into the eighth and both New York runs came as the result of a freak play when Stan Hack and Billy Jurges crashed together trying to field Joe Gordon's slow roller to the left side of the infield. It dribbled through them to the outfield for a fluke double and two runs scored.

In the next five innings, Diz faced only fifteen batters, par for the course. He gave up one hit, a single to Gehrig, but Lou was wrapped up in a double play. George Selkirk opened the eighth with a single but was forced by Gordon who, in turn, was forced by Myril Hoag, pinch-hitting for Gomez.

Frankie Crosetti, batting .143 at the moment, came up. The Crow, as the Yanks call him, was a cagey hitter, if not a great one. He worked Dean to a three-and-two count and fouled off several pitches, each of them taking something from Diz's arm and from his stamina. Frankie was too cute to go for the corner pitches and Dean finally came through with one. Crosetti smashed it into the left field bleachers and the Yanks were in front, 4 to 3.

What happened after that was anticlimactic, although Dean summoned enough life from his dead arm to fan Rolfe and close out the eighth. When the ninth came around, Diz had only two more pitches left in his arm. Tommy Henrich hit the first for a single and DiMaggio hit the next up against a firehouse outside the left field wall. Dean walked sadly from the mound.

It was really the end of the Dean story, although Diz came back to pitch relief in the last inning of the fourth game, which the Yankees won by 8 to 3.

Dean went to the Texas League in 1940, came back to the Cubs, but the old fire was gone. He eventually came back to baseball as a broadcaster and then a telecaster and his fame was such that the Browns hired him to pitch on the final game of the 1947 season, purely as a gate attraction. Diz pitched four innings, allowed

JAY HANNA DEAN

Born January 16, 1911 at Lucas, Ark.
Height, 6′ 3″. Weight, 202. Threw and batted right-handed.

YEAR	CLUB	LEAGUE	G	IP	W	L	PCT	H	R	ER	SO	BB	ERA
1930	St. Joseph	Western	32	217	17	8	.680	204	118	89	134	77	3.69
1930	Houston	Texas	14	85	8	2	.800	62	31	27	95	49	2.82
1930	St. Louis	Nat.	1	9	1	0	1.000	3	1	1	5	3	1.00
1931	Houston	Texas	41	304	26	10	.722	210	71	53	303	90	1.53
1932	St. Louis	Nat.	46	286	18	15	.545	280	122	105	191	102	3.30
1933	St. Louis	Nat.	48	293	20	18	.526	279	113	99	199	64	3.04
1934	St. Louis	Nat.	50	312	30	7	.811	288	110	92	195	75	2.65
1935	St. Louis	Nat.	50	324	28	12	.700	326	128	112	182	82	3.11
1936	St. Louis	Nat.	51	315	24	13	.649	310	128	111	195	53	3.17
1937	St. Louis *	Nat.	27	197	13	10	.565	200	76	59	120	33	2.70
1938	Chicago	Nat.	13	75	7	1	.875	63	20	15	22	8	1.80
1939	Chicago	Nat.	19	96	6	4	.600	98	40	36	27	17	3.38
1940	Chicago	Nat.	10	54	3	3	.500	68	35	31	18	20	5.17
1940	Tulsa	Texas	21	142	8	8	.500	149	69	50	51	19	3.17
1941	Chicago †	Nat.	1	1	0	0	.000	3	3	2	1	0	18.00
1947	St. Louis ‡	Amer.	1	4	0	0	.000	3	0	0	0	1	0.00
	Major League Totals		317	1966	150	83	.644	1931	776	663	1155	458	3.03

WORLD SERIES RECORD

YEAR	CLUB	LEAGUE	G	IP	W	L	PCT	H	R	ER	SO	BB	ERA
1934	St. Louis	Nat.	3	26	2	1	.667	20	6	5	17	5	1.73
1938	Chicago	Nat.	2	8⅓	0	1	.000	8	6	6	2	1	6.75
	World Series Totals		5	34⅓	2	2	.500	28	12	11	19	6	2.88

ALL-STAR GAME RECORD

YEAR	LEAGUE	IP	W	L	PCT	H	R	ER	SO	BB	ER
1934	National	3	0	0	.000	5	1	1	4	1	3.0
1935	National	1	0	0	.000	1	0	0	1	1	0.0
1936	National	3	1	0	1.000	0	0	0	3	2	0.0
1937	National	3	0	1	.000	4	2	2	2	1	6.0
	All-Star Game Totals	10	1	1	.500	10	3	3	10	5	2.7

* Traded to Chicago for Pitchers Curt Davis and Clyde Shoun and $185,000, April 16, 1938.

† Released as player and signed as coach with Chicago Clubs, May 14, 1941; retired as coach to accept baseball broadcasting job in St. Louis, July 12, 1941.

‡ Signed by St. Louis Browns to pitch final game of 1947 season as gate attraction.

no runs and made a single in his only time at bat to be credited with a batting average of 1.000 in his only American League appearance.

It was a fantastic finish, but then Dizzy was a fantastic guy!

CHAPTER VI

THE YANKEE CLIPPER

Joseph Paul DiMaggio

THINGS WERE pretty hilarious in the Yankee dressing room after the second game of the 1947 World Series. The Dodgers had been easy in the first two games and the general belief was that there would be no more baseball in Yankee Stadium that fall. The three games in Ebbets Field should wind it up. Maybe, even, three wouldn't be necessary. It could be wound up in two, in the traditional four-game sweep of the Bronx Bombers.

Relaxed and pleased, but not exactly hilarious, Joe DiMaggio sprawled on a stool in front of his locker, the second from the last on the right-hand side. He had loosened his baseball trousers and unbuttoned his blouse. He was drawing lazily and contentedly on a cigarette, the picture of a man who was taking his ease after a job well done. The shower could wait.

One of the reporters in the little knot clustered around DiMaggio wanted to know if he had any explanation for the troubles which had beset the Dodgers' Pete Reiser in center field that afternoon. Pete, and the rival left fielders, Gene Hermanski of the Dodgers and Johnny Lindell, seemed bedeviled by the sun.

Quickly DiMag went to the defense of his brother outfielders, explaining that in the late fall afternoons the shadows in Yankee Stadium were very tricky and that the situation was complicated with a big crowd, since the combined smoke from sixty or seventy thousand fans threw a haze before the stands which gave the left and center fielders a difficult background.

Bob Cooke, of the New York *Herald Tribune,* took this as a logical explanation for the troubles of Reiser, Hermanski and Lindell but a thought struck him. He said:

"Well, Joe, how about yourself? Doesn't this haze and tricky background bother you?"

DiMaggio looked at Cooke almost without expression. He waited a second or two and then said, grinningly, "Now, Bob, you aren't going to start worrying about the 'old boy' now, are you?"

It was the first time, perhaps the only time, anybody ever heard DiMaggio refer to himself in the third person. "I realized then," said Cooke in retelling the story, "that Joe had been explaining about the hazards the background presented to *ordinary* outfielders. It never even occurred to him that he might have trouble out there."

DiMaggio had no desire to see Reiser, or any ballplayer, criticized for defensive lapses which could be excused. He could excuse those lapses but, of course, he couldn't excuse them in himself. In fact, he never even thought about the possibility of a lapse and, therefore, of the need of an excuse for one.

DiMaggio was one of baseball's picture hitters. He employed a wide open stance, standing well back in the box, feet planted firmly and well apart. His stride was short, five or six inches, and he did a minimum of preliminary bat-waggling. His right elbow was fairly close to his side, the bat held at the extreme end and on his right shoulder. If Joe were to take the same stance, discard his bat and extend his left arm straight out, he would look like an old boxing print of John L. Sullivan with the right hand cocked close to his breast.

The stance was the same one Joe used when he was a preteenage kid, playing on the old Horse Lot of San Francisco. The only advice the Clipper ever received on batting was a tip or two from Lefty O'Doul, when the latter was managing the Seals just before Joe came to the majors. And these did not alter his stance but consisted of advice on how to pull the ball. Since DiMaggio batted with his feet apart, he pulled almost every pitch to left field.

A right-handed pull-hitter such as DiMaggio was at a disadvantage at Yankee Stadium, which was custom-built for Babe Ruth and the many left-handed pull-hitters the Yanks have had since. Once in a great while, Joe hit to right field but most of his hits into that territory were the result of late timing, with only a few being deliberately placed to right.

"I'm paid to hit the long ball," DiMaggio explained one time, "and I can hit the long ball only to left. If I tried to hit to right, I'd probably lose the groove of my swing and wind up being able to hit to neither field."

DiMaggio's stance made him the picture of nonchalance at the plate. He seemed completely relaxed and comfortable, which he insisted was the only recipe for a satisfactory stance. Joe didn't say other batters should copy his stance but that no batter should employ a stance in which he felt uncomfortable. The very nature of DiMag's stance made him a late swinger. Some of Joe's best hits came, as the players phrase it, "right out of the catcher's glove."

One ball game DiMaggio invariably referred to when seized upon by a soul-searching interviewer was the All-Star game of 1936, played at Braves Field. That was DiMag's freshman year and he entered the game with a feeling that the world, or at least, the American League, was his oyster. Joe always thought that that game, in which he played an uncertain outfield, went hitless, popped up and hit into a double play, was the poorest he ever played, considering its importance.

"I was just over-confident," he declared. "It was the first setback I had ever received in baseball, barring injuries, of course. On the ball field everything had run smoothly in my three years on the Pacific Coast League, and there was no appreciable difference during my half-season in the American League. I was going great and it looked as though the game had been invented for my special benefit.

"When that 1936 All-Star game was over, I was the saddest, bluest guy you ever saw in the clubhouse. I'd been up five times without getting the ball out of the infield, had gummed up two balls in the outfield and left several runners stranded. The papers did a pretty good job on me, which I deserved. This was my first national game, so to speak, and I turned out to be a Grade A bust."

Joe McCarthy, who managed the Yankees during DiMaggio's first eight seasons, was the American League All-Star manager that afternoon and he stopped by DiMag's locker for a brief moment. "Don't let it get you down, kid," said McCarthy. Just that and no more.

DiMaggio didn't let the incident get him down but he never let himself forget it, either. He learned an invaluable lesson that day, the lesson being that nothing comes easily. For all of his seeming nonchalance at the plate, his facility in hauling down drives in the outfield, DiMag never ceased to bear down. He made it look easy but he never took it easily.

No better proof of what the public expected of the Clipper can be offered than the fact that writers frequently refer to 1946 as Joe's "bad year." It was the only time in his first eleven years with the Yankees that he failed to hit .300, failed by a matter of seven base hits. He batted .290, knocked in 95 runs and hit 25 home runs. And that was in his first season back after three years in service, a season in which he was beset by personal troubles, as an attempted reconciliation with his wife failed, and harassed by a tangled financial status. It was DiMag's "bad year," all right, but 80 per cent of the players in the majors today would settle for one like it at the plate.

For a person who came from humble beginnings, DiMaggio had a strange disregard for a dollar. He wasn't a coal-oil Johnny but he always acted as though there were plenty more where it came from. It was after the 1947 World Series that DiMag got his first big contractual raise. It was then, at thirty-three, that he realized nobody could go on forever and then that he developed a consciousness of the need for security.

Joe was born in Martinez, California, on November 25, 1914, the eighth of nine children. His father, a Sicilian immigrant, moved his brood to San Francisco shortly after Joe was born and before the arrival of the ninth DiMaggio, Dominic.

The DiMaggio income stemmed from the fishing ventures of Papa DiMaggio and the older brothers and was precarious, to put it mildly. The Clipper looks back on those days without self-consciousness.

"We weren't poor in the sense that we were ever cold or hungry," he says, "but there never was any extra money in the house for luxuries. I can remember having to miss two movies which I wanted very much to see, Al Jolson's first talking picture, *The Jazz Singer*, and a war picture, *All Quiet On The Western Front*. I think they were charging two-bits in the movie houses in my neighborhood at that time but they might as well have been charging ten dollars. And I can remember walking two miles, or maybe more, to play ball and then walking back after the game was over. Even carfare was in the luxury class when I was a kid."

The queasy stomach which was to plague DiMaggio with ulcers when he was an adult was present even when he was a kid. He couldn't help out on the family fishing expeditions because the roll of the small boat and the odor of the fish made him ill. His part of the family chores was to clean and repair the boat and the fishing nets.

Joe, as well as all of his brothers, sought extra work to augment the family income. Restless, DiMaggio bounced around as an errand boy, odd-job "man" and the other run of the mill tasks by which boys acquire pocket money. With the DiMaggios, however, it wasn't pocket money, it was table money. Every cent he earned was turned over to the household. Joe recalled that his most lucrative job was selling newspapers, at which he sometimes made as much as a dollar a day. "Counting tips, of course," he added seriously.

On a balmy afternoon in March, 1949, DiMaggio, Phil Rizzuto, Yogi Berra were sipping beers at Egan's Grill on St. Petersburg Beach. Practice was over and throughout baseball a bottle of beer after a workout, or a game, is regarded as relaxing. Only DiMaggio didn't seem in the least relaxed. Rizzuto and Berra left to shoot a game of pool next door and a reporter asked Joe what made him so moody.

"That thing is growing back again," he said. "I can feel it every time I try to run hard. Maybe I'm through."

DiMag said more than that but that was the gist of it. Joe had played through most of the 1948 season with an excruciating pain in his right heel as the result of a calcium deposit known as a bone spur. He had been operated on for it in November, leaving the hospital in Baltimore on Thanksgiving Eve. Until after the New Year, he was practically a hermit in his hotel room, getting around on crutches. When the cast was removed and the crutches discarded, Joe was able to walk without pain and there was no reason to believe that the operation had not been 100 per cent successful.

When spring training opened March 1, at St. Petersburg, DiMaggio discovered he couldn't run without the same pain in his heel which had existed the year before. He flew back to Johns Hopkins immediately for X rays and was told that the spur was not growing back, as he feared. He returned to St. Pete but the evidence of the X rays and the opinions of the doctors did not convince the Clipper that the spur was not there. The same pain was there and that seemed more convincing to Joe than any amount of medical explanations.

It was after his return to St. Petersburg that he had the foregoing conversation at Egan's, the first time he ever voiced the fear that he might be through. That fear was to remain with DiMaggio for the rest of spring training and for nearly half of the American League season. Indeed, before the barnstorming tour on the way home was completed, Joe had again left the club, flying from Dallas, Texas, where he had to quit after two innings of exhibition play, to Baltimore for further treatments.

Casey Stengel, back from the minors to manage in the majors for the third time, handled DiMaggio with great understanding. Throughout the training period he allowed DiMag to judge when he should play and when he should not. When the regular season opened and it was apparent that DiMaggio was a cripple of uncertain status, Joe went into a blue funk.

Alone in his hotel room, DiMaggio brooded about being through. He began to wonder about his eyes going back on him, as well as his legs. He could get no satisfaction from doctors, for only rest could be prescribed. And Joe couldn't even rest, for he tossed wide awake half the night, ridden by nightmares in which he faced a future without baseball.

The miracle happened without advance signs. One morning his heel pained him when he put his foot upon the floor for the first time and the next morning it didn't pain him. He reported at Yankee Stadium, took batting practice until his palms were blistered.

Slowly he began to spend more time at the plate and finally took an outfield workout.

When Joe felt that he was ready, he told Manager Stengel he would like to play a few innings in a night exhibition game against the Giants. Casey told him to go as far as he liked and Joe, to his own surprise as much as that of anybody else, went the full nine innings. It was characteristic of DiMaggio, perhaps the greatest ballplayer of his time, that he chose to give himself his big test in an exhibition game. The Yankees were surprisingly leading the league and Joe didn't want to do anything to handicap them!

After the exhibition the Yanks moved on to Boston, to meet the Red Sox, their strongest rivals and a team, as it turned out, they were to beat for the pennant in the final game of the year. DiMaggio got a single on his first time at bat against Maurice McDermott, after having missed the first 66 games the Yankees played that year. Later in the game Joe blasted a home run over the left field fence and sent the Yankee bench into ecstasies. In the next game of the Series Joe hit two more home runs and in the third game he hit his fourth!

It was the most spectacular comeback in baseball history. DiMaggio became the most talked of person in baseball, maybe in America for the next few weeks. *Life* made him its cover boy, devoted six pages to his comeback and purportedly paid him $6,000 to put his by-line over the story.

Once back in the lineup, DiMag never let up. He was the outstanding player in the All-Star game at Ebbets Field with a double and single which drove in three runs and, proportionately, from his return in late June until he was stricken with virus pneumonia in mid-September, Joe's work matched that of any of his early years.

Two weeks before the end of the season, when the Red Sox began inching uncomfortably close to the Yankees, DiMaggio ran a fever and had to take to his bed. His ailment was diagnosed as virus pneumonia but there were rumors that he was a polio victim, so great is the power of exaggeration. And so mighty was the legend of the Clipper's hard luck.

With DiMaggio again in sick bay, the Red Sox caught and passed the Yankees in the last week of the season. Joe McCarthy's team came into Yankee Stadium on a Saturday, the penultimate day of the season, holding a one-game lead. The pennant was theirs if they could split the two remaining games.

It so happened that this Saturday had been designated as "Joe DiMaggio Day," a day conceived before he fell before the onslaughts of the virus. Weak, gaunt and haggard, 15 pounds underweight, Joe stood at home plate with his mother, his brothers and Little Joe by his side. He received gifts which ranged from a speedboat to an oil painting, from rosary beads to a gold belt buckle. And, of course, the customary automobile. Mayor William V. O'Dwyer and other civic dignitaries advanced on the public address system and told Joe how good he was. And then the game started and Joe went out and proved it!

Too weak to pull the ball, DiMag dropped a couple of hits into right field and the Yanks went on to win and tie up the pennant race. And, on Sunday, again with Joe hitting to right field instead of left, they beat the Red Sox again and won the pennant.

On the momentum of those two games with the Red Sox, the Yankees stormed through the World Series to defeat the Dodgers in five games. And, in the fifth game, played in Brooklyn, DiMaggio whaled a home run into the upper deck at Ebbets Field. The game, and the Series was over by then but the crowd stood as one man to give the Clipper an ovation as he trotted around the bases. Joe had come a long way since that March afternoon in Egan's Grill when he voiced the fear that he was through.

About the only period in DiMaggio's life when baseball wasn't the alpha and omega of his existence was when he was twelve years old and, inflamed by the exploits of two fellow San Franciscans, Maurice McLaughlin and Bill Johnston, he decided to become a tennis player. Within a year or two, Joe had forgotten about tennis and was firmly set on a baseball career. His older brother, Vince, was playing week-end ball and getting a couple of bucks for it and Joe decided that sandlot baseball would be the ideal medium through which to increase the family's bankroll.

Spike Hennessey, a scout for the San Francisco Seals, invited DiMaggio to work out with the club at the tag end of the 1932 season. Vince already had been recalled from a farm club where the Seals had him under contract. Augie Galan, the club's regular shortstop, received permission to leave for a Honolulu vacation before the season ended and Vince told Ike Caveney, the Seals' manager, that his kid brother Joe could fill in. Joe did just that and hit a triple off Ted Pillette, a former major leaguer, on his first time at bat in organized ball.

What DiMaggio showed at short in those few games was good enough for the Seals to bring him to training camp in 1933 and sign him to a contract, calling for $225 a month, before the season opened. Although listed as a shortstop, Joe got his first chance in the outfield and he's been there ever since.

All DiMaggio had at eighteen was a natural ability to hit a baseball. The niceties of the game were to be acquired later. "I was really pea-green," confessed Joe looking back through the years. "I remember a reporter asking me for a 'quote' on something or other and I was so dumb I didn't even know what a 'quote' was. I thought it was some kind of soft drink."

DiMag wasn't pea-green up at the plate, however. In his freshman year, 1933, he batted in 61 consecutive games in the Coast League, breaking a record set by Jack Ness in 49 games, nearly twenty years before. The streak by the rookie turned the spotlight on Joe and he hasn't escaped its glare since. Major league scouts swarmed around San Francisco like locusts.

Charley Graham, the San Francisco owner, was one of baseball's pioneers. He had sold ballplayers to the majors before, and was to keep selling them until his death many years later. He stood off the bids, reasoning that Joe was a natural and that another season with the Seals would help the club in the race, and at the gate, and would put a higher value on DiMaggio.

The 1934 season had scarcely opened when the now notorious DiMaggio jinx struck for the first time. Stepping out of an automobile, in which he had been riding in a cramped position, Joe's left knee popped on him. He tried to dismiss it to Manager Caveney as a Charley horse but it was obviously more serious. Eventually, DiMag had to spend six weeks in a splint.

Bill Essick and Joe Devine, the Yankee scouts for Pacific Coast territory, saw that DiMaggio was favoring his knee for the balance of the season but refused to believe he was washed up. Essick told Graham that if a San Francisco physician, a Dr. Spencer, were given permission to examine and treat DiMaggio, the Yankees would be willing to give $25,000 and four players for Joe and allow Graham his services for 1935.

Dr. Spencer's treatments were efficacious and the Yanks completed the deal after the close of the 1934 season, Joe being purchased for delivery in the spring of 1936. That the Yankees acted when they did was a fortuitous break for their exchequer, for all DiMag did in his final season in the Coast League was bat .398, making 270 base hits, of which 34 were home runs. By that time, San Francisco could have got as much as $100,000 for DiMaggio but he was Yankee property. And was for a long time afterward.

In 1941, when DiMaggio made American League history by hitting in 56 consecutive games, he was in danger of having his streak halted by the Browns, after he had hit in 36 straight games. Bob Muncrief had stopped him three times but on the fourth try, Joe cracked him for a single.

Since the Yankees were well ahead at the time, DiMaggio's hit meant nothing except to his streak and there was some discussion afterward as to why Muncrief didn't walk the Clipper.

"I couldn't have done that," said Bob. "It wouldn't have been fair to him or to me. He's the greatest player I've ever seen."

That Muncrief was not alone in this viewpoint was demonstrated two days later, in the third game of the Brownie series. Again Joe was held hitless coming up to the ninth and this time there were three Yankees slated to hit before he did. The leadoff hitter singled and the next batter sacrificed to avoid the double play contingency and assure DiMag of coming to bat. With two out, a man on second and first base open, the dictates of strategy are to walk the batter. Manager Luke Sewell ordered Elden Auker to pitch to Joe and the Clipper smacked out a two-bagger.

When Joe was sidelined in the spring of 1949, Manager Stengel adopted a you're-the-boss attitude toward him. He told DiMag that whenever he felt ready to play, he'd use him and that Joe could bench himself at any time he felt his injuries bothering him.

The temptation to use DiMaggio, crippled heel and all, as a pinch-hitter must have been strong. The Yankees had one key-player injured after another and Stengel must have felt that there were times when a pinch-hit by DiMaggio would have worked wonders but he refrained. Asked about it, Casey replied in a manner that showed he, too, was not lacking in big league class.

"Why use the fellow on one leg?" said Stengel impatiently. "When he's ready, he'll let me know. He's been too great a ballplayer to be wasted or make a fool of." Casey ended his sentence on a preposition but on a sound proposition.

When the Yankee Clipper faced a battery of television cameras, photographers, reporters and interested bystanders in the swank Yankee offices in the Squibb Building on December 11, 1951 and announced that he was through as an active player, he may have surprised some people but he really didn't shock anybody.

The end of the trail had been looming for Joe all through the season. His biggest value to the Yankees was that he, Joe DiMaggio, wearing No. 5, was playing center field and batting clean-up. He wasn't the old Joe, by any means. He couldn't get around on the ball, fast balls were too quick for his reflexes and he couldn't cover ground or throw as he once had. Nevertheless, just being DiMaggio he looked good out there; the Yankees felt better with him and the opposition still worried over him.

When the Yankees squared off with Leo Durocher's amazing Giants in the World Series, Joe was held hitless on his first dozen trips to the plate. It wasn't until the fourth game, against Sal Maglie at the Polo Grounds, that the Clipper began to pull the ball. He hit a sharp single to left on his second trip and a homer into the upper left field seats the next time at bat. He hit safely in each of the next two games and wound up with an average of .261 for the Series.

It was only natural that the writing boys should let themselves go when DiMaggio called it a career. There were some fine columns written and Arthur Daley of the *New York Times* did one of the most interesting, for he put his finger on what undoubtedly was the straw which tipped the scales—the publication in *Life* of the scouting report Andy High had made on the Yankees. It was meant to be used by the Dodgers against the Yanks but the fates decided that the Dodgers weren't to make the Series, so High's report was turned over to his fellow National Leaguers.

The report, of course, was supposed to be top-secret. Garry Schumacher, promotional director of the Giants and a lifelong friend of High's, had obtained it from Andy. When Durocher reported how helpful it had been, mention was made of High's generosity but nothing of the contents of the report.

Clay Felker, an enterprising young man connected with the Giant broadcasts, finally wrangled a copy of the report from the Dodger offices—not the Giants—and sold it to *Life* for a fat fee, plus a job in the magazine's sports department.

JOSEPH PAUL (JOE) DIMAGGIO

Born Nov. 25, 1914, Martinez, Calif.
Height 6' 2". Weight 205. Bats and throws right-handed.

YEAR	CLUB	LEAGUE	POS	G	AB	R	H	2B	3B	HR	RBI	BA
1932	San Francisco	P. C.	SS	3	9	2	2	1	1	0	2	.222
1933	San Francisco	P. C.	OF	187	762	129	259	45	13	28	169	.340
1934	San Francisco	P. C.	OF	101	375	58	128	18	6	12	69	.341
1935	San Francisco	P. C.	OF	172	679	173	270	48	18	34	154	.398
1936	New York	Amer.	OF	138	637	132	206	44	x15	29	125	.323
1937	New York	Amer.	OF	151	621	*151	215	35	15	*46	167	.346
1938	New York	Amer.	OF	145	599	129	194	32	13	32	140	.324
1939	New York	Amer.	OF	120	462	108	176	32	6	30	126	*.381
1940	New York	Amer.	OF	132	508	93	179	28	9	31	*133	*.352
1941	New York	Amer.	OF	139	541	122	193	43	11	30	125	.357
1942	New York	Amer.	OF	154	610	123	186	29	13	21	114	.305
1943-44-45	New York	Amer.					(In Military Service)					
1946	New York	Amer.	OF	132	503	81	146	20	8	25	95	.290
1947	New York	Amer.	OF	141	534	97	168	31	10	20	97	.315
1948	New York	Amer.	OF	153	594	110	190	26	11	*39	*155	.320
1949	New York	Amer.	OF	76	272	58	94	14	6	14	67	.346
1950	New York	Amer.	OF-1B	139	525	114	158	33	10	32	122	.301
1951	New York	Amer.	OF	116	415	72	109	22	4	12	71	.263
	Major League Totals			1736	6821	1390	2214	389	131	361	1537	.325

WORLD SERIES RECORD

YEAR	CLUB	LEAGUE	POS	G	AB	R	H	2B	3B	HR	RBI	BA
1936	New York	Amer.	OF	6	26	3	9	3	0	0	3	.346
1937	New York	Amer.	OF	5	22	2	6	0	0	1	4	.273
1938	New York	Amer.	OF	4	15	4	4	0	0	1	2	.267
1939	New York	Amer.	OF	4	16	3	5	0	0	1	3	.313
1941	New York	Amer.	OF	5	19	1	5	0	0	0	1	.263
1942	New York	Amer.	OF	5	21	3	7	0	0	0	3	.333
1947	New York	Amer.	OF	7	26	4	6	0	0	2	5	.231
1949	New York	Amer.	OF	5	18	2	2	0	0	1	2	.111
1950	New York	Amer.	OF	4	13	2	4	1	0	1	2	.308
1951	New York	Amer.	OF	6	23	3	6	2	0	1	5	.261
	World Series Totals			51	199	27	54	6	0	8	30	.271

ALL-STAR GAME RECORD

YEAR	LEAGUE	POS	AB	R	H	2B	3B	HR	RBI	BA
1936	American	OF	5	0	0	0	0	0	0	.000
1937	American	OF	4	1	1	0	0	0	0	.250
1938	American	OF	4	1	1	0	0	0	0	.250
1939	American	OF	4	1	1	0	0	1	1	.250
1940	American	OF	4	0	0	0	0	0	0	.000
1941	American	OF	4	3	1	1	0	0	1	.250
1942	American	OF	4	0	2	0	0	0	0	.500
1947	American	OF	3	0	1	0	0	0	0	.333
1948	American	PH	1	0	0	0	0	0	1	.000
1949	American	OF	4	1	2	1	0	0	3	.500
1950	American	OF	3	0	0	0	0	0	0	.000
	All-Star Totals		40	7	9	2	0	1	6	.225

*—Led league   x—tied for lead

Everybody hollered bloody murder, the Giants, Dodgers and Yankees, together. The report had this to say about DiMaggio: "He can't stop quickly and throw hard. . . . You can take the extra base on him. . . . He can't run and won't bunt. . . . His reflexes are very slow and he can't pull a good fast ball at all."

As Daley said, "This must have cut him to the quick." It did. Joe wasn't going to take that sort of criticism—not even for $100,-000 a year.

CHAPTER VII

THE FIREBALLER

Robert William Andrew Feller

CONVERSATION among the writers traveling with the Giants was brisk and stimulating that Easter Sunday morning in 1937 as they moved from Jackson, Mississippi, to Vicksburg for an exhibition game with the Cleveland Indians. They were going to get a look at Bob Feller, the schoolboy who broke in so sensationally with the Indians late in the preceding season. The kid had fanned eight Cardinals in three innings in a July exhibition game, struck out fifteen of the St. Louis Browns in his first major league start, but so far none of the writers with the Giants had seen him.

The ball park at Vicksburg was built with an eye to convenience. Home plate was within fifty feet of the first row of the grandstand and the press box was in the first row. There were three writers accompanying the Indians and ten with the Giants. The press box was built to accommodate about a half-dozen and the overflow press sat on a bench on the playing field. When Feller cut loose with his first warm-up pitch, somebody tipped the bench and everybody keeled over. It was a gag, of course, but one which had its foundations in truth, for Robert William Andrew Feller, of Van Meter, Iowa, was the original blow-'em-down kid in those days.

It didn't take the New York writers more than a few pitches to realize that their Cleveland brethren weren't kidding when they said young Feller was out of this world. He had a fast ball as explosive as any they had ever seen—Dazzy Vance, Walter Johnson, Lefty Grove or Van Lingle Mungo. And the boy was only eighteen years old!

Feller pitched the first three innings, held the Giants without

72

a hit, fanned six, four of them in succession. For once, a sports writer could employ the adjective "sensational" and be well within the bounds of accuracy. Bob walked only one man, facing a total of ten in the three innings he worked.

Bill Klem, the veteran National League umpire who worked behind the plate that afternoon in Vicksburg, was loud in his praise of Feller after the game. "The boy has a chance to be the greatest of them all," said Bill. The Giants, for the most part, agreed with Klem. Manager Bill Terry cautiously added the phrase "if he has control" to his encomia of Feller. Mel Ott admired his curve ball and Carl Hubbell said he thought Bob was "about as fast as anybody I've ever seen."

There was one dissenter—Dick Bartell, the Giant shortstop. Batting against Feller in the first inning, Dick popped out. While taking fielding practice between innings a ball took a bad hop and hit Dick in the face, so he was excused from further duty. Maybe it was the fact that his acquaintance with Feller was thus curtailed which warped Dick's judgement but the shortstop was unimpressed.

"We've got several guys in our league who can throw just as hard," stoutly maintained Richard. "I know he isn't as fast as Mungo."

The Giants saw a great deal more of Feller that spring, for the tour with the Indians carried them through many stops— New Orleans; Tyler, Texas; Shawnee, Oklahoma; Pine Bluff, Arkansas; Thomaston, Georgia; Decatur, Alabama, and Fort Smith, Arkansas, to name a few.

Feller continued to strike out the Giants, seemingly leveling at Bartell. He fanned Dick something like thirteen times in eighteen turns at bat. As the late Bill Slocum wrote, "Bartell went all the way to Fort Smith before he got so much as a loud foul against Feller."

No ball player in modern times broke in as sensationally as Feller. He was an unknown who burst into national prominence with his exhibition performance against the Cardinals. Harry Grayson, sports editor of the Newspaper Enterprise Association, which then had its home office in Cleveland, was the first to bring word East of Feller's fireball. Harry burst in on a group of New York writers in Pittsburgh's Schenley Hotel one night and began to sing the praises of Feller, whom he had seen in the night exhibition against the Cards.

"You never saw anything like this kid!" sputtered Grayson excitedly. "He practically steps toward third base when he throws, and the ball just explodes.

"I was sitting on the bench with Frisch the other night when he brought the Cards to Cleveland. Feller started warming up and Frank said 'Who in the hell is that fireballer?' I told him he was a kid Cy Slapnicka had picked up and that he was selling peanuts. 'Peanuts,' Frisch screams. 'That kid's the fastest pitcher I ever saw.' Then he turns to Stu Martin and says, 'Stu, how'd you like to play second base tonight?' He turned aside to me and winked, saying, 'They're not gonna get the old Flash out there against that kid.'"

The first batter to face Feller, Bruce Ogrodowski, the St. Louis catcher, bunted and was out and then Bob faced Leo Durocher, who became the first major leaguer he ever fanned. He got Leo twice during his three inning stint and also Les Munns, the Card pitcher. The woods are probably full of pitchers who struck out Durocher and Munns twice, but Bob also managed to bag four other Cardinals, Pepper Martin, Charley Gelbert, Rip Collins, and Art Garibaldi.

Feller went on from that night exhibition game against the Cardinals to face the Browns in an American League game and fanned fifteen of them, an impressive total and one which hasn't been topped by many pitchers. This was in late August, 1936, and Rapid Robert's achievement was a sensation, but not for long, because he tangled with the Athletics only three weeks later and fanned seventeen! This tied the National League strikeout record, which had been set by the great Dizzy Dean only three years earlier, and it was the first time an American League pitcher, any American League pitcher—Johnson, Grove, Waddell or the rest —ever had scored so many strikeout victims.

Young Bob had nothing but speed in those closing weeks in 1936, speed and what little he was able to remember of the advice Steve O'Neill gave him. Stout Steve, who was Feller's first manager, even co-operated to the point of catching the fireballer in the exhibition game against the Cardinals, so as to give him additional confidence. And Steve, then fat and forty, took no inconsiderable risk in getting behind the plate to handle the explosive fast ball of the kid.

After this spectacular beginning, it was only natural that the writers with the Giants should be all worked up over the prospect of actually seeing the phenom in the flesh. So far only the Cleveland writers really had any idea of what Feller could do. In the spring of 1937, the Indians trained in New Orleans, which was off the beaten path for the itinerant scribes, and it wasn't until Easter Sunday in Vicksburg that the New York writers got their first look at young Bob.

From that day until this, the New York writers, particularly those who were at Vicksburg, have vied with the Cleveland writers in singing praises of Rapid Robert. Nowhere outside of Cleveland has Bob enjoyed a better press.

Feller broke in with the greatest of all natural gifts for a pitcher—the ability to fire a baseball as though it were jet-propelled. Uncle Wilbert Robinson, who managed the Dodgers for so many years, was adjudged a great handler and developer of pitchers, whatever opinions may have been held on his strategic maneuverings. It was Uncle Robbie who claimed that a pitcher could develop anything he needed, control, a curve, fielding skill, anything except a fast ball.

"Only God can give a man a fast ball," said Robbie.

Although Feller had only one attribute, he had the most important. He was to develop the others as time went on, to develop them painstakingly, through perseverance and practice. Bob was fortunate that his first manager was O'Neill, for there was something of Uncle Robbie in the brawny Irishman from the anthracite country of Pennsylvania. Like Robbie, Steve had been a catcher, and like Robbie, Steve appreciated good pitching. He saw from the beginning that Feller had a chance to become one of the greatest.

Bob, at the outset, didn't have much of a curve and tipped off when he was going to throw it. A change of pace was merely a bit of baseball nomenclature to him, and on the subject of holding base runners to their bases, he knew rather less than a Hindu. Players stole second—and even home—while Feller was holding the ball in his hand. He was the biggest green pea baseball had ever seen—and he was to become one of its greatest pitchers.

It is a moot question whether Feller's lack of control in the early days was a curse or a blessing. To be sure, the bases on balls he issued got him into many a jam, but the fact that nobody, not even Bobby, ever was quite sure where any given pitch was going, certainly padded his strikeout records. Nobody took any toeholds when Feller's forked lightning began striking around home plate.

To quote Uncle Robbie once again, the roundest of all the old Orioles had a phrase for this lack of control in a fast ball pitcher, a phrase which was so much the *mot juste* that he used it over and over when he spoke of Dazzy Vance. Robbie called this trait, "pleasingly wild," which meant that while the pitcher's wildness wasn't enough to get him into serious trouble, it was sufficient to keep the batters foot-loose and fancy free at the plate.

Feller's fireball hardly had burst upon the baseball horizon when Bobby found himself a *cause célèbre* for entirely different reasons. Lee Keyser, who owned the Des Moines franchise in the Western League and who, it irrelevantly must be noted, was the first man to play organized baseball under lights, filed a protest with Commissioner Kenesaw Mountain Landis, that Cy Slapnicka had illegally signed Feller to a Cleveland contract.

At the time it caused a dandy rhubarb, for Feller completed his first season with five victories in eight decisions and the amazing number of 76 strikeouts in 62 innings, which gave him an average of better than eleven per regulation game! If the Commissioner were to declare him a free agent, Feller could have commanded at least $100,000 on the open market.

The circumstances under which Feller became Cleveland's property were not uncommon for that period, even though contrary to baseball law. Bob had been pitching sandlot ball in Iowa when Slapnicka signed him to a contract to pitch for Fargo-Moorehead (North Dakota) in the Northern League. Bob, who came up with a sore arm in the winter, probably as the result of playing basketball at Van Meter High, never reported to Fargo-Moorehead. Instead, he was brought to Cleveland and worked out at League Park when the Indians were on the road and pitched for the Cleveland Rosenblums, under the watchful eye of Slapnicka. Cy was ready to transfer Feller's contract to another Cleveland farm, New Orleans in the Southern League, when Bobby burst like a bombshell on the Cardinals.

After that, Slapnicka decided the boy had to stay with the Indians. Keyser's beef to Landis opened a fine kettle of fish, but by December of 1936, the Judge ruled that Bobby was to remain the property of Cleveland, although he ordered the Indians to pay Keyser and the Des Moines Club $7,500 as damages. The Judge went further than that—he rescinded the rule which forbade major league clubs to deal with sandlot players, since he realized that many of them were doing so anyway.

Slapnicka, who had been a minor league pitcher of the "cute" type, breathed more easily and slept better nights when the Landis decision was announced. He was the first to spot the greatness in Bobby—aside from Bob's dad, who may have been just a mite prejudiced—and he was now ready to reap the rewards of his foresight.

It wasn't to be as easy as Cy hoped, despite Feller's sensational work in the barnstorming games against the Giants in the spring of 1937, when he fanned 37 in 27 innings and climaxed the tour by drawing 31,486 into the Polo Grounds when he faced Carl Hubbell in the finale.

Feller pitched against the Browns in Cleveland's second home game of the season, April 24. On his first pitch of the ball game, Bobby tried to break off a curve against Bill Knickerbocker and almost broke off his arm instead. Before the inning was over, Feller had walked four, given up two hits and had been scored on four times. He contemplated walking off the mound but instead tried to get by with his fast ball alone.

Bob lasted until the sixth, when he tried another curve, with the same searing pain in his right elbow. He told Manager O'Neill he was through, explaining that he had injured his arm in the first inning and had believed he pitched out the soreness until he tried another curve.

It is doubtful if any pitcher in baseball got more publicity than Feller did by *not* pitching. His arm refused to respond to treatment and he wasn't able to pitch again until July 4, an absence of more than two months from the firing line. All sorts of treatments were tried but nothing proved effective until a bone and muscle manipulator a few blocks from the ball park, one A. L. Austin, restored Bobby to normalcy by deciding that Feller's ulna bone was out of its socket and snapping it back into place. He told Bobby to get 24 hours' rest and then go out and pitch.

The kid with the plowboy's walk did just that. He didn't pitch well but he got back into the swing of things. He concluded the season with a record of nine wins and seven defeats, after losing his first four decisions. Feller was on the way back.

Feller's dead arm was a tremendous strain on a youth of eighteen. First of all, he was beset with the morbid fear that his pitching career was over before it started. Secondly, his every visit to a doctor, osteopath or chiropractor was subjected to pitiless publicity. Even when he went home to Van Meter to receive his high school diploma, his sore arm was the principal subject of conversation.

In addition to his dad, Feller had two men to lean upon, the tireless Slapnicka and the patient and generous Steve O'Neill. Although a slovenly season by the Indians had placed Stout Steve's job in jeopardy, he stuck by Bobby and paid as much attention to the kid as if Feller already were the established star he was destined to be, instead of a boy who had won precisely five major league games and who wasn't able to throw a ball at all, let alone throw it hard.

Feller was a baseball anomaly—a pitcher who was a star before he ever starred in the popular conception of the term. His spectacular break-in at the exhibition with the Cardinals in 1936, his strikeout performances in the closing days of the American League season, his involvement with Judge Landis, his great spring series against the Giants and his sore arm—incurred in a game in which he fanned eleven in six innings, including Rogers Hornsby—all these put Bobby in the public eye and he never was out of it again.

It was in 1938, under a new manager, the dynamic Oscar Vitt, that Feller really started to move. Feller played under four Cleveland managers before he came under the guidance of Al Lopez in 1951—O'Neill, Vitt, Roger Peckinpaugh and Lou Boudreau— and he gave them all the same loyal service. The chances are Bobby was closer to O'Neill than any of them, for the paternal Irishman stayed with him during the rough spots of his arm trouble in 1937.

Beginning in 1938, Rapid Robert fanned the amazing number of 1,007 American League hitters in four years, while pitching 1,238 innings and winning 93 games. Then he entered the Navy, not to return to the uniform of the Indians again for almost four full seasons, four seasons when he assuredly would have been at the peak of his career and in a position to challenge all of the all-time strikeout records. He almost certainly would have moved into the select circle of pitchers who have won 300 games.

There was a curious pattern through all of Feller's pitching, an over-all greatness, tinged with frustration. Throughout his career, Bobby was consistently balked on the threshold of his finest achievements. The sore arm he developed in 1937 was a fore-runner of things to be. His entrance into the Navy at the height of his career was symbolic.

Nowhere was the Feller jinx more noticeable than in the World Series of 1948, which Bobby finally reached a dozen years after he first burst upon the baseball scene. The fireballer didn't have a particularly good season—good for him, that is—as the Indians won their first pennant in 28 years through the virtue of Lou Boudreau's hitting in the first play-off game in American League history, which broke the tie with the Red Sox.

Bobby won nineteen games that year, the first full season since 1938 in which he failed to reach twenty. His winning percentage, .559, was the poorest he had ever had up until that time. Although he led the American League in strikeouts for the seventh time, his total, 164, was the lowest he had had for a full season in ten years. And he gave up more base hits than any other pitcher in the league.

Nevertheless, Feller was magnificent in the opening game against the Braves in Boston. He gave up only two hits, yet bowed to Johnny Sain by a score of 1 to 0. It was the first 1–0 World Series decision since Casey Stengel had beaten the Yankees with a home run when he was playing with the Giants, a quarter of a century before. And it was the first 1–0 Series opener since Babe Ruth had pitched the Red Sox to a victory over Hippo Jim Vaughn and the Cubs thirty years earlier.

Marvin Rickert—who played the outfield for the Braves through special dispensation after Jeff Heath sustained a fractured leg in the last week of the season—made the first hit in the fifth, and the second and last hit, a single by Tommy Holmes, beat Feller in the eighth, one of the most controversial innings in World Series history.

Bill Salkeld, Boston catcher, opened the eighth by drawing

Feller's second pass of the game. Phil Masi went in to run for Bill and was sacrificed to second by Mike McCormick. Manager Boudreau ordered an intentional pass for Eddie Stanky, with the obvious aim of setting up a double play situation for Sain.

Boudreau also was setting up something else, the famed pickoff play of the Tribe which had proved effective quite frequently during the regular American League season. While pitching to Sain, Bobby suddenly whirled and threw to Boudreau covering second. It seemed from the stands that Masi was definitely picked off, that Lou had the ball on him before he could dive back into second base. National League umpire Bill Stewart, who, after all, was closer to the play than anybody else, ruled that Masi's headlong slide had beaten Boudreau's tag, that Lou had put the ball on Phil's upper arm after the runner's hand had reached the bag.

When the excitement subsided, Sain flied for the second out, but Holmes, a left-handed batter, singled home Masi from second with the only run of the ball game, and Feller was beaten, although far from disgraced, in his first World Series appearance.

Cleveland took the next three straight, Bob Lemon winning 4 to 1 in Boston, while Gene Bearden won the first game in Cleveland by 2 to 0. For the Saturday game in Cleveland, Boudreau pulled Steve Gromek as a surprise starter and Steve came through with a 2–1 triumph. In four games, the hapless Braves had scored exactly three runs and Feller seemed a cinch to wind up the Series when he made his second start on Sunday before the largest World Series crowd of all time—86,288. Thousands of the spectators must have been motivated by civic pride for, crowded behind the fences in the outfield of the vast Municipal Stadium, they assuredly could see nothing but the backs of their neighbors necks. It is doubtful if they even glimpsed a baseball uniform during the game.

Feller simply didn't have it that day, although Boudreau, with an eye on history's pages, persevered with him far longer than he would with an ordinary pitcher. Bobby was being well belted, but Nelson Potter, the desperation pitching selection of Manager Bill Southworth, wasn't exactly a puzzle and Lou kept hoping that Feller would get a grip on himself.

Bob Elliott tagged Feller for a three-run homer over the right field screen in the first inning and then hit a homer into the left

CHAPTER VIII

THE MARYLAND STRONG BOY

James Emory Foxx

So FAR as is known, a man named Will White, a Cincinnati pitcher, was the only professional ball player to wear glasses for almost the first half century of the game's existence. Then another pitcher, Lee Meadows, reported to the Cardinals in 1915 wearing spectacles. He was, with no great originality, nicknamed "specs," as was George Toporcer, the first infielder to make major league plays behind eyeglasses.

As the years wore on, eyeglasses no longer stood between a player and the game. Scouts didn't hesitate to recommend a player because he wore glasses and many players who had not worn glasses adopted them for remedial purposes.

Such a one was Vernon (Lefty) Gomez, the gay caballero of the Yankees. The great southpaw attempted to aid his fading arm by the experiment of wearing bifocals. The experiment was short-lived. Pitching against the Red Sox one day, Gomez called time, walked from the mound to the Yankee bench, removed his glasses and put them down, never to wear them again.

"I just got a look at Jimmy Foxx through the glasses," explained Lefty. "It's enough to frighten a man to death."

It was a typical Gomez exaggeration but there was the essence of truth behind it. Few hitters contrived to look as menacing at the plate as James Emory Foxx, the Maryland Strong Boy. And Jimmy was every bit as tough as he looked. His straddle-stance, his powerful biceps showing beneath the abbreviated flannel sleeves of his shirt, his broad back and square jaw gave him a purposeful, almost vengeful, appearance. And no American League pitcher ever accused Jimmy of putting on airs with this pose. He wasn't flexing his muscles for show but coiling them to hit the ball out of sight.

Gomez had good reason to respect Foxx. One of the longest home runs ever hit in Yankee Stadium—or in any other ball park —was hit by Foxx against Lefty. It landed in the last section of the third tier in left field. The ball struck about five or six rows back and still had enough force to break the back of a seat.

"I thought it was a fast ball when I threw it," said Lefty ruefully, "but it was going a lot faster after Foxx hit it. After the game it took me twenty minutes to walk to where he had hit the ball in a split second!"

Gomez wasn't the only pitcher victimized by Foxx, although he was among the best in the American League. Jimmy treated them all alike and hit them all as far as he could. It is probable that Foxx hit as many extraordinarily long home runs as any player who ever lived, including Babe Ruth. Jimmy was raw power at the plate. He was a power swinger and frequently struck out but even a pitcher who fanned Foxx had the feeling that he was living on borrowed time. Like Ruth, Jimmy frequently led the league in strikeouts. For three straight years, Foxx was high man in the American League in strikeouts.

During the seasons of 1929, 1930 and 1931, Foxx struck out a total of 220 times, yet in those three seasons Mr. Double-X also hit a total of 100 home runs and his team, the Philadelphia Athletics, won three straight pennants and two World Series. In those seasons, too, Foxx batted in 493 runs, so you can see that the pitchers who had fanned Jimmy were inclined to take a dim view of the achievement, knowing that sooner or later, they would have to pitch to him again. As Gomez so graphically put it, it was enough to frighten a man to death.

Although Foxx was gifted with one of the finest personalities in professional sports, the respect and awe in which this mighty man of muscle was held by his contemporaries is revealed by their pet nickname for him. He was known simply as "The Beast."

John Franklin Baker is the only ballplayer in the history of the major leagues who gained the awe-inspiring nickname of "Home Run." He became known as Home Run Baker during the course of the 1911 World Series between the Athletics and the Giants.

In Philadelphia in the second game, Baker hit a home run

against Rube Marquard to win for the Athletics and even the Series. Christy Mathewson and/or his ghost writer commented the next day that John McGraw had specifically ordered Marquard not to pitch low to Baker and that Rube had disregarded the orders and thus cost the Giants the ball game.

Mathewson pitched the third game and held a 1 to 0 lead with one out in the ninth when Baker came to bat. Frank whacked one into the lower right field stands in the Polo Grounds, now no more than a mashie shot, but then a tremendous wallop. It tied up the score and the A's went on to win the game in extra innings.

Naturally, Marquard's ghost writer had a field day as he wondered what had happened to McGraw's instructions as interpreted by Matty. Rube's ghost writer, just for the records, was Frank G. Menke, author and editor of *The New Encyclopedia of Sports*.

Baker came from Maryland's Eastern Shore, as did Foxx, who was born in Sudlersville, Maryland. Frank saw Foxx playing with Easton in the Eastern Shore League in 1924. Jimmy had not yet reached his seventeenth birthday but a couple of looks at Foxx convinced Baker that this brawny lad was not going to remain in the bushes much longer.

Baker told Mack about Foxx but Connie almost lost interest when he heard the kid was a catcher. He pointed out that he already had two of the American League's outstanding catchers in Mickey Cochrane and Cy Perkins.

"This boy has as much power as any hitter I've ever seen and that goes for Ruth," declared Baker. "You can play him someplace. There must be room on any team for a fellow who can hit like this kid."

Mack soon learned that room had to be made for a hitter like Foxx. He purchased Jimmy in 1925 and farmed him to Providence, the club to which Babe Ruth had been farmed as a rookie pitcher just eleven years earlier. And that was the last time Foxx was farmed out.

Foxx spent two seasons trying to find his spot on the A's but by 1928 he had abandoned the tools of ignorance, as ballplayers call the pad and mask, and was shuttling between third base and first base. He finally settled down at first base, although he wasn't above making excursions to other positions. Where Foxx played never was as important as where Foxx hit.

On the strength of his total home runs alone, Foxx must be assayed as a great hitter. Fewer than ten players in the history of baseball have hit over 300 home runs and Jimmy hit almost twice that many. He twice touched 50 and, along with Hank Greenberg holds the record of coming closer to Ruth's mark of 60 than any other hitter. Foxx hit 58 home runs in 1932 for the Athletics, six years before Greenberg hit the same number for Detroit. And Jimmy hit 50 for the Red Sox the same reason Greenberg was threatening Ruth's record. The half-hundred home runs Foxx hit that season was the biggest total of home runs ever hit by any Red Sox player, just as his 58 is, of course, the seasonal high among Athletic sluggers.

Once Foxx got his sights adjusted to the American League barriers, he kept on the beam. Beginning with the 33 home runs he hit in 1929, Jimmy went for a dozen consecutive seasons in which he bagged 30 or more home runs. Ruth went 30 or better for thirteen seasons, but they were not consecutive being split by 1925, the year Commissioner Kenesaw M. Landis slapped a sixty-day suspension on him.

Foxx had a great shot at Ruth's record in 1932. He missed by two homers but two baseball historians, Fred Lieb and Al Hirshberg, each taking different cases, have written that the fates (and the fences) were against Jimmy. Lieb explains that a screen was erected in front of the right field pavilion at Sportsman's Park that season and that Foxx hit that screen five times. Had Foxx the open target to shoot at which Ruth had in 1927, Jimmy would have had 63 home runs. Hirshberg writes that Cleveland erected a screen in front of the left field bleachers at League Park that same season and calculates that Foxx hit this screen at least three itmes during the season, which would have been enough to break Babe's mark. Taking these combined explanations, Jimmy would have totaled 66 home runs in 1932.

Foxx needs no apologists. His total of 534 homers is impressive enough but even more so is the fact that in the period of twelve seasons from 1929 to 1940 Jimmy smashed 484 home runs, an average of better than 40 per season.

Jimmy's power range was wide, as the explanations of Lieb and Hirshberg attest. In St. Louis, Foxx lost home runs because the right field fence was screened and in Cleveland he lost them because the left field bleachers were screened. Incidentally, those bleachers in old League Park were 375 feet from home plate.

Of the many outsize home runs hit by Foxx in his career, I remember two with startling clarity. One was in the 1935 All-Star game, played in Cleveland's vast Municipal Stadium. There were no wire barriers there in the pre-Veeck era and the outfield was so huge that it was like playing on a parade grounds.

The annual All-Star game is a touchy subject with National Leaguers and none can bring the hackles out more quickly than the 1935 game. It was, at the time, the record attendance and gate receipts game of the set, drawing 69,812 fans.

There was considerable criticism that the National League managers all had used their star pitchers the Sunday before the game. Frankie Frisch, managing the Nationals, started Willie Walker, a left-hander who was scarcely a first-string pitcher at that time, although he had been a star with the Giants earlier in his career.

Before Walker really got warmed to his task, the game was blown out of sight. With one out, Charley Gehringer walked and was forced by Lou Gehrig. Up came Foxx and away went the ball game. Jimmy hit the ball about as far into the left field stands as it was possible to clout a ball, a drive that still had great force when it landed among the customers. That was two runs and it was no trouble at all for the Americans to go on from there and win by 4 to 1.

Foxx always was a fine money player. In the three World Series in which the played, he never was held without a home run and he had a Series average of .344. Jimmy played in seven of the inter-league All-Star games and had an average of .316.

In the 1930 World Series, the Athletics won the first two games from the Cardinals in Philadelphia but when the Cards returned to Sportsman's Park they made things rough for the Mackmen. Bill Hallahan shut out the Athletics in the third game and Jesse Haines held them to one run in the fourth game as the Cardinals evened the Series at two games each.

Burleigh Grimes, the truculent spitballer, hooked up in a tight pitching duel with George (The Moose) Earnshaw. It was scoreless until the eighth when Connie, hoping to take it all, lifted Earnshaw for a pinch-hitter. Although the A's had the bases filled with only one out, the gritty Grimes wriggled off the hook. Mack then called on Lefty Grove who retired the Cards scoreless in their half of the eighth.

Mickey Cochrane was walked to start the ninth but Al Simmons popped up. Foxx came to bat. He had made one of the four hits Grimes had allowed but he knew he was facing a crafty competitor. Burleigh had been tagged for a triple by Jimmy in the first game but had struck him out later in that game with a three-and-two curve when Jimmy was looking for the spitter. In this game, too, Grimes had fooled Foxx by throwing a fast one by him for a third strike.

Grimes, of course, faked a spitter on every delivery. After the first game Connie had warned Foxx to be ready for the curve. Burleigh, the poised veteran, stalled around in the box to get Jimmy on edge. Foxx stepped out of the batter's box and rubbed dirt on his hands and then stepped in again. Grimes put his hands to his mouth, as he did before each ball he pitched. Then he fired the ball toward the plate. "Curve," said Foxx to himself and curve it was. It also was the ball game. The ball shot deep into the distant left field bleachers. There wasn't a doubt in anybody's mind as to its being a homer the instant it left the bat.

There's a man who tells an interesting story about that fifth game of the 1930 World Series. He had come on from Kansas City to see the three games in St. Louis and was driving back with a party of friends immediately after the game. As they passed through a town on the outer fringes of the city, a passerby called to them and asked the score.

"Jimmy Foxx: 2; St. Louis: 0," yelled this chap who was then a judge in the Jackson County Court of Missouri but later became president of these United States. Harry S. Truman is the name.

It was a penny postal card from Home Run Baker which started Foxx's professional career and just eleven years later Jimmy was the key figure in a $150,000 deal, when Mack, dismantling the pennant winning team, sold Foxx to Tom Yawkey, millionaire owner of the Red Sox. Most of the others had been sold before him—Lefty Grove, Mickey Cochrane, Al Simmons, Mule Haas and Jimmy Dykes. Jimmy was carrying on almost alone at Philadelphia, still clouting homers.

Foxx gave the Red Sox full value for their money. He drew a bead on the inviting left field fence at Fenway Park and kept plastering it until a sinus infection impaired his efficiency. There were days when he could barely drag himself to the plate and then barely see when he got there.

It was one of these days, June 6, 1938, that Foxx established a modern record by drawing six bases on balls in a nine-inning game. Jimmy felt so miserable before the game that he was going to ask Manager Joe Cronin for the day off. He knew the Sox needed him and he played, even though he said afterward he couldn't see the pitches coming to him.

Foxx was hit with a pitched ball in an exhibition game in Winnepeg after the close of the 1934 season while on his way to Japan. Many were inclined to blame this for Foxx's aggravated sinus condition. Certainly, he never was plagued with it before being hit.

Whatever the cause there were many times, particularly the damp days shortly after the season opened, when it was misery for Foxx to be on a ball field. Yet, up until 1939, Jimmy missed mighty few games. He was out of 30 that season but he batted .360 and hit 35 home runs.

Foxx is one of three major leaguers who received the award of the Baseball Writers Association as the most valuable player on three different occasions. Jimmy was chosen in 1932, 1933, and 1938, all non-pennant winning years, for the clubs with which he was playing. Joe DiMaggio, the only other American Leaguer to be tapped three times, won in 1939, 1941 and 1947, all years in which the Yankees won pennants and World Championships. Stanley Musial, the only National Leaguer to be picked as the most valuable player three times, won in 1943, 1946 and 1948. The Cardinals were pennant winners in 1943 and 1946.

Baseball was Foxx's lifeblood. It also was the only medium through which Jimmy made any money. He was phenomenally unfortunate when he turned his hand to other business ventures. He lost most of his savings in the stock market crash in 1929 and then, years later when he had put some money together again, he made an investment in a golf course in Florida which became almost worthless when the war broke out and travel was curtailed.

In the middle of the 1942 season, it was obvious that Foxx's sinus condition was making him useless to the Red Sox. Waivers were asked on Jimmy and he was claimed by the Chicago Cubs in the National League, the team he had plagued in the first World Series in which he had played thirteen years before. He hit a couple of homers for the Cubs but it was plain that he was through.

Since nothing had panned out for Foxx in his investments and since baseball was all he knew, Jimmy sat out the season of 1943 in the hope that the year's rest would improve his health. It didn't. Foxx's health was sound enough for the ordinary professions but not for the only trade at which he was skilled, that of belting a baseball out of sight.

Nevertheless, Foxx gave it another try in 1944, after he had passed his thirty-sixth birthday. Jimmy could do nothing for the Cubs and Jim Gallagher, the general manager, took him from the active list and gave him a coach's job. It was a fine gesture by Gallagher, a former sports writer, who felt perhaps that a man whose career had been as great as that of Foxx deserved something more than the pink slip.

After Foxx had served briefly as coach, Gallagher sought to find further outlets for his baseball knowledge by sending him out to manage the Cub farm at Portsmouth, Virginia, in the Piedmont League.

Foxx was released at the end of the 1944 season and signed by the Phillies, where he managed to hit seven more home runs, although he was only a part-time player. After the 1945 season, the major league box scores knew his name no longer. His big league career ended in the same field where it had started—Shibe Park, two decades, three clubs, two leagues and 534 home runs later.

Few stars have ever been more popular with their fellow ballplayers than Foxx. Jimmy's moonface was ever ready to break into a mirthful grin. It is to the everlasting credit of the Maryland Strong Boy that he wore the same smile out of the majors which he carried into the big show. Even the pitchers were sorry to see him go, incredible as it may seem.

JAMES EMORY (JIMMIE) FOXX

Born Oct. 22, 1907, Sudlersville, Md.
Height 5′ 11½″. Weight 195. Batted and threw right-handed.

YEAR	CLUB	LEAGUE	POS	G	AB	R	H	2B	3B	HR	RBI	BA
'24	Eastern	East. Sh.	C	76	260	33	77	11	2	10	—	.296
'25	Philadelphia	Amer.	PH-C	10	9	2	6	1	0	0	0	.667
'25	Providence	Int.	C-1B-OF	41	101	12	33	6	3	1	15	.327
'26	Philadelphia	Amer.	C	26	32	8	10	2	1	0	5	.313
'27	Philadelphia	Amer.	1B	61	130	23	42	6	5	3	20	.323
'28	Philadelphia	Amer.	C-3B-1B	118	400	85	131	29	10	13	79	.328
'29	Philadelphia	Amer.	1B	149	517	123	183	23	9	33	117	.354
'30	Philadelphia	Amer.	1B	153	562	127	188	33	13	37	156	.335
'31	Philadelphia	Amer.	1B-3B	139	515	93	150	32	10	30	120	.291
'32	Philadelphia	Amer.	1B-3B	154	585	*151	213	33	9	*58	*169	.364
'33	Philadelphia	Amer.	1B	149	573	125	204	37	9	*48	*163	*.356
'34	Philadelphia	Amer.	1B	150	539	120	180	28	6	44	130	.334
'35	Philadelphia (A)	Amer.	1B-C	147	535	118	185	33	7	x36	115	.346
'36	Boston	Amer.	1B-OF	155	585	130	198	32	8	41	143	.338
'37	Boston	Amer.	1B	150	569	111	162	24	6	36	127	.285
'38	Boston	Amer.	1B	149	565	139	197	33	9	50	*175	*.349
'39	Boston	Amer.	1B	124	467	130	168	31	10	*35	105	.360
'40	Boston	Amer.	1B-3B-C	144	515	106	153	30	4	36	119	.297
'41	Boston	Amer.	INF-OF	135	487	87	146	27	8	19	105	.300
'42	Boston †	Amer.	1B	30	100	18	27	4	0	5	14	.270
'42	Chicago	Nat.	1B-C	70	205	25	42	8	0	3	19	.205
'43	Chicago	Nat.						(Did not play)				
'44	Chicago ‡	Nat.	3B-C	15	20	0	1	1	0	0	2	.050
'44	Portsmouth §	Pied.	PH-P	5	2	0	0	0	0	0	0	.000
'45	Philadelphia	Nat.	1B-3B	89	244	30	60	11	1	7	38	.268
	Major League Totals			2317	8134	1751	2646	458	125	534	1921	.325

WORLD SERIES RECORD

YEAR	CLUB	LEAGUE	POS	G	AB	R	H	2B	3B	HR	RBI	BA
'29	Philadelphia	Amer.	1B	5	20	5	7	1	0	2	5	.350
'30	Philadelphia	Amer.	1B	6	21	3	7	2	1	1	3	.333
'31	Philadelphia	Amer.	1B	7	23	3	8	0	0	1	3	.348
	World Series Totals			18	64	11	22	3	1	4	11	.344

ALL-STAR GAME RECORD

YEAR	LEAGUE	POS	AB	R	H	2B	3B	HR	RBI	B
1934	American	3B	5	1	2	1	0	0	1	.4
1935	American	3B	3	1	2	0	0	1	3	.6
1936	American	3B	2	1	1	0	0	0	0	.5
1937	American	PH	1	0	0	0	0	0	0	.00
1938	American	1B-3B	4	0	1	0	0	0	0	.25
1940	American	1B	3	0	0	0	0	0	0	.00
1941	American	1B	1	0	0	0	0	0	0	.00
	All-Star Game Totals		19	3	6	1	0	1	4	.31

(A) Traded with Pitcher John Marcum to Boston Red Sox for Pitcher Gordon Rhode Catcher George Savino and $150,000, December 10, 1935

† Released on waivers to Chicago Cubs, June 1, 1942

‡ Released as player and signed as coach, July 6, 1944; released to Portsmouth a manager, August 25, 1944

§ Released by Portsmouth, December 1944, and signed by Philadelphia Phillies, February 10, 1945

* Led League

x Tied for lead

CHAPTER IX

THE IRON HORSE

Henry Louis Gehrig

IT WAS a clear, crisp Sunday in January, 1944, and Paul Krichell was at his entertaining best as the train rolled through New Jersey on its way back from Atlantic City. Paul's best is pretty good, too, if you know the Yankee scout. He has a fund of stories and goes back so far in baseball that there are those who say he remembers when the World Series was played with real Indians.

Yankee brass and the reporters had just finished a week-end tour of inspection of Atlantic City, which was to be the training quarters of the world champions for the next two springs. Having beaten the Cardinals in the World Series the previous fall, the Yankee officials felt pretty bright about the future. And nobody felt brighter than Krichell. A round, little man, whose whole world was built around the Yanks, Krich was spinning ceaseless yarns behind a big cigar.

As the train slowed down entering New Brunswick, Krichell looked across at the tops of the buildings which make up Rutgers University. He was suddenly solemn as he looked out the train window.

"New Brunswick," he almost whispered, in the tones a pilgrim might have used to mention Mecca. "That's where I first saw Lou Gehrig."

It wasn't difficult to understand Krichell's reverence. As a baseball scout it was his profession to discover new talent, yet it comes to a scout only once in a lifetime to discover a player of Gehrig's capacities. Krichell had scouted for the Yankees for more than a score of years and unearthed many a diamond in the rough, yet if he had discovered nobody before Gehrig and nobody after him, he could feel that his mission on earth had been completed. Paul had hit the ivory jackpot.

"Funny thing," recalled Krichell, "was that when I found Gehrig I didn't know who he was. I always follow the local colleges and Fordham and New York University weren't playing that day. I noticed where Columbia was scheduled to play Rutgers here in New Brunswick and came down to see what I could find out.

"By accident, I ran across Andy Coakley and the Columbia squad on the train coming down. I asked Andy if there was any-body worth-while on the squad and he told me about a big left-hander he had who might pitch that day and who hit a long ball.

"When I went into the stands, I noticed Andy had a right-hander warming up, so I figured the boy he was talking about wasn't going to play that day. I thought I'd catch the pitcher later on. Columbia has a big kid in right field, a left-handed hitter, who really laid into the ball every time he came to bat. He hit two home runs into the woods outside the ball field. He wasn't much in the field, kind of clumsy-like, but, brother, could he hit that ball!"

It wasn't until after the game that Krichell learned the right fielder was the left-handed pitcher Coakley had mentioned. Andy, who had been a major league pitcher himself, told Paul that he was using the boy (by now Krich had learned that the young fellow's name was Lou Gehrig) against Pennsylvania later in the week in New York. Krichell promised to be there.

That night Krichell was babblingly incoherent when he reported by phone to Ed Barrow, Yankee general manager. He raved about the long drives Gehrig had hit at New Brunswick and said that he thought maybe he had found "another Ruth." It was neither the first time, nor the last, that a general manager heard that from a scout, but never before nor since was a scout as close to being right as Krichell was.

"Go to bed and sleep it off," chuckled Barrow indulgently. "You'll be all right in the morning."

Columbia hadn't yet moved uptown to Baker Field and was playing its baseball and football at South Field when Krichell took his second look at Gehrig. Lou, pitching for the Lions, was in a 2–2 tie with Penn in the ninth when he tore into a high hard one and drove it out of the park and across the street to the pedestal of a monument on the steps of the library. That was the convincer for Paul.

The next day Gehrig agreed to join the Yankees at the end of the school term. It may shock some of the bonus babies of today to learn that the Yankees paid precisely $1,500 for Lou's signature and gave him a contract of $3,000 for the balance of the 1923 season.

In view of Gehrig's glorious record with the Yankees, it is easy to understand the affection Krichell holds for his memory. Lou was the perfect ballplayer as far as a scout was concerned. A hitter of great ability and tremendous power, Gehrig was always trying, an eager beaver for all of his major league career, a man of model habits and great team spirit. Although any personal fire he may have had was concealed, Lou had a tremendous enthusiasm for baseball and never let his manager down. He was Manager Joe McCarthy's favorite ballplayer, although Joe never intimated as much while Lou was an active player.

Consistency was the keynote of Gehrig's career. His incredible record of 2130 consecutive games in the American League, from June 1, 1925 to May 2, 1939 in Detroit when he asked Manager McCarthy to bench him, is a testimonial to Lou's consistency as well as his durability. It is a record which should stand unsurpassed, like Babe Ruth's home run total of 714. Indeed, it has an even better chance of survival. If the ball keeps getting livelier and the fences shorter, somebody may pass the Babe in total homers. It is difficult to see, however, what artificial means can be contrived to keep a ballplayer in the lineup, day in and day out, over a period of years, unless they shorten the game to three innings.

Gehrig has been labeled a plodder. In many respects he was, if plodding means thorough and painstaking application to the job at hand. Terribly green and awkward when he came up to the Yankees in 1923, Lou was an accomplished first baseman before his star had set.

When Gehrig started as a ballplayer at New York's High School of Commerce, all he had was weight, power and willingness. He could hit a fast ball but he had to learn to hit the curve.

And learn he did. Then he had to learn to field. That he learned, too, one phase of it at a time. One of his most exacting mentors was Wally Pipp, the man whose job he had taken with the Yankees. Pipp, one of baseball's finest characters, knew his career had run its course when he first saw the big kid from Columbia come up, yet Wally worked many hours with Lou teaching him the niceties of first baseball.

Methodically, Gehrig set about mastering the art of first base. In high school and college he had pitched and played the outfield as well as first base and he hadn't too much actual experience around the bag when the Yanks optioned him to Hartford in the Eastern League. One of the last faults Lou had to overcome to become a flawless first baseman was to curb himself on balls hit to his right. This last fault was indicative of Gehrig's character. He couldn't do enough work, so he repeatedly went so far to his right that he was fielding balls which properly belonged to the second baseman and there was no one to cover first after Lou had fielded the ball. It was a fault born of overeagerness.

Gehrig conquered this in characteristic fashion. Before each pitch, he mentally calculated how many steps he could go to his right for ground balls, taking into consideration the batter, the speed of his own pitcher, etc. He didn't work it out to a precise mathematical formula but it worked. As Pipp said of him, "He didn't learn quickly but he learned thoroughly. He sweated each detail out and mastered it before he moved on to the next."

Pipp, Gehrig's predecessor, had a genuine fondness for Lou and even today Wally never tires of telling the story of how Gehrig took his job at first base. According to Wally, he was bothered with a headache before a game in the Stadium one day and asked Doc Woods, the trainer, to get him a couple of aspirin tablets.

Miller Huggins, the Yankee manager, overheard the request and told Wally to take the day off and he would start Gehrig at first base.

"Maybe you need a rest, Wally," remarked Hug solicitously.

" 'A rest,' " grins Wally when he tells the story now. "What I got was a vacation! Gehrig went to first base and stayed there for fifteen years. The next time I played first base it was for Cincinnati in the National League, a year later!"

Gehrig's consecutive game record actually began the day before he replaced Pipp, when he had pinch-hit for Pee Wee Wanninger, the Yankee shortstop of the moment. The Yankees never again played an American League game without Lou's name in the batting order until May 2, 1939, in Detroit when he told Joe McCarthy it would be better for himself and for the team if he were benched. He never played in another ball game and was dead twenty-five months later.

One day, late in September, 1934, Gehrig was talking with a reporter in his room at Chicago's Del Prado Hotel. It was a rainy, miserable day and it just suited the conversation. It was apparent that chasing the Tigers in the few remaining days of the pennant race was physically hopeless, if not yet mathematically so.

Lou talked of next year, a topic you rarely heard with McCarthy's Yankees. He thought Red Rolfe would be shifted to third base and would prove a much better ballplayer there than at short. Gehrig was right on that count, for the switch was made next year and Rolfe went on to be the best of all the American League third basemen. Lou maintained that Tony Lazzeri wasn't washed up at all but suffering from bad arches and that a winter of podiatric treatments would give him another few seasons with the Yanks. He was 100 per cent right on that detail, too.

Then the talk switched to Babe Ruth. The big fellow had slowed down to a walk and was obviously on his way out. This was the year one of the younger, and brasher, Yankees endeavored to get up a petition to have Ruth benched for the good of the team. He was promptly sat upon but it was obvious the Babe no longer could help the club.

"I don't suppose Jidge will be back," volunteered the reporter.

"No, I guess not and it's a shame," replied Gehrig sincerely. "That fellow did a great deal for this ball club and for all baseball."

"Well," said the reporter putting into words what everybody felt, "when Babe goes, you should get your share of the headlines."

"I'm not a headline guy," said Gehrig simply. "I know that as long as I was following Ruth to the plate I could have gone up there and stood on my head and nobody would have noticed the difference. When the Babe was through at the dish, whether he hit one or fanned, nobody paid any attention to the next hitter. They were all talking about what Babe had done."

No incident illustrates more clearly what Gehrig meant when he said he wasn't a "headline guy" than the events of June 3, 1932, the greatest day in Gehrig's baseball life. On that afternoon in Shibe Park, Philadelphia, when the Yanks were convincing Connie Mack's Athletics, pennant winners for three straight seasons that the boat had left, Gehrig gave the greatest batting demonstration of modern times.

Lou wasn't facing any ham-donny when he clouted George Earnshaw for home runs on his first three times at bat. The Moose was to win 19 games for Connie Mack that season. When Lou came up for the fourth time, in the seventh, Lee Roy Mahaffey was pitching for the A's and Gehrig hit another out of sight. It was the first time anybody had hit four home runs in one game in the Twentieth Century—and Gehrig had done it on four successive times at bat. He hit one off the top of the score board his fifth time up, just missing five-for-five.

It was a terrific baseball story but it got the No. 2 spot in the headlines that evening and next day. Why? Well, it seems that a fellow named John Joseph McGraw picked that day to resign as manager of the Giants after having been their boss-man for three decades. He resigned without warning and news of it was learned just about the time Lou was tearing into the Philadelphia pitchers for the first of his four home runs.

In 1927, Gehrig was red hot for homers from the start of the season. He had batted only 16 the previous season but now they roared off his bat in an ever-increasing crescendo. He was giving the Babe a great battle for the home run honors. In midsummer, now one was ahead, now the other, now they were tied. Ruth was having things pretty much his own way in those days but shaking the tenacious Gehrig was no cinch. Yet, in August an editorial paragraphist, H. I. Phillips of *The Sun* made a revealing remark with the prediction that "Gehrig would be known as 'the fellow who hit all those home runs the year Ruth broke the record.'" It was even so, for Lou hit 47 and the big Bambino hit his all-time high of 60.

Another instance of the Gehrig luck, in its relation to headlines, occurred on a gloomy Easter Sunday in 1931 in Washington's Griffith Stadium. It had been raining in the morning and the game was an hour or so late getting under way but the seats were sold and the teams were going to play if it were humanly possible. Or even if only subhumanly possible.

It was early in the game with Lyn Lary on first base when Gehrig boffed one into the far distant concrete bleachers. The ball hit with such force that it rebounded back on the playing field. Lary had rounded second and he jogged to third, Gehrig jogging along some paces behind him. When Lyn reached third, he made his turn and then suddenly veered from the basepath into the Yankee dugout, which was on that side of the field. Gehrig didn't notice Lary's defection, nor did any Yankee, and Lou continued his dogtrot across home plate.

All of a sudden, there was hell to pay, as the players say. The Senators were screaming that Gehrig was out for having passed the preceding base runner and that, since there were two out when the ball was hit, the inning was over. Lou's "home run" was technically transformed into a triple.

Neither Lary nor Joe McCarthy who was coaching at third, ever had a satisfactory answer for what happened. It was the last time McCarthy ever appeared on the lines for the Yanks, but the fault was not Joe's since Lary already had passed him on his way to the plate, had touched third properly and Joe had turned to face Gehrig who was just coming into the bag. Lary said he thought the ball was caught, an excusable optical illusion since it had bounded all the way back to the center fielder. That doesn't explain why he went to the bench, since if the ball were caught it was the third out and Lyn should have gone back to his position at short. It may have been that he was going to pause in the dugout for a drink of water before taking the field.

It was pretty much of a joke at the time but six months later, when the averages were added up, Gehrig had 47 home runs and so did Ruth. Since Chuck Klein had hit only 41 in the National League that season, Gehrig not only would have passed Ruth in home run production but would have led the majors in homers. Lou eventually did pass Ruth in later years but he never did lead the majors in home runs. Headlines were hard for Lou.

Although the headlines did not often fall to Gehrig, Lou had more than his share of statistics. The agate type, of course, isn't as eye-catching as the scareheads. Lou established some mighty marks in World Series play, including four home runs in three successive games against the Cardinals in 1928. He holds the American League record for runs batted in, 184 in 1931, the same season Lary's aberration on the baselines cost him the major league home run title.

To get the true worth of Gehrig's batting prowess it is preferable to take his runs batted in marks rather than any of his other figures. For instance, in 1931, when he set the American League record there were at least 47 times when he came to bat with no chance to drive in a run, except by a homer, since Babe Ruth, batting ahead of him, had hit a home run which meant there was nobody on base when Lou came to bat. And any time Ruth, or whoever batted third for the Yanks in his place, made the third out in the first inning, Gehrig had to lead off the second inning with the bases empty.

When you consider that Gehrig batted home no fewer than 1991 runs in his time with the Yankees and that for ten of those seasons Ruth was hitting home runs to empty the bases ahead of him, you get some idea of the devastating power Lou packed in his bat. Since 1920, when records were first kept on this form of endeavor, Lou totaled more RBI's than anybody except Ruth himself.

Gehrig's power was evident early, even before Scout Krichell saw him powder the ball into the woods against Rutgers or blast one out of South Field against Pennsylvania while playing for Columbia's Lions. It probably was evident from the first time this sturdy son of German immigrants took a bat into his hands.

Perhaps the first person to realize the raw power of Gehrig was Harry Kane, a high school coach of note around New York who had Gehrig as his first baseman back in 1920 on the High School of Commerce team. Commerce won the Greater New York P.S.A.L. title and with it the right to a trip to Chicago to play Lane Technical High, the Chicago champions.

With the score tied at 8–8 and the bases filled with New York high school kids in the ninth, Gehrig hit one clean out of Wrigley Field. Probably the least surprised person in the park was Coach Kane. Harry had seen Lou bust 'em before, and for farther distances, too. It was this blow, however, which first focused the national spotlight on Gehrig. Nobody could believe then, though, that a dozen years later Gehrig would be teamed up with Babe Ruth blasting home runs in that same ball park in a World Series.

Because of his great physique, Gehrig attracted more attention as a football player than a ballplayer at Commerce. He was a great punter and line-smasher and a curly wolf on defense. He had a hatful of college offers but finally settled on Columbia because his parents had been employed at the fraternity house of Sigma Nu there, where Lou had helped to wait on tables. The elder Gehrigs, and young Louie, had formed an attachment for Bob Watts, who was later to be Columbia's director of athletics. Once Bob spoke to Lou and his parents, the other college offers went back into the hat.

A Giant scout persuaded Gehrig to play summer ball at Hartford in the Eastern League but Lou was there, playing under the name of Lewis, for only a dozen games when Columbia authorities realized their star football player, as they thought of him at the time, had jeopardized his eligibility. It was eventually straightened out, not only to Columbia's satisfaction but to that of its opponents and Gehrig was penalized by being ineligible for a year.

Gehrig batted from a wide stance, spread-eagling the plate and taking a short stride. It wasn't as noticeable as it might have been in other players because of his tremendous bulk. Power, of course, was the great characteristic of his hitting, but he had all the attributes of the great batsmen, the eye to follow a curve ball, the judgment to pick out the right ball to hit, the ability to hit through a hole. He didn't have anything but the power at first, of course, but all of these came later, along with the ability to bunt when he had to do so.

Gehrig was called "Buster" by Ruth when he first joined the Yanks and it was a nickname which suited him at the time. He was a buster with the bat and he was boyish enough to merit the tag for affectionate reasons. Whatever Lou was called, even "Biscuit Pants," it was always with affection.

As a matter of fact, it wasn't until after Huggins had passed on and Joe McCarthy had come into full charge that the Yanks began to realize that they had a man, not a boy, in their midst. It was only when Wally Pipp, Waite Hoyt, Benny Bengough, Joe

Dugan, Tony Lazzeri, Herb Pennock and the other regulars of the Huggins regime were traded or retired that Gehrig assumed the stature and status of a veteran.

There were many reasons for this, among them Gehrig's quietness and modesty. He wasn't a pusher, even when he became a regular, and his teammates, all of whom save the great Ruth he was outshining, were still the big Yankees to him and he was the kid from Columbia. The fact that most of the regulars of his own age were married and he was still Mom Gehrig's boy had much to do with his contemporaries treating him as though he were a youngster. It was Lou's mother who accompanied him to spring training, his mother who met him when the club returned from a trip.

Because Gehrig was quiet, sometimes moody, the impression prevailed that he was what ball players call a "loner." Far from it. He was a good bridge player and loved to play, but bridge isn't the noisy, roistering game that poker or that other favorite of the players, hearts, are. Lou loved to fish and you don't fish in front of crowds. He also liked to play billiards and it was something to see that huge frame sprawled over a table, those big paws hiding a cue and Lou nursing the balls in straight rail with a truly deft touch.

Gehrig often said the most remarkable thing that ever happened to him was his marriage to Miss Eleanor Twitchell on September 29, 1933. Eleanor and Lou had met in Chicago and how the shy Lou ever got up enough courage to ask for another date is possibly the best tribute which ever could be paid to the girl who was to be his wife.

Eleanor was the perfect wife for Lou. Big as he was, he needed to be mothered and protected, to lean upon someone for advice and comfort. It was Eleanor who brought out the social side of Gehrig, who enabled him to mix without embarrassment, who directed his reading and who gave him a self-confidence which, if it hadn't been lacking, certainly was never evident. She was a tower of strength to him when he was fighting the hopeless battle against his last illness.

The end came quickly for Gehrig. Not the release from his illness but his end as a ballplayer. He had a sub-par season, sub-par for Lou that is, in 1938 when he fell below .300 for the first time

ball pitching of Grove to aspirin tablets. It was a stock baseball expression to describe a ball which sped plateward so fast that it was almost invisible to the naked eye.

Such was the speed of Grove in those days that National Leaguers were invariably astounded when they got their first glimpse of the star left-hander of the Philadelphia Athletics. The speed of Grove was famous throughout both leagues but it had to be seen to be appreciated.

Cuccinello wasn't the first big leaguer to be amazed when he saw Grove from the proximity of the batter's box for the first time, nor was he the last. The Cubs had a rude shock in the World Series of 1929 when they saw Lefty for the first time.

In the opening game of that Series at Wrigley Field, Mack had pulled Howard Ehmke out of a hat and Ehmke proceeded to make Series history by fanning thirteen Cubs. The next day Connie came up with George Earnshaw, who was relieved by Grove in the fifth. The Big Moose had fanned seven when he needed help from Grove and Lefty struck out another six Cubs to bring the total to thirteen for the second day in a row. And Grove pitched only 4⅓ innings in getting six strikeout victims out of a possible thirteen. In the fourth game, after the Athletics had had a ten-run inning against the Cubs at Shibe Park, Grove came in to pitch the last two innings and fanned four of a possible six, giving him a Series record of ten strikeouts in 6⅓ innings.

There is little question that Grove was the fastest of the pitchers of his time or, at least, until Bob Feller came along. There are those who say that Grove was faster than Feller or that Vance and Mungo rated up with either of the American Leaguers but such arguments are relative. All were far faster than the average and it would take an electric eye to determine which was the fastest.

Grove could throw a ball by a batter as few pitchers ever could. It wasn't only National Leaguers seeing him for the first time who were put into a coma by his speed. It happened to American Leaguers who had seen him time and again and who were simply overpowered, not surprised.

Against the Yankees one day, when the Athletics held a 1–0 lead in the last half of the ninth, Mark Koenig led off with a triple against Grove. With Ruth, Gehrig and Bob Meusel coming up, the customers in Yankee Stadium settled back to await a tie ball game.

Grove simply reared back and flung his fast ball right by the Yankee Murderers' Row, fanning the Babe, Lou and Meusel on nine pitched balls, one of which Meusel came close enough to foul off.

Bob listed that as one of the strikeout achievements he remembered best in an interview with Harold Kaese, Boston sports columnist, and went on to tell him of other games when he was feeding American League sluggers aspirin tablets.

"Another day in Philadelphia I relieved Jack Quinn with the bases filled," Grove told Kaese, "and I struck out Ruth, Gehrig and Tony Lazzeri on ten pitches, all of them strikes. Lazzeri hit a couple of fouls. And in Chicago in 1931, I relieved Roy Mahaffey with men on second and third and fanned the side on ten pitches. The way Johnny Heving froze when he caught the last strike I doubt if he ever saw the ball."

Although Grove was not one to volunteer information nor a particularly articulate player, he could and did speak out whenever anybody made comparisons in favor of old-time pitchers as opposed to modern pitchers. He not only spoke out but he made his point clearly.

Grove was particularly proud of achieving his 300th victory, as well he should be since he was the first since Grover Cleveland Alexander's day to reach that number and will be the last for many years to come. When Cy Young's 511 victories cropped up, in conversation or even the marks of Walter Johnson, Christy Mathewson or Alexander, Lefty was quick to enter a demurrer.

"I might have won 500 games if I pitched forty years ago," he would snort. "Consider all the things those guys had going for 'em that I didn't. First of all they had the dead ball. Guys used to lead the league with a half-dozen home runs. Second, a ball was hardly ever thrown out of play. You could pitch with a discolored ball or a scuffed one. The dirty baseball was hard to follow and the scuffed one 'sailed,' which made it harder to hit. Third, they had the privilege of throwing trick deliveries like the shine-ball, the emory-ball and the spitter."

All of Grove's points were well taken. There isn't any question but the dead ball would have been a great aid to him, while a pitcher with his speed using a baseball that had become discolored through use or with a torn cover would have possessed practically a lethal weapon.

Another point, too, was that in Grove's day—and all 300 of his victories were scored in the era of the lively ball—Babe Ruth had set the style. The choke-hitter had almost disappeared and all the batters were swinging from their heels in an effort to clear the fences. While this was in some ways an asset to a pitcher, since he could get the ball past the hitter who was swinging freely, it also meant trouble if the pitch were the least bit off, if it went anywhere in the zone where the batter had a chance to get the "fat" part of his bat on the ball.

Grove's complaints against comparisons with the pitchers of the pre-Ruthian era may seem conceited but he has a sound argument. To begin with, Lefty is the only pitcher who won 300 games all in the era of the lively ball. Young, Matty and Eddie Plank reached the 300-mark pitching exclusively with the dead ball, while Alexander had a decade with the dead ball and Johnson enjoyed it for thirteen seasons.

Not only is Grove the only jack-rabbit pitcher to reach 300 victories but he has an even more important distinction and one generally overlooked. The lean left-hander won 300 games while losing 141, which gives him the highest won and lost percentage of any pitcher elected to the Hall of Fame at Cooperstown, .680. The closest Hall of Famer to Bob in winning percentage is Babe Ruth with .676, but Ruth was voted into Cooperstown on the strength of his home-run hitting, not his pitching.

Grove had a deep appreciation of what it meant to win 300 games and he hung on until he made it. In 1939, Lefty won fifteen games while losing four for the Red Sox and led the American League pitchers in earned runs with an average of 2.54. Those fifteen triumphs boosted his lifetime total to 286 but it took him two more seasons to get to 300, two seasons in which his overall won-and-lost record was 14–13 and in which his earned-run mark scored at four per nine-inning game and higher.

Robert Moses Grove was born in Lonaconing, Maryland, on March 6, 1900. He was born in circumstances which it would be euphemistic to call "modest." His dad and most of the menfolk in his family worked in the coal mines and Grove, quitting school after his elementary grades, went to work in a silk mill for a half dollar a day, finally working his way, after a couple of years, up to seven bucks a week.

Bob wanted no part of the coal mines and eventually, when he was eighteen, he was working in a glass factory at $5.25 a day. He played ball with other boys in the neighborhood, crude, cow-pasture ball, but finally, in 1919, landed with an organized ama-teur team at Midland, near his home town. Here he was a first baseman simply because no one could handle his blazing fast ball.

Eventually the Midland team obtained a catcher who could hold Grove's speed and his pitching began receiving attention. He was offered a job pitching for Martinsburg, West Virginia, in the Blue Ridge League at $125 a month and he leaped at the chance to get away from the drudgery of manual labor.

Grove was a lean, lanky kid of twenty when he joined Mar-tinsburg and, although he didn't know it at the time, he already was on his way to glory and gold. He was in Martinsburg only a few months when the Baltimore Orioles paid $3,500 for his con-tract and upped his salary $50 a month. The Orioles at that time, managed by the fabulous Jack Dunn, the discoverer of Ruth, were one of the greatest minor league teams in the history of the game.

Dunn had great stars with the Orioles, players who might have been in the majors long before they actually made it had it not been Dunn's whim to keep them in Baltimore where they con-tinued to tear the International League apart, year after year. It was with the Orioles that Grove ran across players like George Earnshaw, Jack Bentley, Max Bishop, Joe Boley, Rube Parnham and Dick Porter.

Baltimore won seven International League pennants in a row, breaking the record for minor league teams set in the Texas League by Jake Atz's Fort Worth team. Grove joined the team when it was in the process of winning its third pennant in that string, and winning it by taking the last 25 games of the season in a row. Lefty stayed with the Orioles while they won the last five of these pennants.

Dunn had sold Ernie Shore, a pitcher, Ben Egan, a catcher,

and Ruth to the Red Sox in 1914 for a grand total of $8,500, with the Babe's price tag reported to be $2,900. Less than six years later, Harry Frazee, the Red Sox owner, found himself caught in a financial squeeze and sold Ruth to the Yankees for $100,000. It was a monumental price for those times and Dunnie, when he arranged to sell Grove, wanted to set a new record for baseball ivory. Connie Mack obliged by tacking $600 extra onto the check. It was the top figure at the time but, of course, has since been exceeded.

With the Athletics Grove not only rejoined some of his Oriole teammates but he was to find himself with a team which shortly was to dominate the American League as Baltimore had dominated the International. Mack had broken up a pennant-winning team after the 1914 season and now was laboriously piecing together another one. He eventually was to have a three-time pennant winner, a club which ended the Yankees' position as baseball's Number 1 team.

Grove, who never had a losing year at Baltimore (he was 12–2 in his first season there), found the American League a little rough at the start. Accustomed to firing the ball past the hitters in the International League, Lefty found that didn't work in the majors. For one thing, big leaguers were more inclined to wait a pitcher out and not chase after bad balls.

At Baltimore, Grove never had to pay much attention to his control. It was nothing for him to fill the bases on walks and then strike out the side. It didn't pan out that way with the A's. In 1925, his first year on the big wheel, Lefty won ten games and lost twelve. He led the American League in bases on balls with 131, the only time he ever won that booby prize but he also led it in strikeouts with 116.

There were several significant items in Grove's first year with the Athletics, not the least of which was the fact that Lefty learned that he would have to alter his pitching tactics. That 1925 season was the only one in Grove's entire career, major or minor, in which he finished with a percentage of lower than .500 and it was the only time he ever walked more men than he fanned. It also was the first of seven straight seasons in which he was to lead the league in strikeouts.

The temperament Grove brought to the majors with him was as remarkable as his fast ball. Dealing with temperamental ball-players was nothing new to Mack, who had handled Rube Waddell and Ossie Schreckengost, fun-loving Rover Boys if ever there were, and Joe Jackson, who threatened to pine away with lonesomeness for the Carolinas. Grove was a different problem. He wasn't a dissipater and he wasn't lonesome. Lefty was merely ornery.

Grove wanted to win but couldn't see that it was his fault when he didn't. In four and a half years with Baltimore, Lefty had won 108 games while losing only 36. When things started to go wrong with him in the American League, when his control was off or when the hitters were tying into his high hard one, Grove took it as a personal insult. He couldn't wait to get the ball back from the catcher so he could fire it at the batters again.

It was Cy Perkins, a catcher out of Gloucester, Massachusetts, who taught Grove patience. Cy served a long time under Connie. He had come to Mack when the 1914 A's were broken up and dispersed over the American League market and he labored with Connie during the long, lonesome stretch when the Athletics spent seven consecutive seasons in the cellar. He lasted long enough to be with the pennant winners of 1929 and 1930, was a coach with the Yankees under Joe McCarthy when they won in 1932, with the Tigers when they were winning in 1934 and 1935 and finally came the full cycle when he was back in Philadelphia under Eddie Sawyer as the Whiz Kids in 1950 won the first National League pennant that city had seen in 35 years.

The cure, of itself, was a simple one but teaching it to Grove was far from simple. Perkins finally made Lefty step off the rubber as he took the throw from the catcher and remain off the rubber while he took the ball in his left hand and plunked it into his gloved right hand three times. You've seen pitchers fiddle around thus on the mound. With most it is merely a reflex action but with Grove it acted as a checkrein. After he had plopped the ball into his mitt three times, then Grove stepped on the mound, leaned forward and took the sign from the catcher.

Having learned to space himself between pitches, Grove taught himself to pace his pitching. No longer did he fire every ball as hard as he could. He saved his fireball for the clutches and found he was able to finish with something in reserve, that he wasn't running out of gas in the closing innings.

With the help from Perkins and the self-study imposed upon him by necessity, Grove had adjusted himself so that he was a winning pitcher in his third year with the Athletics. After his 10–12 season as a freshman, Lefty split 26 decisions right down the middle in 1926, cut his bases on balls down to 101, the last time in the majors he walked more than 100, and managed to lead the American League in earned runs with a mark of 2.51.

Grove won twenty games for Mack in 1927 and for the next six seasons he never failed to win that many. In those seven years before he was sold to the Red Sox, Lefty won a total of 172 games for the A's, an average of nearly 25 per season. This stretch is unparalleled in the era of the lively ball.

Not only was Grove winning twenty or better for Connie, but he was leading the league in strikeouts and in earned runs. The earned-run tabulation was introduced into baseball in 1912 and Grove is the only pitcher who for three straight seasons led the league in both earned runs and won-and-lost percentage. Grove also is the holder of the major league record for the most number of seasons leading the league in earned-run percentage, nine, and the most number of years in leading the league in won-and-lost percentage, five.

Grove had two remarkable seasons in 1930 and 1931, the most amazing pair any modern pitcher has enjoyed. He was 28–5 in 1930, which was sensational enough, but the following year he turned in a 31–4 record. This was the highest winning percentage (.886) ever attained by a pitcher in this century who had twenty decisions. Percentagewise the mark is topped by Freddie Fitzsimmons 16–2 record with Brooklyn in 1940 and Johnny Allen's 15–1 mark with Cleveland in 1937, but neither stands comparison with Grove's record. Indeed, Lefty's 31 victories in that one year equaled the combined victory total of Fitzsimmons and Allen in their record-breaking seasons.

If Grove had his greatest season in 1931—and only one pitcher, Dizzy Dean in 1934, has won as many as thirty games since—it also was the year which led to his most memorable display of temper. At one stretch Grove had a sixteen-game winning streak going and he seemed a cinch to break the American League record which Joe Wood of the Red Sox and Walter Johnson of the Senators had established in 1912.

When Grove set his cap for his seventeenth in a row he had the great power of the Athletics going for him against the lowly St. Louis Browns. The A's were to win 107 games that year and beat the Yankees for the pennant by a comfortable 13½-game margin. Bill Killefer's Browns were to lose 91 games. It didn't seem possible that a better spot could be picked for Grove to write a new page into American League history than Sportsman's Park in St. Louis on that August afternoon in 1931.

Grove's opponent was Dick Coffman, a right-hander with good spirit but nothing like the physical equipment of the Athletic ace. Yet when the smoke had cleared, Dick was the winner by a 1–0 score, the lone run of the game coming when Jim Moore, playing left field for the A's, misjudged a fly ball.

The visitors' dressing room at Sportsman's Park that evening was a shambles. Grove attempted to take it apart, locker by locker. It was the greatest of his towering rages and Lefty's towering rages reached practically into the stratosphere. He was not only mad at everybody present, he was even mad at Al Simmons, who was many miles away in Milwaukee receiving medical treatment.

"If Simmons had been here and in left field, he would have stuck that ball in his back pocket," roared Grove. "What the hell did he have to go to Milwaukee for?"

Despite his ingrown disposition, Grove could adjust himself to conditions—when he was forced to. He proved this by his third year with the Athletics and he was to prove it again with the Red Sox, after Mack had sold him to Tom Yawkey for more than he had paid Jack Dunn for him.

Grove was sold to the Sox after the 1933 season and somewhere along the line during the training session at Sarasota, Florida, the next spring he injured his arm. How or where is a mystery. There were hints that Mack had palmed off damaged goods on Yawkey but the general belief is that Lefty's injury came during training with Boston.

It was a new experience for Grove to find his pitches belted out of the lot. He had an 8–8 record but it was a truly horrible season.

He struck out fewer than fifty hitters and the opposition averaged better than seven runs a game against the once invincible left-hander.

If Grove had been hard to get along with before, the Boston writers found him practically impossible. They had been prepared to welcome a great pitcher and instead found themselves with a great grouch. He talked of quitting and going back to his native Lonaconing. Bucky Harris, then in his first and only year of managing the Sox, persevered with him and by the end of the year old man Mose grumpily allowed as how his arm might be getting a mite better.

It was now that Lefty made the great changeover, that he

ROBERT MOSES GROVE

Born March 6, 1900 at Lonaconing, Md.
Height, 6' 3". Weight, 204. Threw and batted left-handed.

EAR	CLUB	LEAGUE	G	IP	W	L	PCT	H	R	ER	SO	BB	ERA
920	Martinsburg	Blue Ridge											
		P-1B	59	3	3		.500	30	16	..	60	24	...
920	Baltimore	Int.	19	123	12	2	.857	120	69	52	88	71	3.80
921	Baltimore	Int.	47	313	25	10	.714	237	131	89	254	179	2.56
922	Baltimore	Int.	41	209	18	8	.692	146	90	65	205	152	2.80
923	Baltimore	Int.	52	303	27	10	.730	223	128	105	330	186	3.12
924	Baltimore (a)	Int.	47	236	26	6	.813	196	95	79	231	108	3.01
925	Philadelphia	Amer.	45	197	10	12	.455	207	120	104	*116	*131	4.75
926	Philadelphia	Amer.	45	258	13	13	.500	227	97	72	*194	101	*2.51
927	Philadelphia	Amer.	51	262	20	13	.606	251	116	93	*174	79	3.20
928	Philadelphia	Amer.	39	262	*24	8	.750	228	93	75	*183	64	2.57
929	Philadelphia	Amer.	42	275	20	6	*.769	278	104	86	*170	81	*2.81
930	Philadelphia	Amer.	*50	291	*28	5	*.848	273	101	97	*214	60	*3.00
931	Philadelphia	Amer.	41	289	*31	4	*.886	249	84	66	*175	62	*2.06
932	Philadelphia	Amer.	44	292	25	10	.714	269	101	92	188	79	*2.84
933	Philadelphia †	Amer.	45	275	*24	8	*.750	280	113	98	114	83	3.21
934	Boston	Amer.	22	109	8	8	.500	149	84	79	43	32	6.52
935	Boston	Amer.	35	273	20	12	.625	269	105	82	121	65	*2.70
936	Boston	Amer.	35	253	17	12	.586	237	90	79	130	65	*2.81
937	Boston	Amer.	32	262	17	9	.654	269	101	88	153	83	3.02
938	Boston	Amer.	24	164	14	4	*.778	169	65	56	99	52	*3.07
939	Boston	Amer.	23	191	15	4	.789	180	63	54	81	58	*2.54
940	Boston	Amer.	22	153	7	6	.538	159	73	68	62	50	4.00
941	Boston	Amer.	21	134	7	7	.500	155	84	65	82	116	4.37

Major League Totals 616 3940 300 141   .680 3849 INC INC 2271 1187   ...

WORLD SERIES RECORD

YEAR	CLUB	LEAGUE	G	IP	W	L	PCT	H	R	ER	SO	BB	ER
1929	Philadelphia	Amer.	2	6⅓	0	0	.000	3	0	0	10	1	0.0
1930	Philadelphia	Amer.	3	19	2	1	.667	15	5	3	10	3	1.4
1931	Philadelphia	Amer.	3	26	2	1	.667	28	7	7	16	2	2.4
	World Series Total		8	51⅓	4	2	.667	46	12	10	36	6	1.7

ALL-STAR GAME RECORD

YEAR	LEAGUE	IP	W	L	PCT	H	R	ER	SO	BB	ER
1933	American	3	0	0	.000	3	0	0	3	0	0.0
1936	American	3	0	1	.000	3	2	2	2	2	6.0
1938	American	2	0	0	.000	4	2	0	3	0	0.0
	All-Star Game Totals	8	0	1	.000	10	4	2	8	2	2.2

(a) Sold to Philadelphia Athletics for $105,000, November, 1924.

† Traded with Second Baseman Max Bishop and Pitcher George Walberg to Boston Red Sox for Infielder Harold Warstler, Pitcher Bob Kline and $125,000, Dec. 12, 1933.

* Led league.

added pitching artistry to his physical assets. Near the end of the 1934 season under Harris, Grove discovered that there were fewer twinges in his arm when he threw a curve than when he threw a fast ball. He began to develop his curve ball and finally had a good one.

Grove always had a curve ball and it was more than just a wrinkle but since he was winning with his fast ball he neglected it. Now he became a pitcher instead of a thrower. Moe Berg, who was with Grove at Boston, makes a nice distinction of Lefty's changeover. "It wasn't that Grove developed a curve ball after he hurt his arm," explained Moe, "but that he improved the good curve he already had to the point where it was almost a great curve."

Later Grove added a fork-ball to his equipment, a pitch which Bullet Joe Bush had used to implement his own fast ball. It is a pitch which doesn't rotate much, shudders like a knuckler as it nears the plate and usually lures the batter into swinging too soon. The term "fork-ball" stems from the fact that the fingers gripping the ball are spread wide instead of held close together as when pitching a curve or fast one.

Thus when the petulant southpaw went back to Lonaconing 22 years after he set out from there to become a pitcher, he had a complete assortment of pitching equipment. He also had 300 victories and he won them with everything from a blazing fireball to a slow curve. Time, and Grove, had marched on.

CHAPTER XI

THE OUTSPOKEN RAJAH

Rogers Hornsby

AL SPOHRER was a young man with a hairline which receded so rapidly in his youth that it threatened to reach the nape of his neck by the time he attained middle age. Although he once was under a mad delusion that he was a prize fighter, Al was content to make his living catching baseballs, rather than boxing gloves.

An earnest young man, Spohrer attempted the impossible in the summer of 1929. He tried to talk Rogers Hornsby out of a base hit. Catching for the last place Boston Braves against the first place Chicago Cubs at Wrigley Field, Spohrer reached a decision which had been reached in advance of him by many another, and older, head. The decision was that Hornsby couldn't be kept from hitting by ordinary means.

Spohrer, who had been a teammate of Hornsby the year before at Boston, knew of the Rajah's fanatic devotion to steaks. Rogers was the original beef eater and in whatever town he landed, and he landed in several before he was through, he was always on the prowl for a place which served steaks better than any other place in that particular town. The thought struck Al that if he could get Hornsby talking about his hobby it might take his mind off his hitting. Or, rather, off the Boston pitching which, at the moment, Hornsby was finding as appetizing as any steak.

"Say, Rog," began Spohrer conversationally when Hornsby came to bat for the third time, "my wife has discovered a butcher in Boston who sells the finest steaks anyone ever ate."

"That so?" said Hornsby with polite interest.

"Strike one!" bawled the umpire.

"Not only that, Rog," continued Al, really warming to his task, "but my wife can cook steaks better than anybody I know. Grace really has a knack of broiling 'em."

"That sounds good," commented Rogers.

"Strike two!" was the umpire's contribution to the conversation.

"What Grace and I thought," enthused Spohrer, "was that maybe on the next trip up to Boston, you'd come over to the house for dinner some night and try one."

"Crack!" That wasn't the umpire but the bat. The ball disappeared over the left field wall of Wrigley Field and Hornsby began a slow trot around the bases. When he completed the circuit and touched his spikes into the rubber of home plate, he turned to face the chagrined Spohrer.

"What night shall we make it, Al?" Hornsby asked.

The story of Spohrer and Hornsby has been told so often that it has attained the status of a baseball legend and, like so many legends, it may be apocryphal. The chances are, however, it is true but true or not, it serves as perfect example of the fierce concentration Hornsby was able to put in his task of hitting a baseball. Nothing, not even conversation about a succulent steak, could cause any deviation from the course he plotted.

To Hornsby, there was only one way to play baseball and that was by giving it one's full and undivided attention. It was the begin-all and end-all of his existence. Many years after the dinner invitation extended to him by Spohrer, Hornsby was sipping a coke at the bar of the old Auditorium Hotel in Chicago, talking with Bill McCullough, a New York sports writer who was doing publicity in Chicago that fall.

It was a Saturday evening and the abstemious Hornsby was idly turning the pages of the final sports extra of the Chicago *News*. The date was November 13, 1937, and the front page was filled with reports of the Army–Notre Dame in New York. There were stories on Wisconsin-Purdue, Northwestern-Minnesota, Illinois–Ohio State, Michigan-Pennsylvania, Pitt-Nebraska—even one on Chicago and Beloit. There were photos and charts, color stories and play-by-play.

The sports section ran eight pages and was a truly magnificent compilation of the day's doings on the gridiron. As Hornsby looked up one column and down another for some item about baseball without success, he finally put the paper aside.

"Lord, Bill," said Rog to McCullough, "there's *nothing* in the sports pages these days, is there?"

There was always an air of mystery to Hornsby, an air of mystery to his personal comings-and-goings and an air of mystery to his departure from one club to another.

When Hornsby joined the Giants in the spring of 1927, after being traded from the Cardinals when he had brought St. Louis the first of its many pennants, Ferdie Schupp, who had been with Rogers on the Cardinals was questioned as to what manner of man Hornsby might be.

"Nobody knows," answered Schupp honestly. "He never talks to anybody. He just goes out and plays second base and when the game is over he comes into the clubhouse, takes off his uniform, takes a shower and gets dressed without saying a word. Then he leaves the clubhouse and nobody knows where he goes."

Just as nobody knew what Hornsby did between games, neither did anybody know why Hornsby went from club to club. When he was traded by the Cards to the Giants, the civic repercussions in St. Louis were greater than in any city, any time after the trading of a star ballplayer.

Hornsby was traded from the Cards because he wanted a three-year contract at $50,000 to be playing-manager, a job he had held for a year and a half without any pay increase. Why he was traded from the Giants to the Braves after one season nobody knows to this day, least of all Rogers himself. He was traded from the Braves to the Cubs, again after one season, because Judge Emil Fuchs, the owner of the Braves, needed the cash which Hornsby would bring, which turned out to be $120,000, although it was announced as $200,000 when the deal was made. And there is no known reason for the Cubs suddenly releasing Hornsby as player-manager in the middle of the 1932 season.

The opinion here always has been that Hornsby was hurt more by being traded from the Cardinals to the Giants than by any other single factor in his turbulent career. When he came to the Giants he was a player apart. He had been a manager and he never went back to mingle with the rank and file again. John McGraw gave him privileges no other Giant player ever had—or ever was to have again. Hornsby neither flaunted nor abused these privileges but it kept him from being one of the gang.

Hornsby, as has been intimated, always said what he thought and he always spoke for publication. There was no off-the-record stuff with Rog. If you asked his opinion, he gave it and he didn't care whether you printed it or not. It was all one with Hornsby.

When Hornsby reported to the Giants in the spring of 1927, McGraw was absent frequently from the Sarasota camp. He left the club in charge of Rogers. Fred Lindstrom, the third baseman, and Hornsby had an argument over the proper way to make the double play.

Hornsby wanted Lindy to fire the ball to him at second as quickly as possible. (Some said this was to save his own arm, so he wouldn't have to hurry to complete the relay to first base.) Lindstrom said that McGraw always instructed his players to make sure of getting the "head man" on double plays. In other words, McGraw wanted the force-out at second to be certain, preferring to get only one rather than to miss both because the throw to second base was hurried.

"If that's the way the Old Man wants it," snapped Hornsby, "do it that way when he's in charge. When I'm in charge, do it my way."

Lindy, like Hornsby, also could be outspoken. He told Hornsby that once he laid his bat down he was no bargain and not to get puffed up with his own importance.

"I'm not arguing with you, I'm telling you," declared Hornsby. "You'll do as I say. And keep your mouth shut."

Hornsby paused for a moment to look at the other Giants. "And that goes for the rest of you," he barked. It did, too. Whenever McGraw left Hornsby in charge, and he did it several times, not only that spring but during the summer when the club was fighting for the pennant, Hornsby always took charge literally.

Awkward as was his position with the Giants, it was even more so the following season when he was traded to Boston. McGraw fled to Cuba when the trade was made and never did answer any questions about it. With the Braves, Hornsby joined a slap-happy club with a thoroughly confused front office and a manager named Jack Slattery, who had been a college baseball coach the year before.

Visiting newspapermen came to Hornsby for interviews in the spring. They knew Hornsby and they didn't know Slattery. There were rumors that Slattery wouldn't even last long enough as manager to get the club home from spring training. As a matter of fact, Jack mightn't have opened the season had the Boston papers not lined up solidly behind him.

When Slattery finally was let out, Hornsby at first refused to take over the managership. He felt that baseball would feel he had undermined Slattery. As a matter of fact, Slattery was doomed from the start because he never had a ball club. Fuchs argued sufficiently to make Rogers assume the managership and the Braves played the last two-thirds of the season under Hornsby, no better or no worse than they had played under Slattery.

Hornsby felt a genuine fondness for Judge Fuchs and he advised Fuchs to sell him that winter for what he would bring on the open market. It was then that he went to the Cubs, back to the playing ranks again under Joe McCarthy. Hornsby helped McCarthy win his first pennant in 1929 and at the end of the following season succeeded McCarthy as manager. Once again Rogers was on the spot—but he had no more to do with McCarthy leaving the Cubs than he had to do with Slattery leaving the Braves. After the dismal showing of the Cubs in the 1929 World Series, the club was receiving second-guesses in carload lots. And McCarthy, one of the greatest managers the game ever knew, was not one to take second-guessing from the front office.

Hornsby lasted a season and a half as Cub manager and was released outright August 2, 1932. He left behind him a club which won the pennant under Charley Grimm. There was no logical reason for Rog being let out by the Cubs. He was riding the players hard, but he felt that they needed it, that they had the best club and weren't putting out. His contention was borne out when the club won for Grimm. Maybe he should have used sugar instead of vinegar but nobody had ever sugared up Hornsby. In fact, nobody ever had to.

In view of Hornsby's magnificent achievements as a batter, it may come as a surprise to learn that he was purchased by the

Cardinals because that astute scout, Bob Connery, saw fielding greatness in the skinny kid who was playing shortstop for Denison, Texas, in the Class D Western Association.

Another generally forgotten item about Hornsby is that he came up to the Cardinals as a choke-hitter who batted from a crouch, which may explain his .277 average with Denison. It was Connery and Miller Huggins who got him to adopt the stance he later made famous, standing well back in the box, farther from the plate than any ranking hitter ever did.

Hornsby stood with his feet close together and took a tremendous stride, stepping up to meet the ball. "It was impossible to hit me with a pitched ball," said Rogers, "because I always was moving with the pitch."

Because of this stance Hornsby could, and did, hit to all fields. I remember him beating Dutch Ruether with a home run into the right field stands, close to the foul line, at Sportsman's Park one August Sunday in 1924. The score was tied and Hornsby was the leadoff batter for the Cards in the ninth. Wholly irrelevant to the story is that in the second game of that doubleheader, Eddie Dyer pitched for the Cardinals and blanked Brooklyn, 17 to 0. And that then the Dodgers went out and won the next fifteen straight and almost won the pennant.

Hornsby's stance had a lot of imitators, most of them unsuccessful, although Lester Bell, Cardinal third baseman, was a dangerous hitter. It is believed by batting theorists that only a batter who takes a stance with his feet close together, and thus is in a position to hit into the opposite field, can ever achieve the magic .400 figure. The only exception to the rule has been Ted Williams, who batted over .400 in 1941 without hitting to the opposite field very often. Hornsby hit over .400 on three different occasions, holding the modern batting mark of .424, which he set in 1924.

Probably Hornsby was the most devastating hitter baseball ever has seen through the five seasons of 1921, 1922, 1923, 1924 and 1925. Rog's averages for those seasons, respectively and respectfully, were .397, .401, .384, .424 and .403. In those five consecutive seasons, the Rajah went to bat 2679 times and rapped out no fewer than 1078 base hits. His over-all average for the five-year period was .402.

There is no question that the lively ball helped Hornsby. His average jumped from .318 in 1919 to .370 in 1920. And once his average went up, it stayed up until he was through. The fact that Rogers was aided by the lively ball is no reflection upon his hitting skill. The other batters of his time were hitting at the same rabbit-ball but Hornsby was out-hitting them by so far that he led the National League for six consecutive seasons.

Hornsby had gone from Boston a decade before Casey Stengel came there to manage, but the magic of Hornsby's name lived on. Braves Field has the reputation of being one of the most difficult parks in the National League for hitters. The prevailing wind is always from the East and sweeps from the mound to the plate.

One of Stengel's players, in a woeful slump, came back to the dugout, flung his bat from him in disgust and started to revile the ball park, its architecture and its prevailing wind.

"How the hell can they expect anybody to hit up here?" he wanted to know. "The wind is always with the pitcher. Nobody can hit up here."

"All I know," answered Stengel mildly, "is that Hornsby played here one whole season and batted .387."

Although Hornsby generally was not regarded as a great manager, he was a great and inspiring leader for the Cardinals when he won the pennant in 1926 and then upset the vaunted Yankees in the World Series that fall. The general charge against Hornsby was that he was impatient with young players, that things came too easily to him that he couldn't understand others not acquiring the skills which were natural to him.

That may be so but anybody who ever conversed with the Rajah will admit that Hornsby always made sense when he spoke about baseball. And he rarely spoke about anything else. For all of his reputation as a horse player, Rogers never talked about the ponies. He just bet 'em.

Hornsby never went to the movies during the baseball season, rarely read and never attempted to read on a train. He had incredibly clear, blue eyes and was past fifty, before he needed glasses to aid his vision.

Baseball was his abiding passion and his refusal to do anything which might possibly subject his eyes to strain was only part of

THE OUTSPOKEN RAJAH 127

his devotion to the game. In the sere and yellow of his career, Hornsby went into the bushes to manage at Baltimore . . . Oklahoma City . . . Chattanooga . . . Fort Worth . . . wherever there was baseball, there was Hornsby if there was room for him.

Hornsby took over the managership of Oklahoma City in the Texas League in June, 1940. A month or so later, I happened to run across him down there and he told me of the lecture he had given his club when he took over. It is worth retelling, for it is illustrative of his baseball credo.

"I never smoked or drank in my life," began Hornsby to his squad, almost in a Billy Sunday manner. "And you fellows'd be smart if you'd cut out drinking or smoking while you're playing ball. I'm not saying this merely because I don't drink or smoke but merely because it's the best way to keep your legs and wind in shape.

"Don't kid yourselves about baseball. There's only one place to play it—the big leagues. And the idea is to get to the big leagues as quickly as you can and stay there as long as you can. And, if you're in shape, you've got a better chance to get up there and stay up there.

"Anybody who is content to dub around in the minors is a sucker. If you haven't got a chance to make the majors, get out of baseball and go into business or learn a trade while you're still young enough."

It was, to anyone who knew Hornsby, a typical Hornsby talk. One of the Texas sports writers asked Rogers what did a kid need the most if he was to become a successful ballplayer.

"What does a kid need the most to become a successful ballplayer?" repeated the forthright Rajah. "That's a cinch—ability."

In a word, Hornsby summed up his philosophy of life. During his twenty-three years in the majors, the Rajah saw time and again that the race is always to the swift. Baseball pays off only in the major leagues and pays off only on ability. Those who have it, thinks Hornsby, should protect its longevity to the utmost. When he speaks of the evils of drink or the dangers of nicotine, Hornsby is speaking not as a moralist but as the realist he always has been.

No record of Hornsby's career would be complete without a mention of his betting. The Rajah, like millions of other Americans, liked to bet on the horses and he never made a secret of it. As a matter of fact, Rog never made a secret of anything. His life was an open book and those who didn't like it didn't have to read it.

During the 1949 World Series Hornsby revealed that he hadn't made a bet that entire season. His handicapper—the man who figured the horses for him—had died during the previous winter and Rogers merely stopped betting because he didn't have the information he had had in other years.

Hornsby never saw any moral difference between his betting on horses and the owners of ball clubs gambling in the stock market. As a matter of fact, Rog lost more money in the stock market than he did on the ponies, $100,000 in one clip. And that on a tip (*sic*) supplied to him by an owner of a ball club.

Because of differences with various owners, Rog often has been labeled a stormy petrel, a fiery individual. Actually, Hornsby was not hotheaded but a man of cold steel, rigid and uncompromising. He cut his path clearly and never deviated from it by so much as a hair's breadth. No better example of Rog's stubbornly clinging to a point could be cited than the dispute over the stock he owned in the Cardinals and had to sell before he could play with the Giants. It was an issue which threatened to turn the National League upside down until it was settled just before the opening of the 1927 season. And it was settled at Hornsby's terms.

When Hornsby succeeded Branch Rickey as Cardinal manager in 1925, the Mahatma insisted on selling the stock he owned in the club, saying that if he couldn't be manager he didn't wish to hold any stock. The Rajah bought the stock, which had a par value of $30,000, for $50,000. Incidentally the fact that Hornsby, who was then working on a contract calling for $30,000 a year for three years, was able to put up that much money hardly makes him out as the improvident horse player he so often has been pictured.

When Hornsby was traded to the Giants for Frankie Frisch and Jimmy Ring, nobody thought much about the Cardinal stock he owned. It was assumed that Rog would get rid of his stock without any fanfare, that Breadon would be willing to buy it from him.

Hornsby sat still and said nothing, waiting for the Cardinals to come to him with an offer. Breadon finally asked him how much he wanted and almost fainted when Hornsby demanded $116 a share.

"Why you paid only $45 a share for it!" screamed Sam.

"That was before I won the pennant and the World's Championship for the Cardinals," replied Hornsby coldly. "I've had it appraised and have been told it is now worth $116 a share. So that's what I want."

Having had his say, Hornsby added nothing to it while the storm raged all around him. John Heydler, president of the National League, declared Rog couldn't play with the Giants until he had sold the Cardinal stock. John McGraw threatened to go to court and get an injunction restraining the National League from suspending the Rajah.

Breadon was as obdurate as Hornsby and the league finally had to give in to both of them. Sam put up $80,000, the league contributed $18,000 and the Giants $18,000. Rogers took the $116,000 and said nothing.

At the insistence of Branch Rickey, Hornsby was signed to manage the Browns in 1933 and he lasted there four years, although he never had any ballplayers worthy of the name. Nevertheless Hornsby worked as hard for that club as he had for any. He didn't know of any other way, except to go all out.

In midseason of 1935, the Browns came to Yankee Stadium to meet the Yankees and brought up a young second baseman from Rochester, who shall be nameless. Wilbur Wood, sports editor of the since defunct New York *Sun* and Jim Kahn, his assistant, visited Hornsby at the Stadium the day the boy reported.

For some reason, the rookie was two days late in reporting. Hornsby, Wood and Kahn were watching him go through fielding practice at second base. After five or six balls had been hit to him, he tossed his glove away and jogged into the bench, apparently satisfied that he was ready for the majors.

"Look at him!" snorted Hornsby in contempt. "Two days late getting here, fields a half-dozen grounders or less and now he's all set. How the hell does he ever expect to be a major leaguer?

"If that were me and I was called up from the bushes, I'd have been here a day early, instead of two days late. And when I went

out to field my position, I'd stay out there fielding it until somebody drove me out of there."

Thus, the outspoken Rajah.

Although baseball seemingly quit on Hornsby, Hornsby never
quit on baseball. When his various minor league jobs blew up for
one reason or another, the Rajah settled in Chicago, where he
took a fling at television among other things—baseball television, of course.

As a stunt to help its down-state circulation, the *Chicago Daily
News* used to run a traveling baseball school for youngsters.
Sports writers Jack Ryan and John Carmichael handled the mi-
crophone while Hornsby, Tom Sheehan, the former pitcher, and
others gave lessons and demonstrations. During the course of
these Hornsby demonstrated that he could still hit, even though
he was now fifty.

"He gave one exhibition at Wrigley Field before a Cub-Pirate
game," related Tom Sheehan, "that had the players on both
benches standing up, open-mouthed and bug-eyed.

"Carmichael was at the mike and I was pitching. Hornsby, of
course, was batting. What else? 'Mr. Hornsby will now hit to left
field,' announced Carmichael. Bang! Over the fence it went. 'Mr.
Hornsby will now hit to right field,' announced John. Woosh!
Out into the street. 'Mr. Hornsby will now hit to center field,' said
Carmichael. 'If he does,' I said, 'you've got to get yourself another
pitcher. I'm not taking any chances on that son of a gun hitting
one back through the box and killing me.' And I wasn't, either."

The success of Hornsby at the *Daily News* schools may have
influenced his return to baseball. Whether it did or not, he came
back to his native Texas to manage Beaumont and was an immediate success. Then, he moved on to Seattle where he won the
Pacific Coast League pennant in 1951. The upshot of it was an
offer of a job with the St. Louis Browns, to work under Bill
Veeck, the son of the man who fired him as Cub manager in 1932.

Although the players Hornsby had developed at Beaumont and
Seattle swore by him, the 1952 Brownies thought Hornsby was
too harsh a manager. When it came to almost open rebellion in
mid-June, Veeck released Hornsby, saying "It will be easier to get
a new manager than to get 25 new players."

Hornsby, who was replaced by Marty Marion, the popular ex-shortstop of the Cardinals, wasn't idle long. Within a couple of weeks the Cincinnati Reds hired him to take the place of Luke

ROGERS (ROG) HORNSBY

Born April 27, 1896, Winters, Tex.
Height 5' 11". Weight 178. Batted and threw right-handed.

YEAR	CLUB	LEAGUE	POS	G	AB	R	H	HR	SB	BA
1914	Hugo-Denison	Tex. Okla.	SS	113	393	47	91	3	19	.232
1915	Denison	West. Assn.	SS	119	429	75	119	4	24	.277
1915	St. Louis	Nat.	SS	18	57	5	14	0	0	.246
1916	St. Louis	Nat.	1B-3B-SS	139	495	63	155	6	17	.313
1917	St. Louis	Nat.	SS	145	523	86	171	8	17	.327
1918	St. Louis	Nat.	SS	115	416	51	117	5	8	.281
1919	St. Louis	Nat.	2B-3B-SS	138	512	68	163	8	17	.318
1920	St. Louis	Nat.	2B	149	589	96	*218	9	12	*.370
1921	St. Louis	Nat.	2B-3B-SS-OF	154	592	*131	*235	21	13	*.397
1922	St. Louis	Nat.	2B	154	623	*141	*250	*42	17	*.401
1923	St. Louis	Nat.	2B	107	424	89	163	17	3	*.384
1924	St. Louis	Nat.	2B	143	536	*121	*227	25	5	*.424
1925	St. Louis	Nat.	2B	138	504	133	203	*39	5	*.403
1926	St. Louis (A)	Nat.	2B	134	527	96	167	11	3	.317
1927	New York †	Nat.	2B	155	568	*133	205	26	9	.361
1928	Boston ‡	Nat.	2B	140	486	99	188	21	5	*.387
1929	Chicago	Nat.	2B	156	602	*156	229	40	2	.380
1930	Chicago	Nat.	2B	42	104	15	32	2	0	.308
1931	Chicago	Nat.	2B-3B	100	357	64	118	16	1	.331
1932	Chicago §	Nat.	OF-3B	19	58	10	13	1	0	.224
1933	St. Louis	Nat.	2B	46	83	9	27	2	1	.325
1933	St. Louis	Amer.	PH	11	9	2	3	1	0	.333
1934	St. Louis	Amer.	3B-OF-PH	24	23	2	7	1	0	.304
1935	St. Louis	Amer.	1B-2B-3B	10	24	1	5	0	0	.208
1936	St. Louis	Amer.	1B	2	5	1	2	0	0	.400
1937	St. Louis	Amer.	2B	20	56	7	18	1	0	.321
1938	Baltimore	Int.	2B-1B-OF	16	27	2	2	0	0	.074
1938	Chattanooga	South	2B	3	3	1	2	1	0	.667
1940	Oklahoma City	Texas	PH	1	1	0	1	0	0	1.000
	Major League Totals			2259	8173	1579	2930	302	135	.358

(A) Traded to New York Giants for Infielder Frank Frisch and Pitcher Jimmy Ring, December 20, 1926

† Traded to Boston Braves for Outfielder Jimmy Welsh and Catcher Francis Hogan, January 10, 1928

‡ Traded to Chicago Cubs for Infielder Fred Maguire, Catcher Doc. Leggett, Pitchers Percy Jones, Harry Seibold and Bruce Cunningham and $120,000, November 1928

§ Signed with St. Louis Cardinals, October 24, 1932

WORLD SERIES RECORD

YEAR	CLUB	LEAGUE	POS	G	AB	R	H	SB	BA
1926	St. Louis	Nat.	2B	7	28	2	7	1	.250
1929	Chicago	Nat.	2B	5	21	4	5	0	.227
	World Series Totals			12	49	6	12	1	.245

Sewell, who resigned, and the Rajah made a perceptible improvement in the Reds in the last half of the 1952 season.

Hornsby's baseball credo is simple for managing as it was for hitting—direct and forthright.

"If you don't like the way I'm running things, get yourself another boy," he has told more than one owner.

Many—too many—have taken Hornsby at his word.

CHAPTER XII

THE MEAL TICKET

Carl Owen Hubbell

SOME SPORTS WRITER in the long ago hung the tag of "Sinister Dick" on Edward Kinsella, a Giant scout by profession and an Illinois politician by inclination. Dick finished in a photo with Ed Barrow in the matter of luxurious eyebrow foliage, it being the opinion of disinterested and impartial observers that the eyebrows of either would serve as ample cover for a bevy of quail.

Kinsella held a political job in Springfield, Illinois, and in the early summer of 1928 was attending the Democratic National Convention at Houston, Texas, as a delegate instructed to cast his vote for Alfred Emanuel Smith. Sinister Dick had little interest in the long discussions on agrarian relief which preceded the balloting, and one warm, humid afternoon he decided he would be much more comfortable at the ball park.

By any standards, Dick saw a rattling, good ball game. A chunky southpaw was pitching for the Houston Buffs, one Bill Hallahan who was to go on to fame with the Cardinals. Hallahan was opposed by another left-hander working for Beaumont, a tall, cadaverous-appearing chap who pitched with great deliberation and consummate skill.

Back at the Rice Hotel, Kinsella wasted no time calling McGraw in New York. "Mac," reported Dick, "I think I saw another Art Nehf today. Fellow pitching for Beaumont. He worked against Hallahan and beat him one to zero in eleven innings."

"Send him along immediately," ordered McGraw, and thus it was that Carl Owen Hubbell reported to the Giants at the old Auditorium Hotel in Chicago a couple of days later. It was to be a long and profitable association for all concerned.

McGraw knew that Kinsella must have been pretty high on

Hubbell to compare him with Nehf. What nobody knew at the time was that Dick had understated the case. Hubbell turned out to be another Matty, a left-handed Christy Mathewson.

The comparison between Hubbell and Matty is not out of line. Both were pitching heroes of an entire generation of fans and each used an unorthodox delivery to augment his usual pitching equipment. In Matty's case it was called the "fadeaway"; in Hub's it was known as the "screwball."

Matty's fadeaway broke *in* on right-handed batters, whereas the normal right-hander's curve broke *out* and away from right-handers and in on left-handed hitters. Hubbell's screwball broke *in* on left-handed batters and *out* on right-handers. To generalize, Mathewson's fadeaway behaved like a southpaw's curve ball, Hubbell's screwball like the curve ball of a right-hander. If this sounds somewhat confusing, remember that thousands of National League batters were confused by these two pitches through the years.

In throwing a curve, a pitcher lets the ball come off the tip of his index finger as he breaks his wrist. In throwing a screwball (or a fadeaway), the wrist is broken in toward the body as the ball is released, instead of away from the body. Through the years, Hub threw so many screwballs that the palm of his left hand faces outward when he holds his arms at his sides, whereas in any normal person the palms face inward.

In the spring of 1937, the Giants and Cardinals were returning by boat from Havana after the conclusion of an exhibition series in the Cuban capital. Pepper Martin, of the Gas House Gang, was comfortably sprawled in a deck chair, chatting with a reporter as Hubbell went by. The alert Pepper spotted Hub's left palm turned outward.

"Look at the crooked-arm son of a gun," cried Pepper. "His left hand turns the wrong way. No wonder he's such a good pitcher—he's a freak!"

Hubbell wasn't quite a freak in the physical sense implied by Martin but he was indeed a physical rarity, a left-hander with control. Traditionally, southpaws are wild, and it sometimes takes them years to acquire control. Hub had control almost from the day he started pitching. Only once in professional baseball did the number of bases on balls he issued in a season exceed the number of strikeouts he recorded. And that was in 1925, with Oklahoma City in the Western League when Carl walked 108 while fanning 102. In his sixteen years with the Giants, Hub averaged fewer than two bases on balls per nine-inning game.

Such was Hubbell's control that it moved a reformed baseball writer, the late Heywood Broun, to awe. Broun happened to be in Boston in late August, 1933, when the Giants were fighting for their first pennant under Bill Terry. The Giants were in first place but had been jolted by the Cards, three out of five, in their last Polo Grounds series and moved on to Boston, where the surprising Braves had won eight of their last ten to loom as a pennant threat.

The Giants were booked for six games in four days, and Braves Field and the series could have spelled trouble, especially when the Braves won the opening game, 7 to 3, on August 31. Terry called on Hubbell the next day and the Meal Ticket turned in one of his masterpieces to win 2 to 0 in ten innings. The Braves never won another game in the series.

Broun, looking on from the press box, marveled at Hubbell's control as the left-hander pitched his eleventh shutout of the season. Hub not only didn't walk a batter but never was behind on a hitter at any time in the ten innings. He never went to a three-two count once in the ball game.

"Such control in a left-hander is incredible," wrote Broun. "There must be a skelton in Hubbell's closet somewhere, such as a right-handed maternal grandmother."

The second All-Star game was played at the Polo Grounds in 1934, with Bill Terry as manager of the National Leaguers. Terry had won the pennant and the World Series the year before and he had done so by not overlooking any bets. He was a master of detail and he gathered his All-Stars around him in the clubhouse that they might share his pearls of wisdom. Hubbell, who had won 23 games the season before and two more in the World Series, was to be the starting pitcher for the Nationals.

It was a formidable array of hitters the Americans had grouped together and Hub listened respectfully to Terry's suggestions. He tried to keep his first pitch away from Charley Gehringer and it was belted into center for a clean single. Wally Berger fumbled the ball and Charley raced to second. The game was exactly one pitch old and the Americans already had a man in scoring position.

Still pitching cautiously, Hubbell walked Heinie Manush. With men on first and second and none out, the next three hitters were Babe Ruth, Lou Gehrig and Jimmy Foxx. If ever a pitcher was on a spot, Mr. Hubbell was the man.

Catching for the National Leaguers was the ebullient Gabby Hartnett of the Cubs. He halted the game, removed his mask and walked toward the pitcher's box with that ponderous stride that always reminded onlookers of a cop who had halted traffic at a busy intersection to hand out a ticket.

"Look, Hub," admonished Gabby, "never mind all that junk about being careful and pitching this way or that way. Just throw that 'thing.' It'll get 'em out. It always gets me out!"

"That thing," of course, was Hubbell's screwball. Hub fired three of them at Ruth and the Babe was out of there. Three more took care of Gehrig, and the fact that Manush and Gehringer worked a double steal while Lou fanned bothered no one, least of all the cheerful Hartnett.

Having fanned Ruth and Gehrig, Hubbell proceeded to close out the inning by striking out Foxx. Jimmy proved a bit more troublesome than Babe or Lou, however. He managed to hit a foul. Then, in the second inning, Hubbell, still throwing "that thing," struck out Al Simmons and Joe Cronin. It was a demonstration of pitching never equaled before or since. Five straight strikeouts is unusual but the conditions under which Hubbell achieved this feat were even more unusual, for he was facing the flower and power of the American League.

Bill Dickey broke the spell with a single after two were out in the second inning, but Lefty Gomez obligingly became Hub's sixth strikeout victim. It is still a sore point with Lefty that while everybody talks of Hubbell fanning Ruth, Gehrig, Foxx, Simmons and Cronin in succession, nobody ever mentions that Gomez, too, was one of Hubbell's strikeout victims that afternoon.

So remarkable was Hubbell's pitching in this All-Star game that it usually obscures his other great deeds on the mound. In the World Series the fall before, Carl had pitched twenty innings against the Senators without allowing an earned run. He opened the Series and fanned the first three men to face him, Buddy

Myer, Goose Goslin and Heinie Manush. He won that game 4 to 2 and won the fourth game 2 to 1 in eleven innings.

Hubbell won 253 games as a Giant and had five consecutive seasons in which he won better than twenty games each year. From 1933 through 1937, the Meal Ticket won 115 games, an excellent total by modern standards. Those were Hub's glory years, and they were the glory years of the Giants, too. They won three pennants in those five seasons but weren't actual pennant contenders again until 1951.

Two marks the maestro of the screwball left behind him are well known—his 46⅓ scoreless-inning streak in 1933 and the sixteen consecutive games he won in 1936, a string which was still intact when the season ended. Unlike his collection of scoreless innings, this was not a National League record. Another Giant left-hander, Rube Marquard won nineteen straight in 1912, but nobody since Rube has done any better than sixteen. With this string, Hubbell moved into pretty select pitching company— Smokey Joe Wood, Walter Johnson, Lefty Grove and Schoolboy Rowe, all of whom ran their streaks to sixteen.

Since Hubbell's streak was still going when the 1936 National League season ended, there was a chauvanistic effort to regard it as still intact when the 1937 season opened. Nobody can say Hubbell didn't do his part, for he opened with eight straight, a total of 24 consecutive National League games in which he came home first.

There's a story connected with Hubbell's streak that only the writers who were traveling with the Giants in 1936 remember. The all-winning skein started in Pittsburgh on July 17, but those who were with the club on that Western trip believe it should have begun four days earlier at Chicago's Wrigley Field.

The first Cub to face Hubbell that day reached first and was promptly sacrificed to second. Burgess Whitehead came over from second to take the throw at first base for the put-out and then essayed a cute play. He made a snap-throw to shortstop Dick Bartell, covering second, in the hope of trapping the Chicago runner who had rounded the bag. The play was soundly conceived but poorly executed, for the throw went into the outfield and the runner scored. It was the only run of the ball game.

One of the reporters, reminiscing about the streak with Hub, commented on the fact that he had received a tough break due to Whitehead's error. He could have won seventeen straight, a figure nobody in either league has achieved since 1912.

"Mebbe so," observed the realistic Hubbell, "but don't forget we didn't score at all. The best I could have got out of that game would have been a tie."

The most oft-repeated story about Hubbell is that a Detroit manager—some say Ty Cobb, some say George Moriarty—told him that he never would get anywhere throwing the screwball. Actually, it was George McBride, former Washington infielder and a Tiger coach, who told Hub at the Augusta training camp in 1927 that the screwball was a pitch calculated to injure his arm.

"I never threw a screwball while I was Detroit property," declared Hubbell, "after McBride had given me that warning. I pitched for the Tigers with Toronto and with Beaumont but without the screwball."

Carl felt that he was being overlooked by the Tigers, but not because of McBride's admonition about the screwball. In two springs with the Tigers, Hub pitched exactly one inning of one exhibition game—and with the "B" squad against the University of Texas at Austin.

Having discarded the screwball while pitching for the Detroit farm clubs, Hubbell did not employ it when he first came to the Giants. He still remembers distinctly the first screwball he threw in the National League.

"We were playing the Cardinals and I was in a jam with men on base and Chick Hafey at bat," explained Carl. "I consider Hafey one of the best right-handed hitters who ever lived and when the count got to three and one on him, I was plenty worried. Shanty Hogan was catching and he signaled for a fast ball. I threw Chick a screwball and it fooled him. Shanty gave me the fast-ball sign again and I threw another screwball and struck Hafey out."

Hogan encouraged Hubbell in throwing the screwball, and McGraw, who called practically every pitch from the bench, made no objections. Nor, surprisingly enough, any comment. The screwball was, in effect, a secret weapon. Hubbell threw it, Hogan caught it, the batters missed it and nobody ever mentioned it until some years later.

"McBride wasn't kidding about the screwball being a menace to my arm," said Hubbell. "I had arm trouble as early as 1934, although I went on to have a couple of my best years after that. After I pitched a game in 1934, my left elbow would swell up at night and still be swollen and stiff the next afternoon. After I warmed up a little, the stiffness would leave and the swelling would go down.

"I had some X-rays taken and they showed I had chips in my elbow, but they were loose and floating around. Later, when I really had arm trouble, the chips were firmly imbedded and my elbow would 'lock' when I tried to throw the ball."

Hubbell's arm trouble in 1934 resulted in a somewhat mediocre season in 1935, mediocre for Hub, that is, yet it forced him to develop his curve ball, which he threw almost exclusively to left-handed batters. By 1936, Hub was able to throw the screwball again and this, added to his improved curve, made him one of the most effective pitchers in National League history while he was pitching the Giants to pennants in 1936 and 1937. In those two years, the Meal Ticket turned in records of 26–6 and 22–8.

Incidentally, the sobriquet "Meal Ticket" which was hung on Hub at that time didn't sit too well with manager Bill Terry, who seemed to think the appellation was a subtle dig at his strategy. Hub's pitching in those years, however, was of such caliber that even Terry couldn't remain grumpy too long.

Gaunt, lean-visaged, almost Lincolnesque in his angular awkwardness, Hubbell is the soul of modesty. Asked what he considered had been his greatest pitching performance, he didn't leap into the breach and name his sensational five strikeouts in the All-Star game of 1934. He mulled over the question for some time before answering.

"It's like this," he finally said. "I got my biggest pitching thrill out of winning ball games which meant something to the ball club, games when we were fighting for the pennant and they were games we just had to win. That meant something, regardless of the score or the number of strikeouts I got. Those were the games I took pride in winning."

Asked what was the best ball game he ever pitched, Hubbell passed up his 1929 no-hit, no-run game against Pittsburgh and settled for a one-hitter he pitched against Brooklyn at Ebbets Field on Decoration Day, 1940.

"The way I look at it," explained the Meal Ticket, "the best game any pitcher could pitch would be a game in which he got every batter who faced him out—a perfect game.

"This day in Brooklyn, I was getting the Dodgers out one-two-three. I had sixteen in a row when Johnny Hudson came up with one out in the sixth. I had him two strikes and one ball and I tried to waste a pitch, to get it low and outside. Johnny hit it back through the box, a looping line drive just over my head. Our second baseman dove at the ball but he didn't have a chance for it.

"It wasn't too well hit but it was the only hit Brooklyn got. The next batter hit into a double play, and in the last three innings I got the Dodgers out in order, so I faced only 27 men in the whole ball game. It would have been a perfect game except for Hudson but I guess that's what makes perfect games so rare."

Hubbell engaged in some terrific duels with Dizzy Dean when that great man was at the height of his spectacular but short career with the Cardinals. These were "money" games, with both clubs shooting for the pennant, and it is a matter of fact that Hub beat Dean more often than Diz beat him. One of the Meal Ticket's great games against St. Louis was at the Polo Grounds on July 2, 1933, when he beat the Red Birds 1 to 0 in eighteen innings without giving up a base on balls.

It wasn't only against the Cardinals that Hubbell was effective. He had a decided bulge on every club in the league save Brooklyn. This is rather unusual, since in the days when Hub was the Meal Ticket, the Brooks were usually kicking around in the second division. Outside of 1930, when there was a four-cornered fight for the pennant among the Giants, Cards, Cubs and Dodgers, Brooklyn rarely was in contention during Hubbell's good seasons.

One of Hubbell's most amazing defeats was administered by the Dodgers before packed Sunday stands at Ebbets Field in 1930. The southpaw was beaten in ten innings by the veteran Dazzy Vance, 1 to 0, which was far from a disgrace, but the manner in which Hub lost was most unusual. After going through nine scoreless rounds, the Dodgers filled the bases against Carl in the tenth, with Jake Flowers at bat. Flowers, who later became a capable baseball executive, was a steady infielder but not regarded as a dangerous batter. Hubbell made four pitches to Flowers and every one was wide of the plate! The winning, and only run, was thus forced across on a base on balls by the master control pitcher of his time. Hub can't recall another occasion when he forced a run across the plate.

The trouble McBride had predicted for Hubbell so many years before finally caught up with him in 1938. He still was a winning pitcher but no longer the workhorse who had led the Giants to pennants three times in five years. His left elbow was operated on and the bone chips were removed, but when he tried to pitch in 1939, it was obvious that he wasn't the Hubbell of old.

There was one flash left in the Meal Ticket and he came through for his old roommate, Mel Ott, who was elevated to the Giant managership in 1942. In July of that year, the Giants lost 4 one-run games in succession. In the fourth of these, Harry Feldman had the Cardinals beaten 1 to 0 with two out and nobody on base in the last half of the ninth, and the Cards came up with two runs to win before Ott could get anybody ready to warm up.

Ott sat alone in his room in the dark in the Hotel Chase in St. Louis that night, moodily staring across into Forest Park. He had left a note in Hubbell's box that the pitcher was to come to his room that night before going to bed—"no matter what time you come in." This was a touch of dry humor, since Hub was an exemplary athlete during his entire career.

Long before the midnight curfew, there was a rap on Ottie's door and Hubbell presented himself.

"Sit down, Hub," said Mel. "There's something I've got to say to you." Ott then went on to say that the club was in danger of falling apart because of the succession of one-run defeats. Something had to be done to snap the Giants out of it. And the only thing Mel could think of in this crisis was what McGraw and Terry before him had thought of in similar crises—call on the Meal Ticket.

Hubbell went out the next day against Howie Pollet, then one of the most promising young left-handers in the National League. Hub, with only a trace of his former stuff but with plenty of cunning, proceeded to give Pollet a pitching lesson. The Meal Ticket won, 1 to 0, and went on from there to win six straight, the Giants finishing a surprising third, their only first-division finish between 1938 and 1950, when Leo Durocher brought them home third.

By 1943, it was obvious that the Meal Ticket had been punched full. At the winter baseball meetings in the Hotel New Yorker that December, President Horace C. Stoneham of the Giants summoned the press to his room and announced that Hubbell was being placed in charge of the Giant farm system.

CARL OWEN HUBBELL

Born June 22, 1903, at Carthage, Mo.
Height, 6' 1''. Weight, 175. Threw left and batted right-handed.
Elected to Hall of Fame, 1947.

YEAR	CLUB	LEAGUE	G	IP	W	L	PCT	H	R	ER	SO	BB	ERA
1923	Cushing	Okla. St.			(No Records Available)								
1924	Cushing	Okla. St.			(No Records Available)								
1924	Ardmore	West. Assn.	..	12	1	0	1.000	...	...	...	...	...	...
1924	Okla. City	Western	2	15	1	1	.500	19	10	...	3	4	...
1925	Okla. City	Western	45	284	17	13	.567	273	172	...	102	108	...
1926	Toronto	Int.	31	93	7	7	.500	90	42	39	45	44	3.77
1927	Decatur	I. I. I.	23	185	14	7	.667	174	61	52	76	48	2.53
1927	Fort Worth	Tex.	2	3⅓	0	1	.000	7	...	...	0	3	...
1928	Beaumont	Tex.	21	185	12	9	.571	177	69	61	116	45	2.97
1928	New York	Nat.	20	124	10	6	.625	117	49	39	37	21	2.83
1929	New York	Nat.	39	268	18	11	.621	273	128	110	106	67	3.69
1930	New York	Nat.	37	242	17	12	.586	263	120	104	117	58	3.87
1931	New York	Nat.	36	248	14	12	.538	211	88	73	155	67	2.65
1932	New York	Nat.	40	184	18	11	.621	260	96	79	137	40	2.50
1933	New York	Nat.	45	*309	*23	12	.657	256	69	57	156	47	*1.66
1934	New York	Nat.	49	313	21	12	.636	286	100	80	118	37	*2.30
1935	New York	Nat.	42	303	23	12	.657	314	125	110	150	49	3.27
1936	New York	Nat.	42	304	*26	6	*.813	265	81	78	123	57	*2.31
1937	New York	Nat.	39	262	*22	8	*.733	261	108	93	159	55	3.19
1938	New York	Nat.	24	179	13	10	.565	171	70	61	104	33	3.07
1939	New York	Nat.	29	154	11	9	.550	150	60	47	62	24	2.75
1940	New York	Nat.	31	214	11	12	.478	220	102	87	86	59	3.66
1941	New York	Nat.	26	164	11	9	.550	169	73	65	75	53	3.57
1942	New York	Nat.	24	157	11	8	.579	158	75	69	61	34	3.96
1943	New York	Nat.	12	66	4	4	.500	87	36	36	31	24	.491
	Major League Totals		535	3591⅓	253	154	.622	3461	1380	1188	1677	725	2.98

* Led league

WORLD SERIES RECORD

YEAR	CLUB	LEAGUE	G	IP	W	L	PCT	H	R	ER	SO	BB	ERA
1933	New York	Nat.	2	20	2	0	1.000	13	3	0	15	6	0.00
1936	New York	Nat.	2	16	1	1	.500	15	5	4	10	2	2.25
1937	New York	Nat.	2	14⅓	1	1	.500	12	10	6	7	4	3.77
	World Series Totals		6	50⅓	4	2	.667	40	18	10	32	12	1.79

ALL-STAR GAME RECORD

YEAR	LEAGUE	IP	W	L	PCT	H	R	ER	SO	BB	ERA
1933	National	2	0	0	.000	1	0	0	1	1	0.00
1934	National	3	0	0	.000	2	0	0	6	2	0.00
1936	National	3	0	0	.000	2	0	0	2	1	0.00
1937	National	⅔	0	0	.000	3	3	3	1	1	40.50
1940	National	1	0	0	.000	0	0	0	1	1	0.00
	All-Star Game Totals	9⅔	0	0	.000	8	3	3	11	6	2.79

Everybody agreed that it was a nice, sentimental gesture but one cynic remarked what must have been in the minds of several, "What the hell does Hubbell know about the minors? He hasn't been in a minor league in fifteen years!"

Hubbell turned the same thorough concentration on the farm problem that he had turned to his pitching. During the war years, of course, there was little he could do, other than keep the franchises alive, but by 1951, when the Giants finally won the pennant, the fruits of Hub's patient labors became apparent to all. King Karl was still the Meal Ticket.

CHAPTER XIII

THE BIG TRAIN

Walter Perry Johnson

AL SCHACHT owns and operates a thriving restaurant off New York's Park Avenue in the fashionable 50's. It is one of the city's more popular chop houses and Al's old cronies from baseball frequently drop into sneak their teeth into a steak, guzzle a drink and talk over old times with him. A first-time visitor invariably compliments Schacht on the opulence of his place.

"I owe it all to baseball," is Al's usual modest reply, as he waves his arms to encompass the entire joint, upstairs and down.

One day one of Schacht's visitors didn't take Schacht's diffident explanation at face value. He looked at the mirrored bar, the leather-lined booths, the carpeted stairway leading to the private dining rooms and, lastly, he looked at Al.

"All I've got to say, Al," he observed, "is that it's a helluva snazzy layout for a pitcher who won exactly fourteen big league ball games in his life!"

"Well," hedged Schacht, "I really owe it to one of those ball games and to two guys—Clark Griffith and Walter Johnson."

Then came the story and it was one worth hearing, for Schacht really rose to fame and fortune on the result of one ball game— one ball game and the indisposition of Walter Johnson and the kindly disposition of Clark Griffith.

Johnson, universally regarded as the greatest pitcher in the history of the American League, toiled many years for the Washington Senators without ever achieving the distinction of a no-hit game. He won many other honors in the league, about all the pitching honors there were, but the no-hitter eluded him for thirteen long seasons. Finally, he made it on July 1, 1920, at Boston's Fenway Park.

The Big Train was whistling through the day he pitched the no-hitter—and he had to be for the Red Sox battled him right down to the last out. Only one Boston player reached first, Harry Hooper, when Bucky Harris bobbled his grounder at second base for a palpable error. It was the same Harris, however, who delivered the single which won the game for Walter, 1 to 0.

Griff, who was then managing the Senators, saw a great chance to cash in on Johnson's long awaited no-hitter. He advertised the Big Train as his pitcher for the afternoon game in Washington on July 4. The Senators were in sixth place and crowds were few and far between, but with the Yanks and their recently acquired Babe Ruth coming to town to face Johnson, fresh from his no-hitter, the game should be a sellout.

It was, too. Tom Zachary beat the Yanks 4 to 3 in the morning game and there were upward of 25,000 in the stands to welcome Johnson home after his nearly perfect game in Boston. The only hitch was that there was no Johnson!

Johnson phoned from his bedside that morning to say that he couldn't make it. Some historians say it was a sore arm, the only one of his career, others that he pulled a muscle in his groin. At any rate, there were the customers and there was no Johnson.

Griff had advertised Sir Walter in good faith. There was no way out. In desperation he addressed his players before the game and exhorted them to win this one. Only a victory over the Yanks would take the sting out of the disappointment the crowd was going to suffer. Schacht volunteered to be the sacrificial goat.

There was no public-address system in those days and when Lawrence Phillips, the one-armed announcer, bellowed through his megaphone that the battery for Washington would be Schacht and Gharity, the maddened crowd almost tore down the stands.

"They showered the field with cushions, bottles, score cards, everything they could get their hands on," recalls Schacht. "I had to finish my warming up under the grandstand."

Schacht was booed and hooted as he walked to the mound. The leadoff batter for New York was Whitey Witt.

"I walked him on four straight balls," related Al. "They weren't really wild, like, say, pitches thrown by Rex Barney. They just missed the plate an inch or so. But they missed it and, brother, that did it! Down came everything in the house. It took fifteen minutes to get the field cleared—and I hadn't pitched to Babe Ruth, Wally Pipp or Bob Meusel yet!"

Despite this unfriendly reception, Schacht stuck to his knitting and delivered a 9 to 3 victory to Griffith. Griff told Al he could have a job for life with the Senators, if he wished. And lived up to his word, keeping Al on as coach, encouraging him in the pregame clowning which later was to make a comfortable living for Schacht. So, in a way, Al does owe his restaurant to baseball. And to Griff and the Big Train.

When Walter Perry Johnson was at his majestic heights with the Senators—or Capitols or Nats, as they were sometimes called, among other things—vaudeville comics of the day used to get a laugh by striking a dramatic pose and declaiming in resonant tones: "Washington—first in peace, first in war and last in the American League." It wasn't strictly true, for Washington finished last only twice in the 21 years Johnson served there, but it was a second-division team most of the time.

Despite the chronic lowly position of the team, Johnson managed to win 413 games for the Senators. Some records, incidently, still credit Walter with 414, but a recheck by J. G. Taylor Spink, baseball's indefatigable authority, gives 413 as the corrected figure. This is accepted in Mr. Spink's baseball publication, *The Sporting News,* and what is accepted in *The Sporting News* is accepted in baseball.

How many games Johnson may have won with a team which was a habitual contender there is no way of telling. It is known, however, that Walter just missed landing with a contender. Two other clubs had a chance at him before Washington—the Pittsburgh Pirates and the Detroit Tigers.

Johnson would have gone to the 1907 training camp of the Pirates had that club paid his railroad fare from Kansas, where he was living, to Hot Springs, Arkansas. An umpire named McGuire, who had seen Johnson pitch town ball, tipped off the Pirates and George Moreland, one of baseball's early historians, told Fred Clarke, the Pirate manager. However, the Pirates were getting ready to break camp then and Clarke had no time to send for any youngsters.

The original discoverer of Johnson will be forever shrouded in anonymity. The only thing known about him is that he was a cigar salesman. He peppered the Detroit offices with letters about Johnson. Bill Yawkey, then owner of the club, took the matter up with Frank Navin, his partner, and suggested they investigate this phenom, who was pitching in Weiser, Idaho.

"Who is this guy?" asked Navin.

"A friend of mine," explained Yawkey. "He's a cigar salesman and he gets around the country a lot. He knows baseball, too."

"If he knows so much about baseball," snapped Navin, "why isn't he in baseball? What's he doing peddling cigars?"

The letter was pigeon holed, but a few months later, in August of 1907, Navin read where the Detroit team had to go all out to beat some kid Pongo Joe Cantillon had unveiled in Washington, a semi-pro from Weiser, Idaho. The oddly named town rang a bell in Navin's mind. He searched through his desk, found the letter and looked off into space.

The cigar salesman didn't give up when he failed to hear from Detroit. Instead, he bombarded Cantillon with letters. One of the Washington catchers, Cliff Blankenship, was injured and wanted to return to his home in Seattle, Washington. Pongo Joe told him he could take a vacation but that he'd have to stop over in Wichita, Kansas, to look at a young outfielder, Clyde Milan. And then he could look at this kid in Idaho that some crackpot was writing him about.

Blankenship saw Milan and wasted no time in recommending the young outfielder, and then saw Johnson. And when Cliff did his eyes popped as every baseball person's eyes must have popped the first time the blinding speed of Walter Johnson was unfurled. Both were signed and it must go as a credit mark in Blankenship's book that on his first scouting trip, which was really more or less of a sick leave, he signed two players who were to play a total of 36 seasons with the Senators and who were to manage the club at different times.

Around the American League in the period just before, during and after World War I, was a pleasant, voluble outfielder named Bobby (Braggo) Roth. He was only up for eight seasons but he was with the White Sox, the Red Sox, Indians, Senators and Yankees. Braggo was an entertaining talker and more often than not the hero of his stories was himself.

Roth, who came to an untimely death many years ago, owned few batting records but he did have one of which he was quite proud. He singled to beat Walter Johnson in an extra-inning game.

On his first four trips to the plate, Roth didn't get so much as a loud foul off Johnson. Came the eleventh or twelfth, however, with men on base, he managed to get his bat about one third of the way around on one of Walter's pitches. The bat was knocked out of Bobby's hands but the ball sailed in a slow, lazy arc into right field, just over the second baseman's head for the run which won the game.

"Hmph," snorted Roth in the clubhouse later. "Imagine that big Swede trying to sneak his fast one by the ol' doctor!"

It was good for the biggest laugh of the season and understandably so, for Johnson didn't have to sneak his fast ball by anybody, least of all a hitter he had fanned four times that very afternoon. Johnson's speed, like that of Feller, Grove, Dean, Vance and Van Lingle Mungo, was incredible. There are those who say Johnson was able to throw a ball faster than anybody who ever lived. These are not just Washington fans, men who played with or against Johnson, but recognized baseball authorities. Men like Billy Evans, for instance, kingpin umpire of the American League for years.

"I'm not ashamed to admit that I used to blink my eyes when I first saw Johnson's speed," confessed Evans. "He was just unbelievably fast. On dark days ballplayers used to hope that the game would be over before they had to face him again."

"Johnson was the only pitcher I ever saw," declares Schacht, "who would throw a ball out of the game if he found it scuffed or roughed up in any spot on the cover. Other pitchers would try and keep such a ball in play so that they could 'cheat' a bit with it. Scuffed baseballs will 'sail' and are twice as difficult to follow as one on which the cover is smooth. Walter was always afraid of hitting somebody. He knew that with his speed it would be fatal."

Johnson had speed and control—nothing else to speak of. He threw a curve that was no more than a wrinkle but he insisted on throwing it whenever he got two strikes on the hitter. Smart hitters like Eddie Collins used to take the two strikes and wait for the alleged curve. "It's the only way I can hit him," said Eddie.

Ty Cobb, on the other hand, took advantage of Johnson's good nature. Cobb, mellowed through the years, admitted on a recent visit East that he used to crowd the plate against the Big Train, knowing that Walter, fearful of beaning him, would keep the ball outside. Then, with the count in the batter's favor, Cobb knew Johnson would ease up to get the next pitch over and that was the one Ty would hit. Or try to hit. For, as Cobb himself said, "Johnson was no bargain even when he was easing up."

Walter Perry Johnson was born on a farm in Humboldt, Kansas, on November 6, 1887. Eventually the family moved, and the fourteen-year-old Walter with them, to Olinda, California. It was here Johnson became interested in baseball, a sport he had little chance to follow in his isolated farm home in Kansas. He played with various kid teams, with the Fullerton High team and with a semi-pro team in Anaheim.

Johnson's difficulty, as a teen-aged kid, was finding a catcher who could hold the lightning he poured forth. At sixteen, he had a tryout with the Tacoma, Washington, team of the Northwestern League, but he was too green and too young. Eventually, he found a job in Weiser, Idaho, at $75 a month, which was where Blankenship found him.

According to such information as could be pieced together, Johnson pitched 75 innings with Weiser without allowing a run and he fanned 166 in eleven games. It very well could have been so, because it wasn't very long before young Walter was pitching almost that kind of ball in the American League.

Rarely has there been a baseball hero with the innate modesty and decency of Walter Johnson. He neither smoked nor drank, never beefed at an umpire or argued with a teammate. He didn't swear and he never had the faintest semblance of a swelled head. About the only complaint anybody ever could make of him was that he was stubborn—as witness his insistence on throwing the wrinkle he called a curve every time he had two strikes and no balls on the hitter.

The popular nicknames for Johnson were the Big Train, bestowed on him by Grantland Rice, and Barney, after Barney Oldfield, not because of his blinding speed as a pitcher but because of the manner in which he drove one of his early automobiles. Ballplayers, as in the case of Braggo Roth, sometimes referred to him as the big Swede on the theory that anybody named Johnson must, of necessity, be of Swedish extraction. Walter actually was of Dutch, English and Scotch-Irish ancestry. He once was asked why he didn't correct the impression that he was of Swedish descent and carefully explained that Swedes were nice people and he didn't wish to injure their feelings by intimating that he didn't wish to be known as one.

Johnson was an easy worker. He pitched almost sidearm and he worked rapidly. His control was exceptional for a fast-ball pitcher, even as a rookie. The average fast-ball pitcher is wild, particularly in the early stages—Feller, Grove, Vance, Mungo, Parmelee and Barney are examples. Johnson, like Dizzy Dean, was an exception. In one year, 1913, he walked only 38 men in 346 innings, an average of exactly one per nine-inning game!

There is no telling how many strikeouts Johnson might have piled up, and he holds the record with 3,497, had it not been for his persistency in throwing his alleged curve when he had two strikes on a batter, nor how many shutouts he might have compiled had he not been inclined to take it easy any time Washington gave him a two-run margin to work on. The Big Train holds the record for shutouts in the majors with 113 and he also was beaten by 1 to 0 scores no fewer than twenty times, which probably is another record.

Big Barney could always turn on the heat when he had to, the hallmark of pitching greatness. Back in the early days of baseball it wasn't uncommon for ballplayers to bet on themselves to win, a practice which long since has been abolished for reasons which are obvious. The Senators made up a pool one day and bet on themselves with the Red Sox. It was informal stuff—the money was pooled in one clubhouse and an emissary walked into that of the rivals and said, "We got six hundred dollars here that says we can beat you today. How about it?"

The Red Sox accepted the team wager on this particular day and Johnson came into the last half of the ninth carrying a one-run lead. The first two Boston batters hit safely and George Mc-Bride came over from shortstop and began to berate Johnson for his carelessness. The Big Train promptly opened the throttle and fanned the next three batters—and legend has it that they were Tris Speaker, Dick Hoblitzel and Duffy Lewis—on nine pitched balls.

As the game ended and Johnson trudged from the mound, McBride ran up to him and threw his arm around him, but the big pitcher was not to be mollified. "Goodness gracious, McBride," said Walter, "I guess that will teach you to mind your own *darn* business!" From Johnson, that was practically a blast.

Any part of Johnson's record in his 21 years with the Senators yields nuggets when analyzed. Perhaps the most impressive is the string of 56 scoreless innings he put together in 1913. The Yankees, then the Highlanders, scored a run off him in the first inning of a game on April 10 and he wasn't scored on again until the Browns turned the trick on May 15. In between, the Big Train pitched shutouts against the Highlanders, the Athletics, White Sox and two against the Red Sox. During the streak he twice was called on to relieve Joe Engel against Boston, once pitching two and two-thirds innings of scoreless ball and five on another occasion. He had one out in the fourth when St. Louis scored against him.

The Browns were always something of a jinx club for Barney. They halted his 1912 string of sixteen straight, which still stands as an American League record, held by Johnson, Smokey Joe Wood of the Red Sox (who set his the same year) equaled by Lefty Grove in 1931 when the Athletics were streaking to a pennant and by the precocious Schoolboy Rowe in 1934 when the Tigers were winning their first flag in 25 years. Of the four American Leaguers to win sixteen in a row, Johnson was the only member of a non-pennant-winning team to run up such a string.

As befits the ace of the club, indeed, the ace of baseball at that time, Johnson invariably pitched the opening game for the Senators. He holds a record which doubtless will be untouched for all time—seven opening-day shutouts! And the seventh, pitched in 1926, Walter's penultimate season with Washington, was the most remarkable of all, for in this game he went fifteen innings against the Athletics to beat their great knuckle baller, Eddie Rommel, by a 1 to 0 score.

Modern ballplayers, particularly pitchers, shake their heads incredulously when they are told the story of Johnson shutting out the Yankees three times in four days in 1908. The Yankees of those days were known as the Highlanders and there were other differences, too. They weren't playing in spacious Yankee Stadium in the old Hilltop Grounds at 168th Street and Broadway. And they weren't the perennial monarchs of the American League, either. The Highlanders of 1908 finished in the cellar but the Washington team for which Walter pitched finished no higher than seventh.

On Friday, September 6, Johnson beat the Highlanders 3 to 0 on a six-hitter. He looked so good to Manager Cantillon that Joe turned him loose again on Saturday and again he blanked New York, this time on a four-hitter, 6 to 0. Johnson didn't pitch Sunday for the simple reason there was no Sabbath ball in New York those days; but on Monday, which was Labor Day—and never was that holiday more apt—Johnson faced the Highlanders again and once more Walter applied a coat of calcimine, winning 4 to 0 and allowing only two hits. This was the first game of a holiday double-header and legend has it that Johnson hid when Cantillon was looking for a pitcher to start the second game.

While it was a cellar club Johnson blanked three times in four days, it didn't lack for baseball talent. Jack Chesbro, the only pitcher to lead both National and American Leagues, was Walter's opponent in the third shutout; and the Highlanders' batting order had names like Wee Willie Keeler, Hal Chase, Birdie Cree, Kid Elberfeld and Jake Stahl.

As Johnson moved into his prime, another pitcher of note came into the American League with no more preliminary fanfare than the Big Train. His name was George Herman Ruth, and in time his features were to be more easily recognized by more Americans than those of the president of the United States. Babe came up as a left-hander and a rattling good one.

Ruth was a little more than a year out of St. Mary's in Baltimore when he faced Johnson for the first time in August, 1915, and he beat Walter 4 to 3. In 1916, the green southpaw, now with a season's play behind him, beat the great right-hander the first four times he faced him, by 5 to 1, 2 to 1 and twice by 1–0 scores, one of the latter going thirteen innings.

All told, Ruth and Johnson started against each other eight times and Babe won six of these games, three times by 1–0 scores. Walter beat the Babe once in a relief role.

Considering the type of team he usually had behind him, it is not surprising that Johnson had to wait until the sere and yellow of his career to reach a World Series. In 1924, with Bucky Harris, the second baseman, managing the team at the age of 27, the Senators were the surprise team of the American League. The previous season they finished fourth but a cool 24 games behind the pennant-winning Yanks. This year they nosed out the Yanks by two games.

Sir Walter had been a consistent twenty-game winner for the Senators for years but that was in the long ago. Until 1924, it had been five years since Johnson had won twenty. This, however, was Johnson's year, just as it was Bucky's year and a Washington year. The Big Train won 23 while losing seven, led the league in earned runs and was voted its Most Valuable Player.

All the fans in America were pulling for Johnson in his first World Series. It was a better drama than *Nellie, the Beautiful Cloak Model*. There wasn't any question as to Harris's selection for the opening game against the Giants in Washington. It had to be Johnson and it was Johnson. It would be nice to relate that the old master turned in a classic when his World Series chance came at long last, but the truth is that the Giants beat him 4 to 3 in twelve innings.

Although Johnson fanned a dozen Giants, for what then was a World Series record, he was tagged for home runs by George Kelly and Bill Terry, and his pitching opponent, the doughty left-hander Art Nehf, reached Barney for three singles.

In his second start, in the fifth game at the Polo Grounds, Johnson hung in there with another southpaw, Jack Bentley, as his opponent until the eighth, when the Giants scored three times to win 6 to 2. In this game young Freddie Lindstrom, who was born less than two years before Johnson came to the majors, combed the Big Train for four hits.

Sentimentalists throughout the land sighed that Johnson's first

Series after so many heartbreaking years of pitching greatness with inferior teams should come to such a sorry end—two defeats in two starts. They could have saved their tears, for the capricious gods of the diamond were looking after their own.

In the seventh game, played in Washington, the Senators rallied in the eighth inning to score twice and tie up the game at 3 to 3. Again Harris called on Johnson and this time Walter had it. He pitched the last four innings, fanned five, and was the winning pitcher when Earl McNeely's grounder to third took a weird hop over Lindstrom's head to send in the winning run, just as a grounder by Harris took a similar hop in the eighth to send in the tying runs. The breaks were with Sir Walter, sure, but there wasn't a run-of-the-mine fan in America who begrudged him one iota of his triumph. It had taken him a long time.

Johnson was back in a World Series again the following fall and this time in an entirely different role. He won the opening game against Pittsburgh by a 4–1 score, and in the fourth game Johnson gave six scattered hits to completely subdue the Pirates, 4 to 0, no Buc getting beyond first base.

This second victory of Johnson put Washington in front three games to one and it looked like another title. It wasn't, however, because the Pirates stormed through to win the fifth and sixth games, and it was again up to Walter in the seventh game at Forbes Field. It had rained the day before and this game was started in a drizzle and finished in a downpour.

Johnson had what should have been for him commanding leads. He was ahead of the Pirates 4 to 0 at one stage and another time 6 to 3 but he just couldn't hold them off, and eventually Ki-ki Cuyler blasted a ground-rule double inside the first-base bag with the bases filled. The final score was 9 to 7 for Pittsburgh, the only time they were ahead in the ball game.

Johnson had as much bad luck in this deciding game as the Senators had had good luck in the seventh game of the 1924 Series. There were many second guessers who thought Harris persevered too long with Big Barney, that he should have lifted him with Washington in front and counted on one of the younger pitchers to protect the lead.

Among those who felt this way was none other than Byron Bancroft (Ban) Johnson, the president of the American League.

He sent Bucky a scathing telegram which read: "You have sacrificed a World's Championship which the American League should have won to maudlin sentiment."

With characteristic dignity, Harris answered his critics: "If I had to do it over again, I would do the same thing. We went down with our best."

That was the way everybody felt about Sir Walter.

WALTER PERRY JOHNSON

Born November 6, 1887 at Humboldt, Kansas.
Height, 6' 1". Weight, 200. Threw and batted right-handed.
Elected to Hall of Fame in 1936.

YEAR	CLUB	LEAGUE	G	IP	W	L	SHO	H	BB	SO	R	ER	ERA
1907	Washington	Amer.	14	111	5	9	2	95	18	64	33	...	...
1908	Washington	Amer.	36	257	14	14	6	196	52	160	77	...	...
1909	Washington	Amer.	40	297	13	25	4	247	84	164	116	...	...
1910	Washington	Amer.	45	374	25	17	8	269	76	*313	92	...	...
1911	Washington	Amer.	40	323	23	15	6	292	70	209	117	...	...
1912	Washington	Amer.	50	368	32	12	7	259	76	*303	89	...	...
1913	Washington	Amer.	48	346	*36	7	12	232	38	*243	56	44	*1.09
1914	Washington	Amer.	51	371	*28	18	10	287	74	*225	88	71	1.71
1915	Washington	Amer.	47	337	*27	13	8	258	56	*203	83	58	*1.55
1916	Washington	Amer.	48	371	*24	19	3	290	132	*228	105	78	1.89
1917	Washington	Amer.	47	328	23	16	8	259	67	*185	105	84	2.30
1918	Washington	Amer.	39	325	*23	13	8	241	70	*162	71	46	*1.28
1919	Washington	Amer.	39	290	20	14	7	235	51	*147	73	48	*1.49
1920	Washington	Amer.	21	144	8	10	4	135	27	78	68	50	3.13
1921	Washington	Amer.	35	264	17	14	1	265	92	143	122	103	3.51
1922	Washington	Amer.	41	280	15	16	4	283	99	105	115	93	2.99
1923	Washington	Amer.	43	262	17	12	3	267	69	126	114	103	3.54
1924	Washington	Amer.	38	278	*23	7	6	233	77	*158	97	84	*2.72
1925	Washington	Amer.	30	229	20	7	3	211	78	108	95	78	3.07
1926	Washington	Amer.	33	262	15	16	2	259	73	125	120	105	3.61
1927	Washington	Amer.	18	108	5	6	1	113	26	48	70	61	5.08
1928	Newark (a)	Int.	1	0	0	0	0	0	1	0	0	0	0.00
	Major League Totals		803	5925	413	280	113	4926	1405	3497	1906	1106	...

WORLD SERIES RECORD

YEAR	CLUB	LEAGUE	G	IP	W	L	AVE	SO	BB	H	ERA
1924	Washington	Amer.	3	24	1	2	.333	20	11	30	3.38
1925	Washington	Amer.	3	26	2	1	.667	15	4	26	2.08
	World Series Totals		6	50	3	3	.500	35	15	56	3.00

(a) Walked only batter he faced.
* Led league

CHAPTER XIV

NATURE BOY

Napoleon Lajoie

ALONG ABOUT 1915 Leslie Joseph Bush was a young pitcher with the Athletics, fast enough to already have won the nickname of "Bullet Joe." At the same time Napoleon Lajoie was an old infielder with the Athletics. Lajoie was forty years old and his best baseball was all behind him. Nevertheless, Bush watched the veteran with interest. Lajoie was considered to be one of the greatest natural hitters ever to have played ball and young Bush had aspirations as a batter himself.

It wasn't much of a game that afternoon in Shibe Park. Few games were that year, for Connie Mack had sold most of his great stars of the 1914 team and the A's were just beginning a cellar tenancy in the American League, with a seven-year lease as it turned out.

Bush watched Lajoie at the plate. Old Nap stood up there with a magnificent nonchalance, an easy grace. He was old, and he was through, sure, but you had only to look at him to realize that once this man must have been a great hitter. The count went to two balls and no strikes. The pitcher, not wishing to get too far behind, came in with his next pitch. Crack—it disappeared from Shibe Park.

Leisurely Lajoie jogged around the bases. En route to a seat on the bench, he paused for a drink at the water cooler. He sat down beside young Bush. There were a few moments of silence and then Lajoie spoke.

"Never," he said, "let the soft one get by, kid."

For the record it should be noted that that home run was the only one Lajoie hit in the season of 1915. He was washed up, but not enough to make the cardinal mistake of letting the soft one get by.

The inscription on Lajoie's plaque in baseball's Hall of Fame in Cooperstown is unique in that it mentions Larry as "the most graceful and efficient second baseman of his era." It is the only time the adjective "graceful" is mentioned on any of the Cooperstown plaques. There are plenty of "greats" and "greatests" engraved on the bronze tablets which adorn the walls of the museum but only the big Frenchman is singled out for his grace.

Grace was apparent in Larry's ease at the plate, too. He was a natural hitter, some say the best right-handed hitter of all time, a claim that adherents of Rogers Hornsby do not allow to pass unchallenged. Billy Evans, who umpired for many years in the American League, called Larry "the good-to-look-at-hitter." It was a statement no opposing pitcher ever made.

Bush, the young pitcher who was studying Lajoie's batting style, was to have an unusual distinction the next season. On August 26, 1916, Bullet Joe pitched the first and only no-hit, no-run game of his entire career. He did it against Lajoie's old teammates, beating Cleveland 5 to 0. And it was Lajoie's last appearance in a major league box score. Larry made it a good one by tagging Stan Coveleski for a triple. It was the big Frenchman's 3242nd base hit.

"Even then, Larry didn't let the soft one get by," chuckled Bush as he recalled the incident.

Passing the Plaza cab-stand at Central Park recently, an old-timer said, pointing to the Jehu on one of Manhattan's few remaining horse-drawn carriages, "There, but for the grace of God, and a hitting knack, might be Larry Lajoie."

It was a sentimental thought, though fuzzy around the edges, for one doubts that Lajoie would have stuck to hacking, even had not baseball offered a more pleasant and profitable route of travel. The big Frenchman was too adaptable to have stayed long, whip in hand, on the high seat of a hack.

But his true destiny was baseball, and Larry found it soon enough. However, this king of second basemen did have the background of a hack driver, so authentically he takes us back to the last chapter of this country's horse and buggy days.

They were to start Lajoie on his way, so that the major league fame and modest fortune he made, as the country buzzed from the motor car era on into the age of airplanes, would find him sufficiently well fixed so that now, in his mid-seventies, he can spend his time in Florida with his memories, and his golf sticks, tools he had learned to use well.

At his peak, forty or more years ago, the Frenchman was a terrific right-handed hitter, a fast base runner for a big fellow (he was a 6-foot, 1-inch, 195-pounder) and, over and above all, the most graceful player baseball has even known.

There was a flair and a manner about Lajoie: everything he did had an air about it—a distinctive touch. His agile artistry was his true hallmark, although his hitting was memorable enough for him to have thrice led the American League; and in 1901 to have been its first home run champ, with thirteen.

Lajoie was a long-service stalwart, playing 2475 games in twenty-one active seasons, to leave an over-all average of .338 for his major league play.

In each of five different seasons he was good for more than 200 hits, and until Tris Speaker came along, Larry was the American League's top maker of doubles.

The diamond trails carried this New England-born Canuck from Fall River in 1896 to Philadelphia, where he played for both the National and American League; and on to Cleveland, scene of his greatest renown, and longest service, including a hitch as manager, and back once more to the Quaker City, and the A's, where his major league career ended, in 1916, or twenty-one years before he was voted a place in the Hall of Fame.

There was grace in the mere way Larry cocked his cap on the side of his head. He was a handsome fellow, big and dark, with bold features and arresting eyes. The uniform of his early days was equipped with a roll collar, which the Frenchman wore casually, partly turned up, making an attractive frame for his face.

His manner at the plate, habitually drawing a line in the dust alongside the plate with the business end of his bat, as prelude to facing the pitcher, had the flourish of an instinctive artist.

Lajoie's folks, French-Canadians from Montreal, had moved to Woonsocket, Rhode Island like many others from north of the border, and it was in that little New England textile town that

Napoleon (Larry) Lajoie was born, September 5, 1875, when his father was trying to make ends meet as a coal man.

But way back in young Nap's ancestry there must have been a *coureur de bois* heritage, far removed from the dusty makeshifts of life in a tacky industrial town of seventy-five years ago.

On the baseball field, none was ever like Larry, as he threaded the rapids of intricate diamond play with gifted touch that might have been his legacy from some bygone daring canoeist of Canada's early waterways.

He was fluent and unhurried as a second baseman, with an insouciance belying the carefully calculated movements of his big frame, and his wonderfully coordinated, sure fielding hands.

Larry never played on a pennant winner, more's the pity, nor was he ever a high-salaried man, by modern conceptions, yet he set high standards: as with his .405 average for the A's in their first (1901) season, which mark stood out for a decade, or until Ty Cobb began to feel his oats. The Georgia Peach, eleven years Lajoie's junior, had burst on the major league scene in 1905, in Larry's fourth Cleveland season, and his first full year as Cleveland manager.

Larry was an infielder who hit better than most outfielders, and as such was doubly valuable. Some have called him the greatest ever, even above Ty Cobb and Babe Ruth, both outfielders; and Honus Wagner, the peerless shortstop. For twenty-one active years Wagner hit .329, compared with Larry's .338 for twenty-one years.

Ruth was once quoted to the effect that he considered Lajoie the greatest natural hitter of all time, better even than Shoeless Joe Jackson, who came up as an outfielder to Cleveland, during Larry's period there.

Only Rogers Hornsby, who came to the majors as Larry was fading out, compared with the big Frenchman as a hard-hitting second baseman, over a long term of years, though the Rajah was never up to Larry's class as a fielder.

A good share of Lajoie's best hitting not only was prior to the lively ball, but antedated the cork center ball. Also Larry had to cope with pitching at its trickiest; with the spitter and emery ball, as well as squashy, scuffed spheres that were allowed to stay in play for long innings at a stretch.

In Larry's very advent in the majors there was something unusual. This was the circumstance, as reported at the time, that he was tossed in free for good measure in a deal the Phillies were making for another player, and if that is so, then Lajoie must have been the biggest bargain in baseball history.

Since turning seventy, Florida has claimed most of Lajoie's time. He stopped participating in old-timers' games a long time ago, and it was all of twenty-two years back that he paid his last long visit at a big league camp, which was just to cut up old touches, as he hobnobbed at St. Pete, in 1928, with the Yankees.

It was then he gave his version of how his Naps of 1908 had been nosed out for the flag, in what up to that year was the tightest race ever known in the junior loop, coinciding with the dizzy finish the same season in the National League, between the Cubs and Giants.

"It may have been my fault Cleveland lost the flag in 1908; I fear I was too strict with Nig Clarke," said Larry as he sat on a green bench in front of the Princess Martha Hotel, in the Sunshine City, wearing white golf knickers, with a cigar cocked rakishly in his mouth.

"Nig Clarke was one of my catchers. I also had Harry Bemis and Grover Land, but Nig was nifty teaming with Addie Joss . . . You've heard of Joss? A real pitcher: tossed four one-hitters in 1907, and in 1908 he went for a perfect game—not a man reaching first base—not a hit, a walk or an error, in nine innings, against the White Sox.

"Well, late in August of 1908 Nig got the idea that he ought to take a run home and see his new bride. I refused permission. Clarke sulked, then picked up his glove when I told him to work with Joss.

"Know what that silly Nig did? Darned if he didn't deliberately stick his right forefinger into one of Addie's fast ones.

"He came back to the bench bleeding, and the bone could be seen peeking through the flesh of his shattered finger. He stuck his hand out toward me and said, "Well I guess I can go home now, can't I?"

"Clarke was out five weeks, a costly accident for us. Of course, other things hurt us that year, too. The Senators only finished seventh, but they licked us fourteen times in the 1908 season, in-

cluding successive wins over my Naps on September 29, 30 and
October 1, about a week before the race ended. So we could only
blame ourselves, though we sure made it close: 90 won, 64 lost
for us, and 90 won, 63 lost for Detroit."

Larry was not always popular with some of his players. His
method of relaying signs was considered rudimentary. He had a
way of wiggling one finger behind his back, as notice to his outfield, when his pitcher was going to throw a fast ball; and wiggling two fingers for a curve. Enemy pitchers in the bull pen
often could read Larry's signals, and they were never at all any
mystery to Connie Mack.

The burden of managing in 1908 rather got Larry down, and
he hit but .289, which up to then was only the second time in
thirteen major league seasons he had dropped below .300.

But the next year, his last as Cleveland manager, he bounced
back in the old larruping-Larry style to hit .324; and in 1910 he
finished at .384, playing in 159 games, and missing the batting title
of the junior loop by but a fraction of a point, as his old rival,
Cobb, edged him out.

Cobb had been batting king the previous three straight years,
and it was a habit becoming annoying to some, as Ty spared nobody's feelings on his wild careenings around the paths, stretching hits, stealing bases and being a pest generally.

So as it happened in 1910, Lajoie had a lot of folks rooting for
him to beat out the Georgia Peach. The Frenchman nearly did
it at that, aided by some peculiar breaks, in fielding and scoring,
on the final day.

The Indians were to wind up the season in a double-header
with the eighth place Browns. Larry got eight hits out of nine at
bat in the two games, thanks to a half-dozen bunts down the
third base alley, where the Browns had a rookie, John Corriden,
playing very deep.

In the opener, Larry unloaded a triple and then beat out three
bunts to Corriden. In the second game, Larry singled hard his
first time up. His next time, he smashed a deep one to Rhoderick
Wallace, at short, and beat it out, but it was charged as an error
for the Scot.

The boys in the press box were already figuring up the averages, and their scribbling indicated Larry had a chance for the

title, if he could go three-for-three his remaining times at the plate.

Larry did just that, thanks to Rookie Corriden being ordered to play cautiously, which invited Larry to do some more bunting. But with all his hits that day, it wasn't quite enough for Larry, as was proved when the official batting averages were announced.

The league statistics gave the crown to Cobb, and Ty also got the Chalmers automobile that went with the hitting title at that time. Officially Cobb finished the year with a mark of .3848, compared with .3841 for Lajoie.

When much talk developed over Rookie Corriden's strangely deep position on bunts, League President Ban Johnson ordered an investigation, but nothing was ever definitely announced about the findings.

It seems significant that after 1910 Jack O'Connor appeared no longer in the majors. He was succeeded in 1911 by Rhoderick Wallace, as St. Louis manager, and the boys further figured out that had Wallace not drawn an error in that final double-header of 1910 with Cleveland, and had Lajoie instead been credited with a hit on the smash he beat out to shortstop Wallace, Larry rather than Cobb would have been 1910 batting king.

It was in 1910, that Lajoie, who had often astounded pitchers by hitting waste balls, showed to his unprecedented best as a one-handed batter.

It happened when he was facing Russell Ford, of the New York Highlanders. Ford was the cutest of the emery ball tricksters, scratching the horsehide with a piece of emery paper hid in his glove, the roughing-up of the ball making it sail peculiarly. Ford learned the dodge in the Southern League, from where he came up to New York, with his battery mate, Ed Sweeney.

Ford was just one of the many pitchers affronted by Larry's good 1910 hitting, just as there were many batsmen, and managers, too, irked to the extreme by Cobb's high flying spikes.

Ford, finding himself in a tight game with Cleveland at old League Park, decided the best way to avoid trouble was to walk Larry every time he came up. In those days, on an intentional pass the pitchers did not throw so excessively wide as they do at present, with the catcher moving far to his right to prevent any possibility of the batter offering at the ball.

Lajoie, anticipating Ford's intent, crossed him up by reaching out one-handed with his bat for a pitch-out and slapping the ball as only he could do without bringing the left hand into use, for a line double to right.

When Larry next came up there was again a man on base, and again a pass on purpose was indicated. Ford tried to throw as far to the right of the plate as possible but again Larry stretched out one-handed, and doubled to right.

For a third time this embarrassing pass that didn't come to pass resulted in the discomfiture of another one-handed double by Larry off Ford, as the Cleveland score mounted.

But that was all the hits Larry was to get off emery ball Ford that day. Because in his last time facing the versatile batter, Ford crossed up everyone but his catcher by throwing four straight balls behind Larry's back, and finally getting the satisfaction of walking the Frenchman, though by that stage of the game it was too late to save the Highlanders from a licking.

To many fans, one of the keen side features of the 1910 season, when Lajoie was bidding for the batting crown, was his speed afoot. At a time when Larry was thirty-five he had his last big base stealing season with 27 thefts, a total he exceeded on only two previous occasions: in 1897 when he stole 33 bases, as a twenty-two-year-old soph with the Phils (which is more than a modern Joe DiMaggio has purloined in his entire big time career); and in 1904 with Cleveland, when Larry stole 31 bases. That 1904 season, by the way, was when Larry led the American League in batting for the third and last time, having been tops in 1903, at .355; and tops in 1901, for the A's, at a dizzy .405.

Lajoie in twenty-one major league seasons stole 396 bases, not as showy of course as Cobb's 892, in twenty-four years; or Max Carey's 738, in eighteen years, but impressive none the less, and especially so by modern standards, as the steal seems less important now, and low scoring games are comparatively infrequent in this era of exaggerated homer hitting, with parks deliberately tailored to invite slams into the seats and over shortened barriers.

In homers, Lajoie totaled but 79 for his career, compared with 118 for Cobb, who played three years longer than Larry. But Larry's one-season peak of 13, for the A's in 1901, was more than Cobb ever hit in any one year. Cobb's high was 12 in 1921, and repeated again in 1925, which both were seasons after Ruth's rise, and the resultant introduction of the rabbity ball.

It is something always to be remembered to Lajoie's credit that when he was American League homer champ, with thirteen in 1901, it was long, long before any measures had been taken to hop up the ball, which had all the bounce of a doorknob, compared with modern skittish spheres.

Lajoie was on what is believed to have been the first American League team that ever had three men in a row whack homers in one inning. That happened at League Park in 1902 when the Clevelanders put on a scoring party most unusual for that era, when first baseman Charley (Piano Legs) Hickman, Larry, and the tall third baseman, Bill Bradley, came up one after another, each hitting for the circuit.

Larry settled for seven homers that year and considered he had done pretty well. After all, doubles were his trade-mark hits. He made 651 doubles in twenty-one years, with 51 his tops in two-baggers, in 1910, when he came so close to what would have been his fourth batting crown. Probably only Tris Speaker and Honus Wagner were more given to doubles over their long spans of service than was Larry.

Lajoie first worked as a bobbin boy in a cotton mill. His father, the coal man, had died when Larry was five. The boy drifted from job to job in the mills, picking up knowledge of the game on the side, and settling down as a hack driver long before he was old enough to vote.

Hacking was not too profitable, but there was his mother and five brothers and two sisters at home needing support. He thought himself lucky when he could make a little extra money as an occasional Sunday catcher, in semi-pro games.

That led to an offer from Charley Marston, owner of the Fall River team of the old New England League. Marston suggested that Lajoie jump down from his hack seat, and devote all his time to baseball.

"What'd I do with the horse?" Larry wanted to know.

"Turn the nag out to pasture for all I care," said Marston. "And you might do in the pasture yourself. That is, I think you might fit in the outfield. You got too much speed to waste your time catching. Or do you think you'd rather try the infield, if I'd pay enough?"

"You'd pay every week?" Larry asked, incredulous.

"Of course, and every month, too," replied Marston. "Why, I'll promise you $100 a month if you come with me over to Fall River."

"By gar, she's good money," said Larry, lapsing into the French-Canadian type of English of his forebears.

Marston pulled out an old envelope, and an agreement was signed thereon, on the spot, and Larry was a hackie no more.

As a budding pro, and budding second sacker, at Fall River, Larry hit .429 in eighty games during the first part of the 1896 season.

In August, Bill Nash, scout for the Phillies, blew into town on the old Fall River line, announcing that his bosses were interested in outfielder Phil Geier.

Nash landed his man, for $1,200, and Marston was so pleased at the deal that he said he was going to toss in a Canuck kid infielder as good measure.

"You mean that guy 'La-joy'?" said Nash.

"Sure," said Marston. "He's a big growing boy, and might do, but he eats so much that he's wearing out my pocketbook feeding him."

"Well, if you're bound to toss him in on the deal, I guess the Phils won't mind turning him loose in a few lunch wagons while they look him over," said the scout, as he headed back to Philly with two guys, or one more than he had been looking for.

Considering his .429 batting average at Fall River it seems a bit fantastic that Larry was tossed in for nothing on that deal.

One story was that Larry had originally been spotted by Arthur Irwin, and offered to Andy Freedman, then owner of the Giants, for $1,000.

Irwin had managed the Phillies in 1895, and switched to the Giants as pilot in 1896, when he was supplanted as Phillies manager by that club's former secretary, Bill Shettsline.

It may have been in a move to keep Lajoie from the Giants that Shettsline and the Phillies corralled the Canuck in August

1896, in what was a deal ostensibly for outfielder Phil Geier, but actually for Lajoie. Credence was given that view by the fact that Geier never amounted to much in the majors.

By 1899 when Ed Delahanty was pacing the Phillies and the National League with a .408 average, young Lajoie on the same team was not far behind, at .379, and the Frenchman was much discussed as a coming champ.

After one more year with the Phils, hitting a nice .346, Larry jumped from the Phillies and the old league to the new circuit, which had selected the Quaker City as one of its main Eastern shopwindows.

For Ban Johnson had expanded the old Western League into a new major loop called the American League, and Connie Mack had been selected to lead the invaders in Philadelphia with a team called the Athletics. Connie's partner was Ben Shibe, and the pair sought talent.

In a raid on the Phils, to start the A's going in 1901, Lajoie and three pitchers—Bill Bernard, Wiley Piatt and Charley Fraser, quit the Phils for Connie's fledgling outfit.

In retaliation, the Phillies obtained an injunction restraining Lajoie from playing with any other team but their own, inside the boundaries of the state of Pennsylvania. That cramped Larry's home activities with the A's, so the American League found it expedient to transfer his contract from Connie Mack's club to the Cleveland club, for the 1902 season.

Even in 1902 Larry was not able to play with Cleveland on trips to Philadelphia, so he only got in 87 games that year. But he batted a goodly .369, and there was still grief at the park of the A's that such a star had been forced to move West, because Quaker City fans remembered Larry's .405 average for the A's in 1901, when he had astounded the East by getting thirteen homers, after he had run up a streak of hitting in 32 straight games for the Phils, in 1900.

Larry's salary at the time of his transfer to Cleveland was $2,-400 a year, which was considered handsome then.

Bill Armour was Cleveland manager when the Frenchman arrived, but by September of 1904 he was tired of the travails of a fourth place club and Owner John F. Kilfoyl made Larry Cleveland's third American League skipper of record, the pioneer pilot having been Jimmy McAleer, in 1901.

The Cleveland club had been given to a lot of nicknames, back in its National League days and later in Ban Johnson's new league. Cleveland players had variously been known as the Molly Maguires, the Wanderers, the Spiders, and the Blues, the latter their handle when Larry came on the scene.

But just as soon as Nap Lajoie became manager, late in 1904, the Blues were rechristened the Naps, and so they continued until Larry himself threw up the job in the mid-season of 1909, to be succeeded by Jim McGuire.

In the four full seasons Nap was in charge, his Naps of 1905, 1906, 1907 and 1908 finished, respectively, fifth, third, fourth and second.

Larry kept up his batting very well while managing, but he was a fearless contender and often came up with spike wounds, one of which becoming infected threatened his career for a time, and limited his 1905 activities to 65 games.

After giving up the reins as manager in 1909, Larry cheerfully returned to the ranks, and with the load of responsibility off his shoulder in 1910 he was able to make his great try for the batting title, only to be foiled by that fiery new man of destiny, Tyrus Raymond Cobb.

Back in the ranks, Larry not only played in Cleveland under Jim McGuire, but also under George Stovall, Harry Davis and Joe Birmingham.

Stovall, a first baseman from the Pacific Coast, was an impetuous chap, and he once beaned Larry with a chair in a clubhouse argument. It was a mistake, because Larry bashed him back with two chairs, and crowned him with the water bucket. As time went on, the breach closed, and Stovall and Larry became the closest of pals, and George would never listen to anyone who did not agree with his opinion that Larry was the greatest of second basemen.

Joe (Dode) Birmingham, a handsome faced center fielder, who had been exposed to education at Cornell, thought he might improve Larry's batting, when "Birmy," famed for a great throwing arm, moved in as Cleveland skipper in 1912.

That amused Larry no end, but he put on a serious face listening to Dode's advice about shortening up his swing. He even told Dode, with a reasonably straight face, that the Birmingham system had lifted the Lajoie average in 1912 to .368, or three points higher than Larry had hit in 1911.

But by 1914 Larry had passed his peak, hitting only .258 for an eighth place club, and it was arranged for the Lajoie contract

NAPOLEON (LARRY) LAJOIE

Born Woonsocket, R. I., September 5, 1875.
Height 6' 1". Weight 195. Batted and threw right-handed.

YEAR	CLUB	LEAGUE	G	AB	R	H	2B	3B	HR	SB	BA
1896	Fall River	N. Eng.	80	380	94	163	..	..	..	..	.42
1896	Philadelphia	Nat.	39	174	37	57	11	10	4	6	.32
1897	Philadelphia	Nat.	126	545	107	198	36	23	7	22	.36
1898	Philadelphia	Nat.	147	610	113	200	42	9	5	33	.32
1899	Philadelphia	Nat.	72	308	70	117	17	11	6	14	.37
1900	Philadelphia (A)	Nat.	102	451	95	156	32	19	7	25	.34
1901	Philadelphia	Amer.	131	543	145	220	48	13	*13	27	*.40
1902	Cleveland	Amer.	87	352	81	129	34	5	7	19	.36
1903	Cleveland	Amer.	126	488	90	173	40	11	7	22	*.35
1904	Cleveland	Amer.	140	554	92	211	50	14	5	31	*.38
1905	Cleveland	Amer.	65	249	29	82	13	2	2	11	.32
1906	Cleveland	Amer.	152	602	88	214	49	7	0	20	.35
1907	Cleveland	Amer.	137	509	53	152	32	6	2	24	.29
1908	Cleveland	Amer.	157	581	77	168	32	6	2	15	.28
1909	Cleveland	Amer.	128	469	56	152	33	7	1	13	.32
1910	Cleveland	Amer.	159	591	92	227	51	7	4	27	.38
1911	Cleveland	Amer.	90	315	36	115	20	1	2	13	.36
1912	Cleveland	Amer.	117	448	66	165	34	4	0	18	.36
1913	Cleveland	Amer.	137	465	66	156	25	2	1	17	.33
1914	Cleveland	Amer.	121	419	37	108	14	2	1	14	.25
1915	Philadelphia †	Amer.	129	490	40	137	24	5	1	10	.28
1916	Philadelphia	Amer.	113	426	33	105	14	4	2	15	.24
	Major League Totals		2475	9589	1503	3242	651	168	79	396	.33

(A) Jumped to Philadelphia A.L., but Philadelphia N.L. club got injunction and h transferred to Cleveland

† Contract assumed by Philadelphia Athletics, January, 1915

* Led League

Manager, Cleveland, 1904; July, 1909

Manager, Toronto, 1917

Manager, Indianapolis, 1918

Elected to Hall of Fame, 1937

to be assumed by Connie Mack and the A's, with which club the Frenchman bowed out of the majors after hitting .280 in 1915, and .246 in 1916.

During Larry's days as manager in Cleveland he had some spectacular performers whose names should be added to the legend of the great Frenchman. There was the pitcher Addie Joss, former Wisconsin school teacher, who was to die suddenly in his prime. There was right fielder Elmer Flick, who was never without a stopwatch, because he owned a trotter on the side.

Also Harry (Deerfoot) Bay, center fielder, who always carried a cornet on baseball trips, and who wound up in charge of the sirens of the Peoria fire department.

And Bill Bradley, slugging third baseman, a latter day scout for the Cleveland Indians; and the Canadian-born left fielder, Jack Gladstone Graney, still extant and much in evidence in Cleveland as one of the Tribe's, and the town's, most popular sports casters.

CHAPTER XV

BIG SIX

Christopher Mathewson

UNDER A BLAZING SUN at Miami Beach's Flamingo Field in 1935, Adolpho Luque, Giant pitching coach, was teaching two young rookies the art of keeping their curve ball low. One of them, Clydell Castleman, was to develop into a surprise winner for the Giants that season, although the other, Sharkey Eiland, never did make it. Nevertheless, Luque was dividing his time equally between the two, working patiently with them.

Luque, one of the great control pitchers of all time, was an effective relief pitcher at a ripe old age, thanks to his proficiency at keeping his curve ball low, which forced batters to hit it in the ground and set up double-play possibilities.

The workout over, one of the New York reporters strolled from the field with Luque, who spoke a broken English which defied both description and translation.

"Who taught you to keep your curve ball low, Dolf?" inquired the writer conversationally.

"Marti," answered Luque.

"Marty who?" asked the puzzled scribe.

"Marti, you know—Marti, the bestest of everybody," said the Cuban impatiently. " 'Smotter—you no know heem?"

It took a bit of doing but it evolved that Luque's "Marti" was Matty, Christy Mathewson, the greatest pitcher the Giants ever had. In a Cincinnati training camp, when Luque was a rookie, but scarcely a young one or a green one, and Matty was having a fling at managing, Luque carefully absorbed the instructions given him, and now he was handing on the Giant heritage to aspiring rookies, although Mathewson had been dead the last ten years and only Eddie Brannick, the club secretary, had any vivid memories of him.

Luque had made no mistake in copying his style after that of "Marti" and Manager Bill Terry had made no mistake in hiring Luque to pass the art along to the pitchers. There weren't going to be any second Mattys, of course, but any pitcher who picked up even a smidgin of the skill of the man they called Big Six was bound to be a better pitcher.

It wasn't always thus with the Giants and Matty. When John Joseph McGraw jumped the infant American League from Baltimore to come to the Polo Grounds and remain there for thirty stirring seasons, he winced at the first sight he saw. Matty was playing first base!

The Giants, in 1902, were owned by a character named Andrew Freedman, who had a knack of antagonizing the players, and managed by Horace Fogel. It was Fogel's idea that a first baseman's job was just the dish for Matty. When Fogel was replaced by George Smith, an infielder, he remained as an advisor and not only suggested that Smith play Matty at first but also that he try the big right-hander at shortstop.

Mathewson had been a twenty-game winner for a seventh-place Giant team the year before and what could have been going through the minds of Fogel and Smith to try the big fellow as an infielder must forever remain a mystery.

"You can get rid of Fogel," he snorted. "Anybody who doesn't know any more about baseball than he does has no right in a ball park. Trying to make a first baseman out of Mathewson! There's a kid with as fine a pitching motion as I ever saw and as much stuff as any young fellow to come up in years. He'll pitch from now on."

McGraw made many a prophecy during his baseball career but he never called his shot more accurately. "Pitch from now on" was precisely what Matty did. He won better than twenty games for McGraw for the next dozen seasons, topping thirty in each of his first three full seasons under the little Napoleon.

Mathewson was a big man, six feet, one and a half inches, and pitched at 195 pounds. He had such powerful legs, legs which made him a great drop-kicker at Bucknell, that one of the pet names for him was "Gum Boots." For all of his bulk, he pitched smoothly and quickly.

The pitch for which Matty became famous was his fadeaway,

the screwball of today. It was a reverse curve, which broke in on right-handed batters and out on left-handed batters, the diametrical opposite of the orthodox curve ball of a right-handed pitcher.

While Mathewson's fadeaway gained him the headlines, he was one of the great control pitchers of all time. Grover Hartley, a catcher contemporary with Christy who remained in the majors years afterward as a coach, said that Matty could put his curve ball, fast one or fadeaway into an area the size of a grapefruit. And do it consistently. Because he pitched so smoothly, he was forever lulling the batters into a false sense of security. They never really believed he was quite as fast as he was and the ball was upon them before they knew it.

In 1908, Mathewson pitched 416 innings and walked only 42 hitters, an average of less than one per nine-inning game. Five years later, when the Giants were fighting Charley Dooin's Phillies for the pennant, Matty turned in a stretch of control pitching which still stands as a major league record and is likely to remain one for all time, pitchers being what they are today. He pitched 68 consecutive innings without issuing one walk!

In a game at Cincinnati, on June 19, Matty won a raggedy game by an 8–7 score, giving up two passes. He didn't walk another batter until July 18, when he pitched a five-hit shutout against St. Louis at the Polo Grounds. He worked four innings relief against the Phils on June 30, in a game in which the Giants won 11 to 10 in eleven innings to take the lead and keep it for the rest of the season.

All told, in this string Matty started six times and relieved twice without passing one batter. That year Matty won 25 games and lost eleven. He pitched 306 innings and yielded only 21 walks, an even more impressive record than he turned in in 1908, for this figured out to about one base on balls every fifteen innings!

Fred Lieb, the baseball author, tells of an incredible game he saw Mathewson pitch in Cincinnati—a fourteen-hit shutout! Matty was not a pitcher who bore down unless he had to and he had the knack of conserving his stamina for when it was needed.

"I never saw a game such as this one," recalled Fred. "I don't mean the actual game itself, for it was simply the story of a pitcher with a lead pacing himself and taking his work as easily as possible. What was most unusual was the pattern of the game. Throughout the first seven innings, the first two Red batsmen were retired and the next two hit singles. Then Matty disposed of the fifth batter. This pattern held until the eighth when he retired the last six in order. There were no walks."

Sam Crane, veteran baseball writer on the New York *Journal* and who had played with the Giants himself back in 1890, hung the nickname of "Big Six" on Matty. It didn't, as many seem to think, stem from the nickname of a typographical uniform but from a famed New York City fire company. This was supposed to be the champion of all fire companies and, taking that as a cue, Sam called Matty "the Big Six of pitchers." He was so well known by the nickname that he received mail which had been dropped in a letter box with nothing on the envelope but a huge, scrawled "6."

Matty was a strange type for an athlete of that rough-and-tumble period. He won three football letters at Bucknell, where he had a reputation as an excellent kicker. It also was at Bucknell that he first hooked up in his famous pitching duels with that great left-hander, Eddie Plank, who was then attending Gettysburg College, a series of duels which were continued through the World Series between the Giants and Athletics.

Quiet, almost austere, Mathewson was not one to frolic with the boys. He was a keen card player and one of the best checker players baseball ever knew at a time when checkers was a popular clubhouse sport with the athletes.

Mathewson's most productive year as a Giant was 1908, when he won 37 victories, which still stands as a National League record. Yet in many ways it was one of his most disappointing seasons. Matty lost only eleven games that season, yet one of those defeats cost the Giants the pennant. And to make the dose more bitter, it was a game that John McGraw, Matty, and dozens of non-partisan baseball fans, insist never should have been played.

This was the year of what still is erroneously referred to as the "Merkle boner." Fred Merkle, then a kid of nineteen, was in his first full season with the Giants. In the game in which he pulled his alleged rock, at the Polo Grounds against the Cubs, September 23, 1908, Fred was playing his first nine-inning game as a first baseman. The lapse of which he was guilty was standard operating procedure at that time. In his memoirs in *Collier's* in 1951, Bill Klem, supervisor of National League umpires, called the decision Umpire Hank O'Day had made on the play "the worst in the history of baseball."

It is necessary to go back a bit to get the full story of the play. In 1908, the Giants, Cubs and Pirates waged a three-cornered fight for the flag. On September 4, in Pittsburgh, the Cubs lost to Vic Willis and the Pirates, 1 to 0, in the ninth. There were men on first and third with two out when the winning hit was delivered. Warren Gill was the Pirate on first and he left the field as soon as the hit was made.

Johnny Evers, the Cub second baseman, called for the ball from Artie Hofman, the center fielder, and claimed a force at second for the final out. And the rules are specific that no run shall count if the third out of the inning is a force-out. O'Day, who was umpiring that game, refused to allow the claim.

Frank Chance, the Cub manager and first baseman, phoned the owner, Charles Webb Murphy, in Chicago and urged that he lodge a protest with Harry Pulliam, president of the National League. Pulliam denied the protest but admitted that the Cubs had a point.

Evers, and more important, O'Day, remembered all this nineteen days later when Chicago battled the Giants in the Polo Grounds. Matty had allowed his particular nemesis, Joe Tinker, to connect for a home run against him in the fifth, but in the sixth Turkey Mike Donlin singled to score Buck Herzog and tied up the game.

The score stood at 1 to 1 in the Giant half of the ninth, two out, Al Bridwell at bat, Moose McCormick on third and young Merkle on first. Bridwell lined one of Jack Pfeister's pitches, into center and McCormick romped home with what everybody thought was the winning run. Merkle happily dashed to the clubhouse, overlooking the formality of touching second. Evers, with the Pittsburgh incident fresh in his mind, again called for Hofman to give him the ball.

The throw was bad and it got away from Evers at second and

Tinker at short. Floyd Kroh, a relief pitcher on the Cub bench, attempted to retrieve it but was forestalled by Iron Man Joe McGinnity, coaching for the Giants at third base. Joe managed to fight his way clear and fling the ball into the left field stands. From somewhere (some say the Cub ball bag) Evers obtained another baseball and stood on second, claiming the force-out. O'Day allowed it.

By this time, of course, the fans had piled onto the field to celebrate what they thought was a Giant victory. Some of the New York papers next morning actually carried a box score which showed a 2–1 victory for the Giants. McGraw was outraged. He gathered the Giants about him in the clubhouse and told the players under no conditions to discuss the play with anybody. He sent young Merkle to the far-off seclusion of the Hotel Shelbourne in Brighton Beach where he would be safe from inquisitive reporters. There is one story that he told the boy to go out and tag second base at the Polo Grounds in the dead of night so that in forthcoming investigations Fred could truthfully say that he touched second.

McGraw protested the decision to President Pulliam on the grounds that O'Day was enforcing a decision which never before had been enforced in the history of the game. Manager Chance, not content with a tie, went Mac one better and demanded that Pulliam forfeit the game to the Cubs, 9 to 0, since the home club (New York) was responsible for the fact that the field couldn't be cleared so that the 1–1 tie game could be continued.

Pulliam upheld O'Day's decision and ignored Chance's protest, ruling the game a tie. McGraw went over Pulliam's head and appealed to the National Commission, which ruled baseball in those pre-Landis days. The Commission strung along with Pulliam, declared the game a tie and ordered that it be replayed the day after the season ended, if it had any effect upon the final standings.

The effect the tie had on the final standings was merely terrific. Mordecai Brown pitched the Cubs to a 5–2 victory over Willis and the Pirates in Chicago on Sunday, October 4, before 30,247 fans, reported as the largest crowd ever to see a game in the West.

The Cubs thus finished the regular season a half-game in front of Pittsburgh, which also had concluded its season. The Giants, however, had three games left to play with Boston. They played and won all three, which left them tied with the Cubs and a half-game ahead of Pittsburgh.

The play-off game was scheduled for New York on October 8 and, of course, Matty was McGraw's choice. His opponent was the same Pfeister, who had a reputation as a Giant-killer. The attendance was estimated as 35,000 but there never was an accurate count because thousands forced their way into the park by simply smashing down a section of the fence. It was necessary to turn a fire hose on the spectators to keep them from completely engulfing the playing field.

Bottles, cushions and other missiles were showered upon the Cubs when they took the field for practice. It seemed that there would be a full-scale riot before Matty and Pfeister ever finished warming up.

The Giants bounced into Pfeister and knocked him out in the first round. Tenney, who was at first instead of Merkle, was hit by a pitched ball and Herzog walked. Roger Bresnahan fanned but Johnny Kling juggled the third strike and Herzog needlessly broke for second. He was trapped, Kling to Chance, but even this didn't help Pfeister, for Donlin weighed in with a double to score Tenney. When Cy Seymour walked, Chance lifted Pfeister and called on Brown. The three-fingered ace fanned Arthur Devlin and retired the side.

Tinker climbed into Matty for a triple in the third, a drive to center which Seymour played none too well, and Kling singled Joe home. Brown sacrificed the catcher to second, and when Jimmy Sheckard flied out it seemed that Matty was out of danger but Evers drew a walk and kept the rally alive. Wildfire Schulte and Chance followed with doubles and the Cubs were in front by 4 to 1. The best the Giants could do against Brown was make the final score 4 to 2, and the Cubs took the pennant while the Giants tied for second with Fred Clarke's Pirates.

For a truly great pitcher, Mathewson did not have much luck in World Series play. He pitched the greatest number of World Series innings of any pitcher in history—101⅔—and won five games while losing the same number. The fact that Matty's Series record for innings pitched is not an even 102 is the story of another bad break which the great right-hander suffered in his career.

The two most notorious acts of baseball malfeasance are Merkle's failure to touch second in 1908, already described, and the muff of a fly by Fred Snodgrass in the 1912 World Series. In each instance, Matty was the victim. And in each instance, also, there were extenuating circumstances for the personnel popularly accepted as being guilty.

After seven games and nine innings, the 1912 Series between the Red Sox and Giants was still a tie, by virtue of the second game at Boston having ended in a 6–6, eleven-inning tie. Now, again in Boston at the top of the tenth inning, the teams were in a 1–1 tie. Smokey Joe Wood was pitching for the Sox, in relief of Hugh Bedient, when Red John Murray hit his second two-bagger of the afternoon and came home on a single by Merkle.

All Matty had to do was hold the Red Sox for one inning and it seemed a cinch. Indeed, the Sox shouldn't have scored against him at all; a Texas-league double to left by Manager Jake Stahl which fell among three Giant fielders and a pinch-double by Olaf Henricksen which hit the third base bag accounted for the only Boston run against Big Six.

Clyde Engle led off the tenth as a pinch hitter for Wood and lofted an easy fly to Snodgrass in center—which Fred muffed ingloriously. Engle went to second on the error, where he remained as Snodgrass made a remarkable catch of a long drive by Harry Hooper. Then Matty walked Steve Yerkes and brought up Tris Speaker. Spoke raised a soft foul near first base which was allowed to fall between Chief Meyers and Merkle. Either could have caught it.

Perfect baseball in the field would have meant the end of the inning, the game and the World Series. As it was, Speaker, and the Red Sox, were very much alive. Spoke drove a long single to left which sent home Engle with the tying run and put Yerkes on third. McGraw ordered Duffy Lewis passed to fill the bases, but Larry Gardner flied deep to Josh Devore in right and Yerkes scored the winning run.

The muff by Snodgrass, which McGraw excused on the ground

that it was a mechanical error, and the uncaught foul pop, which Mac never excused because it was the result of careless play, should have been enough hard luck for any pitcher in a World Series, but Matty had had Series misadventures even before the Snodgrass muff.

In 1911, against the Athletics, Matty won the Series opening by beating Chief Bender 2 to 1 in an exciting pitching duel. In the second game, when the Series moved to Shibe Park, Jay Franklin Baker started his climb to fame when he broke a 1–1 tie by hitting a home run against Rube Marquard over the right field fence, with Eddie Collins on base.

When the Series returned to New York for the third game, Baker, now on his way to earning his nickname of "Home Run," combed Matty for a home run to tie the score, 1 to 1, in the ninth and the A's eventually won by 3 to 2 in eleven innings.

If Matty had his heartaches in World Series play, he had his moments of glory, too, glory such as no other pitcher has had in the history of baseball—his three shutouts over Philadelphia in the 1905 Series. The Giants won this Series, the first in which they ever played, by four games to one. All of Big Six's starts were shutouts and so were the other two games, in which McGraw started Iron Man Joe McGinnity. Joe was beaten 3 to 0 by Bender in the second game of the Series and in the fourth defeated Eddie Plank 1 to 0.

Plank, who had been a college pitching rival of Matty, faced Big Six in the opener at Shibe Park and was turned back 3 to 0, as Mathewson allowed only four hits. After Bender evened the Series for Philadelphia, Matty returned to Columbia Park and won over Andy Coakley by 9 to 0, the Athletics' pitcher receiving wretched support with five errors behind him.

Matty's second whitewash job put the Giants ahead two games to one and McGinnity made it three to one with his shutout the next day. And then Mathewson, pitching for the first time in New York during the Series, came right back with only a day between starts to beat Bender, Connie Mack's only winner, by a score of 2 to 0. Both the Giant runs reached base by virtue of passes, for the Chief allowed five hits against Mathewson's six. It is worth while noting, for the benefit of current fans used to three-hour ball games, that this World Series classic was reeled off in an hour and thirty-five minutes.

While Matty's Series record is an even five-five, he pitched remarkable ball when the chips were down. All five of his defeats were by hairline margins. In the 1911 Series, the Athletics beat him by scores of 3 to 2, in eleven innings, and 4 to 2. In 1912, he bowed to the Red Sox by 2 to 1, and 3 to 2 in ten innings, the latter the game of Snodgrass's error; and in 1913, the Athletics beat him by a 3-1 score. And Matty blanked them for the last six innings of that game.

Oddly enough, Matty gave out just when he seemed headed for one of his greatest seasons. This was in 1914, the year the Braves under George Stallings made their miracle climb from last place in mid-July to the pennant. On July 19, the Braves were in eighth place, eleven games behind the league-leading Giants. When the season was over, the Braves were ahead with the comfortable margin of 10½ games on the second-place Giants.

Matty started great but soon petered out. He began to complain of pains in his left side after he had pitched, and no reasonable explanation ever was found for these complaints on the side opposite his pitching arm. Despite his weak finish, Mathewson had a record of 24 wins and thirteen defeats for the year, the twelfth consecutive season in which he had won twenty or better for the Giants.

Matty had his first losing season since 1902 in 1915, when he won only eight games while losing fourteen. He had been relegated to the bull pen when, halfway through the 1916 season, McGraw traded him to Cincinnati.

Matty had won three games and lost four for the Giants by mid-July when the trade was made. The Cincinnati fans were hopeful that he would recover his mound magic for them, but even if he couldn't pitch for them, they felt they had gained something, since they were certain he no longer would pitch against them. Big Six's record against the Reds was the most remarkable spell of dominance any pitcher ever held against any club, far surpassing the jinx Ed Lopat of the Yankees held over the Cleveland Indians.

The first time Matty ever pitched against the Reds in his life he beat them by 1 to 0. His career record against them was 64 victories against eighteen defeats and he once turned them off 22 times in succession.

CHRISTOPHER MATHEWSON

Born August 12, 1880 at Factoryville, Pa.
Height, 6' 1½". Weight, 195. Threw and batted right-handed.
Elected to Hall of Fame in 1936.

YEAR	CLUB	LEAGUE	G	IP	W	L	AVE	SO	BB	
1899	Taunton	New Eng.	17	...	5	2	.714	...	...	.
1900	Norfolk	Virginia	28	...	21	2	.956	...	...	.
1900	New York (a)	Nat.	5	30	0	3	.000	15	14	
1901	New York	Nat.	40	336	20	17	.541	215	92	2
1902	New York	Nat.	34	276	14	17	.452	162	74	2
1903	New York	Nat.	45	367	30	13	.698	*267	100	3
1904	New York	Nat.	48	368	33	12	.733	212	78	3
1905	New York	Nat.	43	339	31	9	.775	206	64	2
1906	New York	Nat.	38	267	22	12	.647	128	77	2
1907	New York	Nat.	41	316	24	12	.667	178	53	2
1908	New York	Nat.	56	391	*37	11	.771	259	42	2
1909	New York	Nat.	37	275	25	6	*.806	149	36	1
1910	New York	Nat.	38	319	27	9	.750	190	57	2
1911	New York	Nat.	45	307	26	13	.667	141	38	3
1912	New York	Nat.	43	310	23	12	.657	134	34	3
1913	New York	Nat.	40	306	25	11	.694	93	21	2
1914	New York	Nat.	41	312	24	13	.648	80	23	3
1915	New York	Nat.	27	186	8	14	.364	57	20	1
1916	New York-Cincinnati †	Nat.	13	74	4	4	.500	19	8	7
	Major League Totals		634	4779	373	188	.665	2505	831	419

WORLD SERIES RECORD

YEAR	CLUB	LEAGUE	G	IP	W	L	AVE	SO	BB	H
1905	New York	Nat.	3	27	3	0	1.000	18	1	1
1911	New York	Nat.	3	27	1	2	.333	13	2	2
1912	New York	Nat.	3	28⅔	0	2	.000	10	5	2
1913	New York	Nat.	2	19	1	1	.500	7	2	1
	World Series Totals		11	101⅔	5	5	.500	48	10	7

(a) Joined Giants mid-season, 1900. Turned back to Norfolk at end of campaign, bu drafted by Cincinnati and traded to Giants for Pitcher Amos Rusie.

† Traded with Outfielder Edd Roush to Cincinnati for Infielder Charles Herzog an Outfielder Wade Killefer, July 20, 1916.

* Led league
x Tied for league lead

Mathewson pitched only once as a member of the Reds and it was a remarkable game for several reasons, not the least of which was that it was the only National League game he ever pitched in any but a Giant uniform. It also was one of the few games in the major leagues which saw a left-handed second baseman perform —Hal Chase, the regular first baseman, playing that position for Cincinnati and accepting seven out of eight chances.

The game was against the Cubs, the second game of a Labor Day double-header, and it pitted Matty against his ancient foe, Mordecai Brown, who had beaten him in the memorable play-off game in 1908. This time, with nothing hanging in the balance, the honors went to Matty by a score of 10 to 8. Although hit freely, both old-timers stuck it out to the end.

It was the last game for Brown also, the old three-fingered star never pitching again in the majors. Mathewson's control was good, even at the end, for he gave up only one base on balls.

The importance of Big Six's only victory in a Cincinnati uniform wasn't realized for nearly three decades. It was then a figure filbert, checking through the records, discovered that in May of 1902 Matty had beaten the Pirates by a score of 4 to 2, but that the game, through an error, had been entered as a defeat. When this correction was made it was discovered that Matty had a total of 373 victories, precisely the same number as Grover Alexander won in the National League. Both are tied for National League honors in games won, with nobody else even close or threatening to be close.

CHAPTER XVI

THE MAN

Stanley Frank Musial

MAN AND BOY, Tom Sheehan has been around baseball parks most of his life. He has been on the pitching mound and the batters' box, the coaching box and the dugout. He has been in the bull pen and in the bleachers, in the grandstand and the front row boxes. He was in one of the latter when the 1946 World Series opened at Sportsman's Park, St. Louis.

While others might loll in the luxury of their box seats, our hero leaned forward, almost bug-eyed in his intentness to catch every move on the field. Other people are fans and spectators but Tom is a student of baseball.

With particular interest, Sheehan watched the Red Sox pitcher, Tex Hughson, face Stan Musial, the Cardinal slugger who had led the National League that season with a .365 batting average. Tom had been away from the majors for some years, toiling in such places as Minneapolis and St. Cloud, Minnesota, and hadn't had much chance to study Musial.

He watched as Musial took his stand in the left-handed side of the batter's box, noted carefully that Stan gripped the bat down at the end, his right hand just above the knob. Tom noted with approval that Musial stood in the box with his feet close together, the stance of a batter who can hit to either field. Sheehan's eyes really popped, however, as Stan placed his right foot a little closer to the plate than his left, bent his knees slightly and turned his right shoulder toward the pitcher. He watched as Musial grounded crisply to Bobby Doerr at second base to end the inning.

"Well," said Tom as he turned to his new employer, Horace

Stoneham, president of the Giants, "no wonder nobody can pitch to that guy. He hits at you from around the corner."

It was an apt description of Musial's stance. Stan almost has his back turned to the pitcher as the latter starts his delivery. The bent knees and the crouch give him the appearance of a coiled spring, although most pitchers think of him as a coiled rattle-snake. And when he unwinds and lashes into the ball, it spells trouble for somebody.

As is the case with any extraordinary hitter, Musial's timing is excellent, his vision perfect. With Stan, once more we encounter the feet-together theory, which says that only a batter who stands with his feet together and thus is able to hit to both fields ever can have a shot at a possible .400 average. The .376 average with which Musial led the league in 1948 was the highest compiled in the National League since Bill Terry hit .401 for the Giants in 1931, seventeen years earlier.

Musial's crouch and his habit of turning his right shoulder toward the pitcher created a great deal of comment in 1946. This set some inquisitive baseball writers to wondering and when baseball writers wonder they always ask questions. Terry Moore, the Cardinal team captain and one of the greatest ball hawks who ever played, supplied the answer.

"That crouch is something Stan picked up in the Navy," explained Moore. "He used to stand up straighter before he went into service. And now when he crouches, it exaggerates that shoulder he turns toward the pitcher. Although only the crouch is new, it makes him look entirely different."

Oddly enough, Musial doesn't think that he crouches any more now than he did before he went into service after the 1944 World Series. This isn't too unusual with ballplayers, who frequently alter their batting styles during the course of their careers without being aware of it themselves. The chances are that Musial had been modifying his stance during all the years he was with the Cardinals. Had it not been that he was in the Navy in 1945, the change might have been so gradual as to not have been noticed by even the most observant of his teammates.

Like Babe Ruth, George Sisler, Lefty O'Doul, Bill Terry and

many another great hitter, Stanley Frank Musial began his professional career as a southpaw pitcher. And, like another slugger, Lou Gehrig, the insistence of Musial's immigrant parents upon the college education which they themselves never had almost kept him from professional baseball.

Musial was a fine athlete in high school at his native Donora, Pennsylvania, the same Donora High at which Arnold Galiffa was to star some years later before going to West Point to become one of the country's outstanding quarterbacks. Western Pennsylvania always has been fertile ground for high school stars and Musial could have had his pick of several colleges with room, board, books and tuition were it not that he had his heart set on baseball.

To Papa Lukasz Musial, America was the land of opportunity where every man had a right to an education. He wanted his oldest boy to have the best. And here was the boy with a choice of the very best turning it down to play some silly game which would pay him little money and that for only six months of the year. It was almost the same argument which Papa and Mom Gehrig used when Paul Krichell tried first to tell them of the gold and the glory that awaited their boy Louie as a Yankee.

Young Stan had been piling up the strikeouts as a skinny left-hander at Donora High. He had worked out with Monessen in the Penn State League and both the manager, Ollie Vanek, and the business manager, Andy French, thought the boy had possibilities. Pie Traynor, of the Pittsburgh Pirates, had one of his scouts, Johnny Gooch, chasing after the boy, too. Monessen was in the Cardinal chain and French had learned something of the spellbinders' art from Branch Rickey but he was getting nowhere fast with Papa Musial.

After French had spent several evenings in vain pleading with the elder Musial, young Stan saw it was a losing battle. Only seventeen at the time, he began to cry softly. Stanley's tears worked where all of French's oratory had failed. Reluctantly, Papa Lukasz allowed Mr. French to sign his boy to a Monessen contract.

As a left-handed kid starting out in organized ball, Musial was just about what you would expect, ordinary but promising. He had a fair curve and better control than could reasonably be expected from a southpaw of his inexperience. He finished the 1938 season with Williamson, West Virginia, in the Mountain State League and stayed there for all of 1939.

It was after that first full season when Musial married his school-days sweetheart, Lillian Labash, whose dad ran a grocery store in Donora, where Stan worked winters. The pair married on November 21, 1939, Stan's nineteenth birthday.

The married man of nineteen was moved up in the Cardinal organization in 1940, being sent to pitch for the Daytona Beach Islanders in the Florida State League. It was here he got the best and the worst breaks of his career. The best was when he met Dickie Kerr, one of the white White Sox of the 1919 World Series, the pitcher who won two games from Cincinnati while some of his teammates were trying to throw the Series. Kerr was an intelligent, understanding man and he polished Stan's pitching. Kerr also decided that the power of Musial could be utilized in the outfield and began playing Stan there on days when he wasn't pitching.

Musial was going well both as a pitcher and a batter when he ran into the bad break. By mid-August he had won 17 games for the Islanders and was hitting over .300. He essayed a diving catch of a sinking line drive in center and while he caught the ball, he injured his left shoulder so severely that he lost his pitching touch completely. More than that, he lost the ability to throw with any power at all. Stan still could hit but he was a dead-armed outfielder.

Still months short of his twentieth birthday. Musial was face to face with the harsh facts of life. His wife was going to have a baby, his salary was $100 a month, six months of the year, and his baseball future seemed washed up. It seemed as though he were headed for the very fate Papa Musial had sought to avoid by having him enter college—a life in the steel mills of his native Donora.

J. Roy Stockton, the able St. Louis author and the first of Stan's many biographers, relates that Manager Kerr came to Musial's rescue in more ways than one. Dickie advised Stan not to quit baseball and told him he still had a chance to make the big wheel as an outfielder, that he was a natural hitter and that hitting covered more sins than charity ever did. Besides, there was no reason to believe that the shoulder injury which impaired his throwing was going to be permanent.

Kerr did more than merely bolster Musial's morale. He gave him material aid as well. The Kerrs rented a larger house in Daytona Beach and moved Stan and his young bride in with them. This cut down Musial's expenses and enabled him to finish the season with the Islanders. He wound up with a batting average of .311—and a dead arm.

Horatio Alger wouldn't have dared to put down on paper the rags-to-riches story of our hero Stanley in 1941. It would have frightened even Burt L. Standish, the creator of the Merriwells. In March, there wasn't a manager in the far-flung baseball empire of the Cardinals who wanted him. By July, the New York Giants offered to buy him for $40,000 and by September, he was hitting better than .400 in the National League.

Branch Rickey, then the Cardinal brain, was the first to establish baseball camps, as distinguished from training camps. Some years before he had tried out the plan at St. Joseph, Missouri, and he felt it possessed distinct advantages. He since carried it to the point where it is virtually a baseball assembly line.

Briefly Rickey's plan was to establish a common pool of the Cardinals' minor league ballplayers under a faculty of minor league managers and coaches. Since the minor league seasons usually open much later than the major league the camp usually was held at a site different than that used for training by the parent club.

Columbus, Georgia, was the spot Rickey selected for his 1940 proving grounds. Musial was one of more than two hundred young ballplayers. He soon showed that he had lost nothing of his batting skill. He had the same level, rhythmic swing, the same keen eye. And he was getting more distance to his drives than ever before. On the other hand, Stan couldn't throw for beans.

After the long afternoon workouts, the brain trusters would gather in solemn conclave in the evenings to compare notes. The opinion was unanimous that Musial could hit but nobody was willing to say that he ever would be able to throw again. Or that his hitting skill would be sufficient to offset the liability of his lame arm.

Eventually Ollie Vanek, managing Springfield, Missouri, in

the Class C Western League, took the dead-armed Musial. Ollie had been managing Monessen when Stan worked out with that club before being signed to a Cardinal organization contract. Vanek knew the boy could hit but before he took him he exacted a promise from Rickey that Musial would be replaced with an able-bodied outfielder at the first opportunity.

Whether Rickey ever did dig up the able-bodied outfielder nobody knows, for Musial started hitting from the first day he put on a Springfield uniform and he hasn't stopped yet. At one stage, Stan was tearing the Western League apart with a batting average which at one time touched .440. Even when he tapered off, it was to a robust .379 before he was shifted to Rochester in the International League.

From Class C to Class AA, which was the alphabetical classification of the International League then, is a big jump but Musial took it in stride. The first time he went to bat for Manager Tony Kaufman he hit a home run and he was batting .326 when he was called in to bolster the Cardinals in their ding-dong battle with the Dodgers for the pennant.

Nobody around the National League had heard about Musial and nobody knew how to pronounce his name when he joined the Cards on September 17, 1941. When he wound up the season with an average of .426 for a dozen games, everybody around the National League knew who he was and how his name was pronounced, everything about him, in fact, except how to pitch to him.

Musial won no batting crowns in 1941 for all of his great hitting simply because he played in no league long enough to be a contender for the title but his average in the Western Association, International League and National League was higher than that of the leader in each of those circuits. Nor did he have the satisfaction of being with a pennant winner in any of the three leagues.

The Cardinals that year were just nosed out by the Dodgers, who went into St. Louis and won two games out of three a few days before Musial joined the club.

It was on September 13 that the Dodgers played their last game against the Cardinals and on September 17 the name of Musial appeared in a St. Louis box score for the first time. And from the very first day there always were one or two, and sometimes more, hits posted after his name.

"We got out of town just in time," was the philosophical observation of Dodger manager Leo Durocher.

Although Musial won neither batting crowns nor pennants in his rags-to-riches year of 1941, he soon was to win more than his share of them. In each of his first three years as a regular with the Cardinals, the National League pennant went to St. Louis and by 1943 Stan was the batting leader of the league with a mark of .357. He was in the Navy in 1945 but when he returned in 1946, there was another batting championship for Musial, another pennant and another World Series triumph for the Cardinals.

The season of 1946 was one of the most sparkling in all the glamorous history of the Cardinals. For the first time there was a playoff for the National League pennant and the Cardinals beat the Dodgers twice to meet the Red Sox in the World Series and score a stunning upset victory by capturing both the sixth and seventh games. It was a great season for Musial, too, for he was switched to first base by his new manager, Eddie Dyer, and performed around the bag with the grace and skill of one to the manner born.

If 1946 ended in a blaze of glory for Musial, 1947 started in a most deplorable fashion for Stan and for his fellow Cardinals. The Cardinals won only two of their first thirteen games and Musial was hitting not only below .300, which was unprecedented for him, but actually below .200! By mid-May, Musial was clocked at .140, a mark rarely achieved in the majors, even by third-string pitchers with defective vision.

Eventually Musial's trouble was traced to an unruly appendix. An immediate operation was advised while the club was in the East. Stan rebelled at being cut while the season was in progress and flew to St. Louis where he consulted with Dr. Robert F. Hyland, baseball's surgeon general. He asked Dr. Hyland if the appendix could be frozen for the duration, so to speak. Dr. Hyland said it could be done and, after a brief hospitalization, Musial returned to the wars.

The climb to the heights was slow for both Musial and the Cardinals. It wasn't until mid-July that the champions of the year before escaped from the dank precincts of the second division, even then Stan, although his average had climbed more than 100 points, still was hovering around the .250 mark. By now, however, he no longer was a slumping hitter. Like a horse which begins to roll in the stretch, Musial was now coming fastest of all, although there was plenty of distance separating him from the leaders. In the month of August, he batted well over .450 and by the time the season ended, his average was a respectable .312. And he then went on to lead the league with .376 in 1948, "taper off" to .338 in 1949 and to lead the league for each of the next three seasons.

It was the fans of Brooklyn who gave Musial the only nickname he has had in baseball, save the semi-family one of "Stash," a diminutive of "Stashu" which his dad called him. With the simplicity which his greatness deserves the fans of Flatbush refer to Musial as "The Man." It is from this that he sometimes is mentioned in print as Stan (The Man) Musial.

Musial's hitting against the Dodgers, particularly at Ebbets Field has been amazing. It is nothing for him to hit .400 there for a season, or even .500. National Leaguers consider Musial the best clutch hitter in baseball and it is principally because of his hitting against the Dodgers. Rarely is there a Brooklyn-St. Louis series which doesn't have a highly important bearing on the race and rarely is there a series between the two in which Stan the Man doesn't leave his imprint upon the Brooklyn pitching.

Bob Broeg, who covers the Cards for the St. Louis *Post-Dispatch*, tells of the time Musial came to Ebbets Field not feeling up to par—something any Dodger fan would find hard to believe. In the course of the game, in addition to getting his customary quota of hits, Musial had made some elegant catches in the outfield, one of them a bit of larceny which necessitated an acrobatic dive. Stan injured his shoulder on the play but said nothing about it until there were two out in Brooklyn's half of the ninth, with a man on second, the score tied and Pete Reiser at bat.

Musial called time and came into the Cardinal bench to speak to Manager Dyer. "Skip," said he, "I think you'd better take me out and put Chuck Diering in. My shoulder hurts and if Reiser should hit one to the outfield, I couldn't make the throw to the plate in time to keep the winning run from scoring."

The substitution was made, much to the mystification of the fans. For the records, Musial knew when he asked Dyer to take him out that he was the leadoff batter for the Cards in the top of the tenth should the game remain a tie. It turned out the precautions were unnecessary, for Reiser tagged the next ball on a line into right field and the game was over.

For all of his great clutch hitting, which is attested to by his annual runs-batted-in totals, Musial has batted .300 only once in his four World Series. He never, however, has had a bad Series and in 1942 he made a spectacular catch against Joe Gordon in Yankee Stadium when he went into the boxes in left field to take a home run away from the Flash.

Musial is one of the few current players who sets up a nervous tension among the fans, even his own fans, whenever he comes to bat. The sight of Stan, coiled to strike and looking over his right shoulder at the pitcher carries with it a thrill of anticipation. This is true even when Stan is in one of his so-called "slumps." He is, as the ball players inelegantly phrase it, "liable to bust loose at any time." The fans know this and the pitchers know it—how they know it!

After the death of his father in late 1948, Musial entered into a partnership in a restaurant business in St. Louis, where he now has established a permanent home for himself and his family. When he came East for the first time with the Cardinals in 1949, he wasn't hitting well, which is to say he was hitting well enough for a mortal but not for a Musial. A story was printed that he was worried over his restaurant business, which was reported losing money, and that it was being reflected in his hitting.

Musial was genuinely perturbed over the story. When St. Louis came to Ebbets Field he asked me if I had seen the article and would I please inform the writer, and all the writers, that there wasn't any truth to it.

"I only wish I was going as well as the restaurant," said Stan honestly. "We're doing capacity every night at the dinner hour."

When the game started, Musial proceeded to do "capacity" himself, getting two home runs and a single against the Dodger pitching. Afterward, he was told that his batting display that afternoon should end the rumors about both his restaurant and his slump.

"Yes," he smiled modestly, "this always has been a lucky park for me."

Nobody will ever convince Brooklyn fans that Stan the Man is lucky. They happen to think he is simply great—and he proves it almost every chance he gets against their pitchers.

One of the big complaints against Musial is that he is "colorless." He doesn't stand on his head, unless in an effort to catch a fly ball, but he is neither a stoic nor a dead-pan. There is always the trace of a smile, if not a full-blown one, playing about his face as he waits his turn to hit and he is one of the most easily approached ball players in the game, great or small.

If colorless means paying strict attention to business, staying in shape, being obliging and courteous, then the adjective fits Musial. If it means apathetic, then it belongs to somebody else.

Musial never has forgotten the kindness of Dickie Kerr at Daytona Beach in 1940, when he thought seriously about chucking it all and going into the steel mills of Western Pennsylvania. It was then Dickie, treated shabbily himself by baseball, convinced Musial that you don't just up and quit the game. And he convinced Stan, too, that he had a future as a hitter, if not as a southpaw pitcher. Musial named his first son, Dickie, after Kerr.

If Musial has not forgotten Kerr, neither did the game little White Sox pitcher forget him. In 1947, when Musial was plagued by poisoned tonsils and an obstreperous appendix and was hitting under .200, he received a letter from Kerr.

"You know you can hit," was the substance of what Kerr wrote to the ailing and slumping Musial. "Don't let anybody or anything get you down. You're a natural .300 hitter and you'll be one as long as you're young enough to play ball. All you have to do, is to keep trying."

Whether it bolstered his confidence or not, Musial went from that horrendous slump to finish up with a .312 average as already related. And he kept trying, for Stan doesn't know any other way to play ball.

Because he is a natural hustler, Musial sustained the injury which ruined him as a pitcher. He was trying to catch a ball which he could have played on one hop in safety. Yet the injury which ruined him as a pitcher, opened the gates to fame and fortune for him as an outfielder.

Musial's philosophy of baseball and of life is simple, simple but effective.

"Unless you can give it all you've got," he says, "there isn't any sense in playing."

It never has been any effort for Stan to give it all he has. As the song so happily puts it, he's just doing what comes natural.

STANLEY FRANK (STAN) MUSIAL

Born November 21, 1920, Donora, Pa.
Height 6'. Weight 175. Bats and throws left-handed.

YEAR	CLUB	LEAGUE	POS	G	AB	R	H	2B	3B	HR	RBI	BA
1938	Williamson	Mt. St.	P	26	62	5	16	3	0	1	6	.258
1939	Williamson	Mt. St.	P-PH	23	71	10	25	3	3	1	9	.352
1940	Daytona Beach	Fla. St.	OF-P	113	405	55	126	17	10	1	70	.311
1941	Springfield	W.A.	OF	87	348	100	132	27	10	26	94	.379
1941	Rochester	Int.	OF	54	221	43	72	10	4	3	21	.326
1941	St. Louis	Nat.	OF	12	47	8	20	4	0	1	7	.426
1942	St. Louis	Nat.	OF	140	467	87	147	32	10	10	72	.315
1943	St. Louis	Nat.	OF	157	617	108	*220	*48	x20	13	81	*.357
1944	St. Louis	Nat.	OF	146	568	112	x197	x51	14	12	94	.347
1945	St. Louis	Nat.					(In Military Service)					
1946	St. Louis	Nat.	1B-OF	156	624	*124	*228	*50	*20	16	103	*.365
1947	St. Louis	Nat.	1B	149	587	113	183	30	13	19	95	.312
1948	St. Louis	Nat.	OF-1B	155	611	135	*230	*48	*18	39	*131	*.376
1949	St. Louis	Nat.	OF-1B	157	612	128	*207	*41	x13	36	123	.338
1950	St. Louis	Nat.	1B-OF	149	555	105	192	41	7	28	109	*.346
1951	St. Louis	Nat.	1B-OF	152	578	124	205	30	12	32	108	*.355
1952	St. Louis	Nat.	1B-OF	154	578	105	194	42	6	21	91	*.336
	Major League Totals			1524	5844	1149	2023	415	133	227	1014	.346

WORLD SERIES RECORD

YEAR	CLUB	LEAGUE	POS	G	AB	R	H	2B	3B	HR	RBI	BA
1942	St. Louis	Nat.	OF	5	18	2	4	1	0	0	2	.222
1943	St. Louis	Nat.	OF	5	18	2	5	0	0	0	0	.278
1944	St. Louis	Nat.	OF	6	23	2	7	2	0	1	2	.304
1946	St. Louis	Nat.	1B	7	27	3	6	4	1	0	4	.222
	World Series Totals			23	86	9	22	7	1	1	8	.256

ALL-STAR GAME RECORD

YEAR	LEAGUE	POS	AB	R	H	2B	3B	HR	RBI	BA
1943	National	OF	4	0	1	1	0	0	1	.250
1944	National	OF	4	1	1	0	0	0	1	.250
1946	National	OF	2	0	0	0	0	0	0	.000
1947	National	PH	1	0	0	0	0	0	0	.000
1948	National	OF	4	1	2	0	0	1	2	.500
1949	National	OF	4	1	3	0	0	1	2	.750
1950	National	1B	5	0	0	0	0	0	0	.000
1951	National	OF	4	1	2	0	0	1	1	.500
1952	National	OF	2	1	0	0	0	0	0	.000
	All-Star Totals		30	5	9	1	0	3	7	.300

* Led league
x Tied for lead

CHAPTER XVII

THE TRAIL BLAZER

Jackie Robinson

BACK IN THE EARLY 40's, a sports writer who took time out to read an occasional book, as some do, happened upon a felicitous phrase for W. Branch Rickey, then the resident genius of the Dodgers. He called the Brooklyn president "The Mahatma" and the tag stuck. Mahatma in Sanskrit means "great-souled, wise," but the reporter wasn't thinking of the literal definition as much as he was of a line of John Gunther he had read in *Inside Asia* (Harper & Brothers, New York.)

Gunther referred to Mohandas K. Gandhi as "an incredible combination of Jesus Christ, Tammany Hall and your father." It certainly suited Rickey, who was religious, shrewd, devious and paternal.

Rickey has many sound claims to baseball fame but it may be that in the years to come his greatest achievement will have been the erasure of baseball's Jim Crow law. It was Rickey who had the courage to break the bonds of tradition and bigotry, but it was the intelligence and physical skills of Jackie Robinson which made it possible.

For many years the Mahatma had what he might have called in his own circumlocutory style "an academic expression of a passive abhorence of an inexcusable condition." Going back almost to the turn of the century, when Branch was player-coach of the football team at Ohio Wesleyan and a Negro player on the squad had difficulty being housed at a hotel in South Bend, Indiana, Rickey felt that Jim Crowism was an abomination and an anachronism in a democracy. He was a long time getting around to doing anything about it, merely because he wasn't in a position to do anything. Once he moved, he moved with forthright courage.

194

During the winter of 1944–45, Rickey talked about the formation of a new Negro league, the United States League, which would be represented by the Brown Dodgers at Ebbets Field. He had his scouts watch over players in the two Negro loops then in this country and also to scout players in Mexico, Cuba, Puerto Rico and Venezuela.

The story is that the scouts believed they were seeking talent for the Brown Dodgers, but there is evidence that at least one scout knew that he was looking for Negro stars to play in the major leagues. That scout was Tom Greenwade, the discoverer of Mickey Mantle, by the way.

When scouting Latin-American teams, Greenwade had a code in his cables back home. If the first word of his message started with a letter below "M" in the alphabet, he was reporting on a player of Latin extraction. If it started with a letter above "M" in the alphabet, he was reporting on a Negro. It was Tom who "found" Robinson, although he left the Dodgers to join the Yankees before Jackie started in organized baseball.

Rickey felt that he had the ideal spot in which to break in a Negro ballplayer, the Triple-A farm at Montreal where there is no racial discrimination. The trick then was to find the player. He had to have not only the physical skills to make the grade, but he had to have the intelligence and restraint to withstand the insults and humiliations which would be his lot while the racial barriers were in the process of being dismantled. It was no spot for a coward—or a firebrand.

The Negro picked by Rickey had to have the depth of understanding to realize that he would be subjected to a great many indignities for the eventual advancement of his race. When reports by Greenwade, George Sisler and Clyde Sukeforth made it plain that Robinson, then playing shortstop for the Kansas City Monarchs, had the physical assets, the Mahatma conducted his own investigation into Robbie's background to make certain that he was temperamentally fitted for the tremendous job ahead of him.

Robinson was born in Georgia but his family had moved to California when Jackie was less than two. He had gone through high school and played baseball, basketball and football at the University of California at Los Angeles. He had been in the

Army and gone through OCS, becoming a second lieutenant before receiving a medical discharge late in 1944.

It was Sukeforth who finally picked up Robbie in Chicago and brought him to Brooklyn for the meeting with Rickey. This was in the summer of 1945. For three hours, the Mahatma turned on his rhetoric. He made no effort to minimize the hardships, the personal indignities which faced Robinson.

"I put him through the mill that day," admitted Rickey to Bill Roeder of the *New York World-Telegram and Sun* when the latter was gathering material for his biography of Robinson (A. S. Barnes & Co., New York).

"I told him I knew his actions had been resented in California for fighting back at whites," continued the Mahatma. "I told him he would have to curb that aggressiveness, even though he would be a target for all sorts of vilification. I predicted in disgusting detail the name-calling he would have to take and warned him that he would have to turn the other cheek, to take it in silence.

"Every five minutes I barked at him: 'Can you do it? Can I trust you?' Then I would give him examples. 'Suppose 1200 colored people want to make up an excursion to see you play. I say no. I stop it. What will you say?' I told him I feared there would be an over-enthusiastic reaction from the Negro people. I warned him that this might lead to a bad reaction from the press, from baseball owners and the white players."

It was a three-hour tirade. Finally the Mahatma paused and said, "Well? Do you still want to go through with it?"

"Yes," answered Jackie without drawing a deep breath, "I am not afraid to try."

Thus, the beginnings of the Great Experiment. Robinson's natural baseball talent is such that it is a pity that so much of this chapter has had to be devoted to the sociological aspects of his career, but that is one of the penalties Jackie pays for being the trail blazer for baseball equality for his race.

Although then 26, Robbie was in his first year with the Kansas City Monarchs when the Brooklyn scouts picked up his trail. Greenwade, Sisler and Sukeforth all agreed that Robinson was a big leaguer and all were agreed that his arm wasn't strong enough for short, where the Monarchs were using him. Second base was his spot, they declared.

At Daytona Beach, Florida, Robinson went into training with the Montreal Royals. The Dodgers worked out at Island Park and the Royals at Kelley Field over on the mainland, in the Negro section of town. Clay Hopper, the Royals' manager, wanted Robinson at second base—provided he could make it, of course.

Over-anxiousness gave Robinson a sore arm in the beginning and then he had to battle a returned GI, Lou Rochelli, for the job. Rochelli turned out to be the first friend Robbie made among the white players. Even though it was costing him his job, Lou helped Jackie with advice and instruction around second base. It wasn't long before Hopper realized that there need be no fear of Robinson's defensive play. His arm was strong enough to make the double play, he could cover ground, take throws and had the agility to handle himself around the bag.

Robinson, however, wasn't hitting. He bunted well but he wasn't meeting the ball solidly at all. It was Paul Derringer, an ex-National League pitching great, who brought Robinson out of his slump. Paul, Kentucky born and bred, was past 40 at this time and pitching for Indianapolis.

Paul told Hopper that he would knock Robinson down a few times and see what made him tick. Derringer dusted Jackie off on his first trip and Robbie got up and hit a line single to the outfield. He knocked Jackie down again the second time and then came in with a curve ball and Robinson unloaded on it for a well pasted triple.

Derringer then turned to Hopper on the Montreal bench and yelled, "Hey, Clay! This boy's gonna be all right!"

Montreal opened its International League season in Jersey City before an overflow crowd, which was announced at 52,000. Robinson opened with a bang and never looked back. He made four hits, including a home run, and stole two bases. The Royals cake-walked to the pennant, Robinson led the league in batting, topped the second basemen in fielding and stole 40 bases.

Outside of abuse from the Syracuse bench and at first rejection and then acceptance by the fans in Baltimore, Robinson didn't have too much trouble in the International League. The French-Canadians in Montreal received him with open arms and made his stay there a pleasant one, although when the Little World Series opened in Louisville, Jackie found out the depths of abuse to which a baseball crowd can sink.

When the Dodgers trained in Havana in the spring of 1947, Montreal trained there also and Robinson trained with Montreal. Again there were separate ball parks, as there had been at Daytona Beach. Rickey had chosen the Cuban capital because the Dodgers would play most of their exhibition games against native teams, which were predominantly Negro in their make-up and he wanted the players to become accustomed to playing against Negroes.

Robinson's arm was too weak for him to be at short, where the Dodgers already had one of the best in the business and at second base there was Eddie Stanky, a key man on the ball club. The Reese-Stanky combination couldn't be broken up and there seemed no place for Robbie but third base, a position at which he had never played, but one at which it was felt he could adapt himself.

Rickey had other plans, however, deep, dark and devious ones. When the Dodgers flew off to Panama for a series of exhibitions, Mel Jones, the general manager of the Royals, gave Robbie a first baseman's mitt and told him it was Mr. Rickey's orders that he was to work out there. Robinson didn't like it a bit and his manager, Clay Hopper, liked it even less.

The strategy became apparent when the Royals joined the Dodgers in Panama for a series. In seven games, Robbie hit .625, stole seven bases and handled himself with grace and skill around first base. The stage was now set for Rickey's coup d'etat.

There were to be two miscalculations, however, one minor and one major. The first was that the anti-Negro faction among the Dodgers planned to present a petition to Mahatma asking him not to bring up Robinson. The other was that Leo Durocher, who was to make a public plea to Rickey to put Robbie on the Varsity, was inexplicably suspended by Commissioner A. B. (Happy) Chandler the day before he was to make the grandstand play.

Rickey cleared the first hurdle easily. He asked the dissidents whether they could search their souls, one of his favorite projects, and find any valid reason for not having Robinson as a teammate. Investigation disclosed that two players, by reason of birth and heritage, had no desire to play with a Negro. He asked them to re-consider, "for the good of the club," and promised that if, at the end of the year, their feelings hadn't changed, he would see that they were traded to another major league club. When the season ended, one said he had no objections to Robbie and the other said he would prefer to be traded and Rickey granted his wishes.

Consider now the task that confronted Robinson on the eve of his major league debut. Originally a shortstop, he was asked to play second base at Montreal and now he was being asked to play first base in the National League. And the Dodgers were opening the season without a regular manager, with Durocher suspended for a year.

Clyde Sukeforth, who had first brought Robinson to Rickey, was the *pro tem* manager when the season opened against the Braves in 1947. It is indicative of the changing order in baseball that of the other eight men in the lineup that day only Pee Wee Reese was still in the Brooklyn lineup when the Dodgers faced the Yankees in the opener of the 1952 World Series. Even Rickey and Sukeforth were gone from Brooklyn.

Burt (Barney) Shotton was finally called out of retirement by Rickey to manage the 1947 Dodgers. He kept Robbie at first base even when the latter went through a horrendous early season batting slump. It was confidence well rewarded, for Robinson soon snapped out of his slump and went on to become one of the key players as the Dodgers moved to their first pennant in six years.

Robinson batted just under .300, led the league in stolen bases with 29 and played an acceptable, if not an exceptional, first base. *The Sporting News,* baseball's bible, called him the Rookie of the Year and he finished fifth in the Most Valuable Player balloting, a remarkable achievement for a first year man.

Perhaps the most spine-tingling of all Robbie's skills is his ability to steal home. It has repeatedly thrilled the fans around National League cities. For historical purposes, it may be well to record for posterity that the first time Robbie stole home was June 24, 1947 in a night game at Pittsburgh when Fritz Ostermueller, a southpaw, grew a little absent-minded about Jackie's tentative dashes toward the plate.

Since Robinson is the only active major leaguer who makes a specialty of stealing home his own views on the niceties of this particular art are interesting.

"Stealing home is an impromptu thing," Robbie told Bill Roeder, his biographer. "It isn't something you can plan, except to consider doing it when the situation is right. As a general rule, I'd say this about stealing home: Never do it unless there are two out, the run is absolutely needed, the opposing pitcher is pitching an awfully good ball game and there is a right-handed hitter at the plate. A left-handed hitter gives the catcher too much of an advantage. He can see you coming all the way and he can move up on the pitch because he knows the batter isn't going to swing. A right-handed hitter can help you. He's supposed to stand there all the way, blocking the catcher.

"It's a dangerous play because you don't have time to give a signal on it. Usually I experiment with a long lead off third. I'll make one or two fakes but I'm never sure which time I'm going to do it. I keep watching the pitcher and I don't think I make up my mind until I'm about a quarter of the way home. Sometimes I holler to the hitter 'Let it go!' but more often than not there's no time even for a yell. The hitter just has to be alert. Usually he can tell. If you're standing there at the plate and a runner is bearing down on you, you're aware of it even though you're watching the pitch."

Once more Robinson was confronted with a command to shift positions. After his brilliant freshman year at first base in 1947, the Dodger brain trust decided to return him to second base. Training in Santo Domingo in 1948, with Durocher reinstated as manager, Brooklyn caused a spring furor with the announcement that Eddie Stanky had been sold to Boston.

It was not a decision hastily arrived at. Rickey had announced after the 1947 Series, "The best second baseman in baseball is playing first base."

Is wasn't simply a matter of moving Robbie into Stanky's

shoes. The Dodgers still had no assurance that they had a first baseman. Ray Sanders, who came from Boston in the Stanky deal, and Pete Reiser were not adequate. The season was well under way before Gil Hodges, listed as a catcher, was put on first base, there to stay and become one of the home run threats of the National League.

Brooklyn got off badly and there was friction between Durocher and Rickey, with the eventual result that the Lip wound up with the Giants and Shotton came back with his old pal, "Rick." Robbie got along better with Barney than he ever had with Durocher and he probably welcomed the change. He had a good year, even though the Dodgers finished third, and in teaming up with Reese he gave the Dodgers one of the best double play combinations in baseball.

Robbie's career by now had been highly successful but also highly checkered. In '45, he broke into Negro baseball as a shortstop; in 1946 he was second baseman with a pennant-winning Montreal team and in 1947 a first baseman with a pennant-winning Brooklyn team. Now in '48, he was back at second again and working under two managers in the one season.

Shotton may have given Robinson one of the best single bits of help he was to receive at the Vero Beach, Florida, camp in 1949 when he suggested Jackie bat clean-up. Robbie had been batting No. 2 where his bunting ability and skill at hitting behind the runner made him seemingly the perfect choice. The voluminous statistics which Allen Roth kept for Rickey showed that Robbie knocked in an inordinate number of runs for a second-place hitter, 85 in 1948. The Dodgers had been lacking a consistent batter at No. 4 all year and Shotton tapped Robbie for this responsible post.

It turned out to be an amazingly happy choice. Robbie's bat carried the Dodgers to another pennant, their second in his three seasons with them. He led the league with .342, batted in 124 runs, scored 122, hit 16 home runs and led the league in stolen bases with 37 and also led the league in sacrifices, something unheard of in a fourth-place hitter.

Robinson's crowning glory in 1949, however, was that he was voted the Most Valuable Player in the National League, with a total of 264 votes to 226 for Stan Musial and half of the 24 first place votes. He was, of course, the first Negro to be awarded this honor, but Robbie by now was used to "firsts."

It was now, too, that Robbie broke his shell, so to speak. He began talking back to umpires, was tossed out of a highly important game in St. Louis in what threatened to create a baseball incident. There were some who professed to be upset over Robbie's actions, forgetting that these same actions would be taken for granted had they been committed by a white player. Jackie apparently figured that he had taken all he had been expected to take, that it now was his turn to act just like any other ballplayer.

It is difficult for Robinson to achieve his goal of being "just another ballplayer." For one thing his physical skills lift him far above the average and for another, he was the first Negro to break the color line. When he protests a decision it becomes an issue. When Roy Campanella, Sam Jethroe of the Braves, Larry Doby of the Indians or Monte Irvin of the Giants protests a decision not too much attention is paid to it. Robinson is simply paying the price which always accompanies the trail blazer.

Baseball has made Robinson a fairly wealthy man, able to provide comfort and security for his pretty wife, Rachel, his son, Jackie, Jr. and daughter, Sharon, but it is safe to assume that the proudest moment in Robinson's career came away from the ball field, on July 18, 1949 when he spoke before the House Committee on Un-American Activities.

Paul Robeson, who had been a great football player at Rutgers University, a first team All-America choice of Walter Camp in 1918, and later a famed actor and concert singer, made a speech in Paris in which, speaking as a Negro, he said Negroes in the United States would not fight against Russia.

Robeson did not represent American Negroes but the Un-American Committee felt it would be to the improvement of racial relations to have some distinguished American Negroes answer him. Among those invited to deliver a rebuttal were lawyers, professors, doctors—and Jackie Robinson, perhaps the best known American Negro of all.

Robinson had no desire to be drawn into a controversy of this sort but after a conference with Rickey, he decided that it was his duty. The Mahatma pointed out that if Jackie didn't accept the invitation he would lose the respect of many Americans, regardless of color, and that the Communists would be quick to capitalize on his silence as a tacit indorsement of Robeson's speech.

After pointing out that, despite his opportunity in baseball, he realized full well the problems created for his people by segregation and discrimination, Robinson wound up his speech in this manner:

"What I'm trying to get across is that the American public is off on the wrong foot when it begins to think of radicalism in terms of any special minority group. It is thinking of this sort which gets people scared because one Negro, speaking to a Communist group in Paris, threatens an organized boycott by fifteen million members of his race.

"I can't speak for any fifteen million people any more than any other one person can, but I know that I've got too much invested for my wife and child and myself in the future of this country and I and other Americans of many races and faiths have too much invested in our country's welfare for any of us to throw it away because of a siren song sung in bass.

"I am a religious man. Therefore I cherish America where I am free to worship as I please, a privilege which some countries do not give. And I suspect that nine hundred and ninety-nine out of almost any thousand colored Americans you meet will tell you the same thing.

"But that doesn't mean that we're going to stop fighting race discrimination in this country until we've got it licked. It means we're going to fight it all the harder because our stake in the future is so big. We can win our fight without the Communists and we don't want their help."

Robbie and his wife flew back to Brooklyn after he had delivered the speech and he stole home in a game in which the Dodgers beat the Cubs, 3 to 0. Stole it on his own, too, as he had done everything else—with no help from the Communists.

JACK ROOSEVELT ROBINSON

Born Carol, Ga., January 31, 1919

YEAR	CLUB	LEAGUE	POS	G	AB	R	H	2B	3B	HR	RBI	SB	PCT
1946	Montreal	Int.	2B	124	444	113	155	25	8	3	66	40	.34*
1947	Brooklyn	Nat.	1B	151	590	125	175	31	5	12	49	*29	.29*
1948	Brooklyn	Nat.	INF	147	574	108	170	38	8	12	85	22	.29*
1949	Brooklyn (a)	Nat.	2B	156	593	122	203	38	12	16	124	*37	*.34*
1950	Brooklyn	Nat.	2B	144	518	99	170	39	4	14	81	12	.328
1951	Brooklyn	Nat.	2B	153	548	106	185	33	7	19	88	25	.338
1952	Brooklyn	Nat.	2B	149	510	104	157	17	3	19	75	24	.308
	Major League Totals			894	3333	664	1060	196	39	92	501	149	.318

WORLD SERIES RECORD

YEAR	CLUB	LEAGUE	POS	G	AB	R	H	2B	3B	HR	RBI	SB	PCT
1947	Brooklyn	Nat.	1B	7	27	3	7	2	0	0	3	2	.259
1949	Brooklyn	Nat.	2B	5	16	2	3	1	0	0	2	0	.188
1952	Brooklyn	Nat.	2B	7	23	4	4	0	0	1	2	2	.174
	World Series Totals			19	66	9	14	3	0	1	7	4	.212

ALL-STAR GAME RECORD

YEAR	LEAGUE	POS	AB	R	H	2B	3B	HR	RBI	SB	PCT
1949	National	2B	4	3	1	1	0	0	0	0	.250
1950	National	2B	4	1	1	0	0	0	0	0	.250
1951	National	2B	3	1	1	0	0	1	1	0	.333
	All-Star Totals		11	5	3	1	0	1	1	0	.273

* Led league

(a) Voted Most Valuable Player in National League, 1949

CHAPTER XVIII

THE BIG FELLOW

George Herman Ruth

ONE of the great palliatives for insomnia is to pause among a group of baseball men and ask, "Who was the greatest ballplayer of all time—Cobb or Ruth?" You won't have to worry any longer about tossing sleeplessly in your bed for the simple reason that you'll see your bed no more that night. If there are any among the group old enough to have been a contemporary of Ty and the Babe, the chances are you'll never, never be troubled with insomnia again.

Nobody ever will settle the Cobb versus Ruth controversy to the satisfaction of both sides. It isn't the intention here to even try. "Great," and its various gradations, is an adjective used loosely in sports. Today's fine catch is always the greatest ever made until somebody makes a better one tomorrow. Cobb and Ruth represented different types of ballplayers. It is like comparing a skilled master of the rapier with a man wielding a meat axe. Each is deadly with his own medium.

There is no question, however, that Ruth wielded the greatest influence upon baseball of any man who ever played the game. The Babe was the most important ballplayer of all time, important because he radically altered the entire structure of the game, financially, physically and tactically. Cobb was a great star in the American League when Ruth was an awkward orphan kid in St. Mary's Industrial School for Boys in Baltimore. Yet baseball remained basically the same game it had been before the Georgia Peach burst forth from Augusta in the Sally League. It took Ruth, when Ed Barrow decided to switch him from a pitcher-outfielder to a full-time outfielder, just two seasons to change the entire concept of the game as well as the tools with which it was played.

Once the owners saw the box office lure which was in the home run bat of the Babe, they stepped up the resiliency of the baseball to spawn whole generations of newer, and lesser, Ruths. Once the players saw the money Ruth's home runs could command in terms of salary, they abandoned the choke-style of hitting, grasped the bat at the extreme end of the handle, swung from their heels, pulled for the fences and hoped for the best. The baseball became, in Ruth's own words, "a stitched golf ball."

Ruth's home runs not only changed the physical properties of the baseball and the style of batting but they affected the architecture of many baseball parks, a trend which continued even after the death of the big fellow. Comiskey Park in Chicago, a fine symmetrical playing field, altered the contour of its boundaries in 1949, erecting screen fences to make synthetic home runs possible. The experiment was short-lived when it was discovered that the visiting players were hitting more home runs over the shortened barriers than the White Sox could possibly hope to hit.

Out of the home runs of the Babe came newer and larger ball parks, mushrooming attendance and increased salaries. His home runs were to baseball what the forward pass was to football, the knockout punch of Jack Dempsey and Joe Louis to boxing. Baseball owes as much to Ruth as it does to Doubleday, providing Abner actually did invent the game. Regardless of who conceived baseball, it was Ruth who made it big business, Ruth and Barrow, the man who decided to give up a great left-handed pitcher, which Babe was, in order that the Red Sox might have a home run hitting outfielder.

Ruth, if the truth were known, really mastered baseball, even though he never was able to master himself. He was a winning pitcher, first with a blazing fast one and strength, then with cunning. He was a remarkable outfielder and an exceptional thrower, a surprisingly daring and skillful base runner. Babe shifted dexterously around first base on the few occasions when he had to play the bag.

Later, of course, Ruth lost many of his fine skills. As his prodigious appetite caused his girth to balloon, his spindly legs became inadequate for their mammoth burden. In his later years, the Babe was content to rest his case on the sheer power of his bat.

He made few attempts to steal bases and his outfielding verged from mediocre to ordinary, save on the occasions when his natural competitive instincts urged him to put forth an exceptional try. In his later years, these flashes were increasingly infrequent but they served to give the newer fans, players and writers an idea of what the big fellow could do in his prime.

With all of his home runs, Ruth was a scientific batter as well as a swinger. He was a better than average bunter and when the defense overshifted against him, as the Cardinals did in the 1946 World Series against Ted Williams, Babe took advantage of the inviting gaps by shortening up and punching the ball to the opposite field. Most of the time the Babe gripped the bat with the knob in the palm of his right hand and swung from his heels but he could bunt, punch or drag a ball if the defense played him out of position.

There was no particular reason for the Yankees, or the writers traveling with them, to feel elated when they piled aboard the sleepers leaving Detroit for New York in May of 1930. It hadn't been a particularly impressive Western trip. Philadelphia, which had run away with the American League pennant race the year before, was in the process of doing it once more.

It was the first year after the death of Miller Huggins and the Yankees, with Bob Shawkey as a stop-gap manager, were just going through the motions. There wasn't much else they could do, for they weren't going anywhere and everybody knew it.

A couple of the writers selected a berth which hadn't been made up, obtained a card table from the porter and began shuffling the pasteboards. A couple of the Yankees joined them, Henry Johnson for one, Mark Koenig for another. Out from the drawing room came Babe Ruth in all his sartorial magnificence wearing moiré lounging pajamas of apple green, with slippers to match.

Babe dug in the capacious pocket of his lounging pajamas, came up with a five-dollar bill and started to get change from one of the poker players. While the money-changer was stacking up the coins (we were playing a two-bit, four-bit game) Ruth suddenly drew the bill back to him.

"Waddaya know?" he boomed laughingly. "A phoney fin!

Musta got it back at the hotel when I was paying Mrs. Ruth's bill. First time I ever came up with a bad bill in my life."

The bill was passed around and could be seen to be a counterfeit when compared with other five-dollar bills but the chances are that it could have gone through the game without anybody being the wiser had Babe not noticed it when he asked for change. He quickly produced one of Uncle Sam's best and the game continued.

Around midnight the game broke up, the other players retreated to their bunks and Babe hung around to smoke a postmidnight perfecto and chew the fat with the writers, one of his favorite Pullman pastimes. He was ruffling the sheaf of bills before him, counting his winnings or losses, as the case may have been. He was careful to keep the counterfeit five away from the rest of his money. Somebody complimented him on spotting it so quickly.

"Yeah," condescended the Babe, "it was quite a trick at that, considering I was playing ball for Dunnie before I ever saw any kind of a five-dollar bill, genuine or counterfeit."

He exhaled a billow of smoke and began to reminisce about his early days in baseball, something he rarely did. I think that was the only time I ever heard him mention Dunnie (Jack Dunn) or his baseball beginnings unless somebody asked him a direct question. Babe was never one for looking back, for he lived entirely in the present. With the big fellow, yesterday was already gone beyond recall and tomorrow might never come. Today was all that counted.

"Ballplayers don't know how soft they got it today," mumbled Ruth. "A kid comes up to the Yankees, puts a uniform on him with 'New York' across the chest and bam!—he's a big leaguer. It wasn't so easy when I broke in.

"When I was with Dunnie training at Fayetteville, North Carolina, the older players on the Orioles made no move to take me in as one of the gang. I had to make my own way. And later on that year, when I went up to Boston, I ran into the same thing. The Red Sox wanted no part of me, a busher. Because I liked to hit and took my turn in batting practice with the regulars I found all my bats sawed in half when I came to my locker the next day."

Veteran writers who had been with the Yankees before me also were a little surprised to hear Ruth go down memory lane. Men like Bill Slocum and Ford Frick, Charley Segar, Jim Kahn, Fred Leib and Arthur Mann agreed that it wasn't like the big fellow. At that, the Babe made a rather incongruous picture, bulked there against the train window in his snazzy pajamas, smoking a 50-center and talking about how easy everybody had it in these soft and effete days.

It was a most human reaction. Everybody who has reached the top likes to hark back and tell how thorny he found the road when he started the big climb. Babe's beginnings had been rough enough, with no home life to speak of and trips to the home for the homeless commencing when he was seven. He knew little of his parents or relatives, never made any effort to seek out his kin. He was on his own from the time the Xaverian brothers took him in hand at St. Mary's in Baltimore.

In later years Ruth showed a definite sense of gratitude to the brothers who had guided his footsteps. He particularly respected Brother Matthais, somewhat to the exclusion of Brother Gilbert who also had a hand in the development of Babe. It was Brother Gilbert who persuaded Dunn to sign Ruth to an Oriole contract. After Babe had left baseball he showed a tendency to minimize the part Brother Gilbert had played in landing him his first Baltimore contract at $600 a season, a contract which was doubled and then tripled by a grateful Dunn before Ruth was sold to the Red Sox.

There is little question Ruth was a baseball star from the time he first put a glove on—and a right-handed catcher's mitt, at that. Joe Engel, who pitched and scouted for the Washington Senators and later made P. T. Barnum look like a blushing violet when he operated the Chattanooga Lookouts in the Southern Association, saw Babe pitch a game at Emmitsburg, Maryland, and never forgot the blinding speed of the green southpaw.

Ruth pitched a shutout in his first professional game, in April, 1914, beating Buffalo 6 to 0. Joe McCarthy, who was to be Babe's manager in his last four years with the Yankees, played second base for the Bisons that day and went hitless. Paul Krichell, who served the Yankees as a scout during all of Ruth's career in New York, caught for the opposing team. In an exhibition game that spring, Babe had beaten the Athletics, champions of the baseball world by virtue of their victory over the Giants in the World Series the fall before.

One Sunday in June of 1914, the Brooklyn Dodgers played an exhibition game against the Orioles in a fair grounds at Baltimore. Among the Dodgers was Casey Stengel, who nine years later was to star for the Giants in a lost cause against Ruth and the Yankees in a World Series and who, later still, was to manage the Yankees in the House that Ruth built.

"There was no Sunday ball in the East then," recalled Stengel, "and maybe the reason we were playing the Orioles on this fair grounds was that it was outside the Baltimore city limits or something. At any rate, nobody had played there all year it looked like. The ground was uneven, the grass was high in the outfield and a race track ran all around the field.

"Uncle Robbie (Wilbert Robinson) was managing the Dodgers and he wanted to make a good showing in Baltimore. He'd played on the Orioles with McGraw, 'n Jennings 'n Keeler and he'd run a saloon there with McGraw and had owned a butcher shop.

"None of the Dodgers cared much about the game. All it meant to us was that we were being dragged a coupla hundred miles out of way on what should have been our day off. And to make matters worse, Dunnie has some big clown pitching who's making suckers out of our left-handed hitters—Zach Wheat, Jack Daubert and myself. This pitcher was a big skinny kid with the gol-durndest haircomb I ever did see and he was real quick.

"No matter what anybody tells you, there never was a big league team that liked to lose an exhibition to a bush league club. We forgot all about blowing our day off and we were trying to comb this guy and couldn't do anything about it.

"Along about the third inning, this pitcher, who, of course, was Ruth but nobody knew it at the time, comes to bat and he belts one nine miles over my head in right field. Robbie jawed me about it when I came back to the bench, claimed I played the feller too short.

"Well, I was fresh as paint in those days and I sasses right back, saying I played him as deep as I played Schulte or Cravath or Zimmerman or Doyle or any of the good hitters in the National League. 'Besides,' I asks Robbie, 'who is this busher, anyway?' Robbie, of course, didn't know who he was any more than the rest of us.

"The next time this big kid came up, I moved so deep in the outfield you could only see the top of my hat in the grass. I was doing it just to rib Robbie, of course, because no human being could hit a ball as deep as I was playing. No human being 'cept Ruth that is, providing the big guy was human even in those days. He cleared my head, the tall grass and the race track. To this day, it was one of the longest drives I've ever seen. And, remember, he was hitting a beanbag, not the lively ball we had later on."

There was an aftermath to Stengel's story about playing deep for Ruth, the moral of which seems to be that you couldn't play the big fellow too deep. In the 1922 World Series, Bill Cunningham, playing for the Giants, went into the niche behind the Eddie Grant memorial monument in center field and caught a ball at the Polo Grounds. It was the greatest catch of the Series, one of the greatest catches of any Series.

"You know," confided Stengel who alternated with Cunningham, "I caught a couple that Ruth hit pretty deep into center in that same World Series, too. I didn't have to run as far as Cunningham did, of course, because I was already there. I remembered the son-of-a-gun from Baltimore!"

Strangely enough, Ruth hit no home runs as an Oriole. He was sold to Joe Lannin, of the Red Sox, along with Ernie Shore and Ben Egan in July of his first season with Baltimore. The total price was reported to be $8,500 for the trio, with the Babe appraised at $2,900. His only International League home run was hit after the Red Sox shipped him to Providence to finish out the 1914 season. On September 5, in Toronto, the Babe hit the first home run of his professional career and the only one he ever hit in the minors. This homer made considerably less impression on Ruth's Boston employers than the fact that he blanked the Leafs, 9–0, that same afternoon, allowing only one hit.

By 1915, some fourteen months after Jack Dunn had signed papers to obtain Ruth's release from "The Home," as Baltimoreans euphemistically called St. Mary's, the big fellow was a regular pitcher with the Red Sox, a club on its way to a pennant and a world's championship.

The first of Ruth's 714 major league home runs was hit against Jack Warhop, of the Yankees, at the Polo Grounds on the afternoon of May 6, 1915. Characteristically, Ruth hit it into the upper deck in right field, a spot which was to receive many more of his homers in the three seasons he played in that ball park when the Yankees were making it their home grounds. There were few in the stands to witness the launching of Ruth's maiden home run in the majors and none of those who watched, either from the stands or the dugout, realized that they were watching the end of an era in baseball, the beginning of a revolution which hasn't stopped yet.

Nobody present realized that Ruth's homers eventually would result in a stadium being built a little east of the Polo Grounds or that the very Yankees who were being victimized by this home run were one day to become the richest, and most powerful, club in baseball through the medium of many more home runs by the kid who was even then pigeon-toeing his way around the bases to the polite patter of restrained applause. There wasn't a great deal written about Ruth's first homer in the next day's papers, either, since the publications had their hands full with the torpedoing of the Lusitania by a German U-boat off the coast of Ireland.

Most everybody remembers Babe Ruth as a moonfaced, barrel-chested hulk of a man with spindly legs. Indeed, Babe's rotund countenance was his trade-mark. There really were many different Ruths in physical appearance, but the round moonface was prominent in all of them, even to his death when it was lined and ravaged by illness. Babe was always outsize—he was called "Big George" at St. Mary's when he was only fifteen.

Babe had a big head—physically that is. He customarily affected a cap, preferably a brown camel-haired one, because hats looked silly on him. Once Ruth realized that his home runs gave him special privileges, that the rules of ordinary ballplayers weren't for him, the first thing he did was discard hats and take to a cap. He also was one of the first athletes to go bareheaded.

Much has been made of the pipestemmed legs which supported Ruth's Gargantuan body. Their thinness was accentuated by the bay window Ruth accumulated in later years. The longer the Babe played, the more people went to see him and Ruth played until he was past forty. He was in his thirty-third year when he collected his record-breaking 60 home runs in 1927. As a consequence, there is a tendency to exaggerate his spindle-shanked qualities. Had Babe bothered to keep his weight down to normal he wouldn't have looked so much like an egg balanced on two straws.

Ruth's batting style was as distinctive as his build. He took a stance with his feet close together, his body swiveled slightly so that he was looking at the pitcher over his right shoulder. His feet were about four inches apart and his right foot was about an inch closer to home plate than his left. He stood to the rear of the batter's box but not especially deep, being almost on a line with the plate.

As is true with all good hitters, the Babe had exceptional reflexes and muscular coordination. He took a big stride forward with his right foot, planted his back leg firmly, swung forward on a level plane, snapping his wrists into the swing at the moment of impact and pulling the club head "through" the ball. He held the bat long, as already mentioned, with the knob at the small end gripped in his right hand. The force of his follow-through often sent him sprawling when he missed the ball. There was grace and effortless power in his swing when he hit the ball.

Ruth carried his gifts of coordination, quick reflexes and amazing vision into other sports with him, such as bowling and golf at which he was quite adept. He would have been a fine golfer, in fact, if he had the patience but Babe rarely could get through eighteen holes on the links without blowing up at least once. And only his physical gifts kept him from being snuffed out in his prime when he was behind the wheel of a car. He had enough smack-ups and near-misses to kill a score of ordinary persons.

Moe Berg, the Princetonian who came into baseball in 1923 as a shortstop and remained on as a catcher and coach until Pearl Harbor when he entered the OSS, was a student of baseball as he is of life. Remarkably observant, Berg made the statement that Ruth was the only hitter he ever saw who didn't short his grip with two strikes against him. Taking the precaution of moving the hands up a little on the handle of the bat was the regular procedure.

"I never found out whether Babe didn't know he had two strikes on him," remarked Moe, "or whether he didn't care."

There is no doubt that Ruth possessed the war club whose face launched a thousand homers. Babe had 714 to his credit in the major leagues, fifteen in the World Series, one in the first All-Star game ever held and he must have larruped at least 300 in the various exhibition games he played during his career. Of all these home runs, the one for which the big fellow is best remembered is the last one he hit in a World Series, the famous called shot against Charley Root of the Cubs at Wrigley Field in the third game of the 1932 Series.

To this day Ruth's defiant gesture of calling his shot is hotly debated. As recently as 1948, Root refused to play himself in the Hollywood film about the Babe, claiming that it was not a premeditated home run. Or, that if it was, it at least wasn't pinpointed in advance.

Briefly, for the story has been oft told, the situation was this: There had been a great deal of dugout jockeying between the clubs, the Yanks needling the Cubs because Mark Koenig, the ex-Yankee, had been voted only a half-share by them, although his September batting helped win the pennant for Chicago.

The Yanks won both the games played in New York and moved to Chicago for the next two. In the third game, Ruth hit a three-run homer in the first round but when he came to bat again in the fifth, the Cubs had rallied and the score was tied at 4–4. Lemons were pegged at the big fellow from the stands and all the Cub reserves crowded to the edge of the dugout to pour invective at the big Bam.

Root whipped a fast ball right down the middle and Babe, holding up one finger, yelled "Strike one!" in unison with Umpire Roy Van Graflan. Charley came back with another high hard one and Ruth, his moonface split with a grin, held up two fingers. And then he pointed dramatically toward the bleachers in center. It was precisely where the ball disappeared. The home run, Babe's last in World Series play, broke the tie and apparently did something to Root, too, because Lou Gehrig followed with another home run.

As memory dimmed the Babe wasn't sure whether he called his shot or not, but he had no doubt that night that he had hit the ball where he had pointed. And there was no doubt in the minds of his teammates because that night at the Edgewater Beach Hotel they all were full of talk about "Jidge's" nerve in calling his shot. "Jidge," incidentally, was the pet nickname for Babe with the Yankees, a nickname which began to die out around the clubhouse as his teammates of the Miller Huggins era began to drift away, to other clubs or out of baseball entirely.

Although Ruth tended more and more to disassociate himself from the players in his final years with the club, he was very much one of the boys in the early days. He was one with the team in the days of Waite Hoyt and Wally Schang, Joe Dugan and Wally Pipp and the others of the Huggins era. When the widowed Babe remarried in April, 1929, his second wife made all the road trips with the Yankees which tended to have a chastening effect upon the big fellow. Since Mrs. Ruth was the only wife along on the trips, it was natural that the Babe spent more of his time with her and less with his teammates.

Ruth and Joe McCarthy, who came to manage the Yanks in 1931, never really got along. The Babe felt that the job should have been his by divine right. McCarthy wisely gave Ruth his head, recognizing him as a player apart and realizing that he would get the maximum value from Ruth's fading glory by letting him run without a rein. Neither ever was openly critical of the other until Babe's famous blow-up after the 1934 season when he said he never again would play for the Yankees except as manager. Colonel Ruppert released him to the Braves the following spring and Babe played out the last few months of his major league career in an opera bouffe setting in Boston, the town where he had first known national fame.

Paraphrasing scripture, it was written that Ruth, crushed to earth, shall rise gain. He had his moments with the Braves, one on opening day when, before the governors of the six New England states, he hit a home run against Carl Hubbell, then considered the greatest southpaw extant. Another was shortly before he quit when he hit three home runs in a single game in Pittsburgh, one of them clearing the roof of Forbes Field, the record distance blow in that park. It was the big fellow's last major league home run.

When the Yankees paid Joe DiMaggio $100,000 for the 1949 season it was recorded as the largest salary ever paid to a ballplayer. It was, too, but it wasn't as great, in value, as the $80,000 Ruth received for the seasons of 1930 and 1931. Babe's "take-home pay" was the highest any ballplayer ever received—or is likely to receive in the foreseeable future.

Without again going into player vs. player controversies, Ruth was the most popular figure the game ever knew. He ran to superlatives in hitting and in salary, in living and in playing. Persons who never saw a baseball, let alone a baseball game, knew who Ruth was. And many persons saw baseball games only because they could thus see Ruth. His home runs restored the faith of the public in baseball after the shocking disclosures of the 1919 World Series scandal but his home runs did more than that—they carried baseball to the forefront in the wave of sports enthusiasm following the end of World War I.

When Babe Ruth died August 16, 1948, more than a decade had elapsed since his last home run. Yet millions mourned his passing as that of a national figure, which he was. Children who hadn't been born when Ruth was a home run star filed tearfully past his bier as he lay in state at Yankee Stadium, the ball park his home runs had built.

The late Lloyd Lewis, distinguished Lincolnophile and Chicago author and editor, made this comparison of Babe Ruth and the times in which he lived and flourished:

"Ruth's heyday, 1921 to 1933, was in relation to the American era of which his incredible home run performance was so spectacular a part if not, indeed, symbol—the era of soaring prices, high scores, huge and huger crowds, bigger and bigger stadia, two chickens in every pot—and the mastodonic Babe lumbering through it, overeating, reckless of his health, indifferent to the names of players on his own team, good-humored, kind-hearted, reveling in his prowess and front-page fame, loving small children, throwing away the wealth that had been showered upon him, childlike, sentimental, supremely sure that this glorious day would last forever.

"He had come up from a grinding poverty and was now like the America which was abolishing poverty. He was the American success story of the 1920's.

"And like it, too, his paunch finally grew too heavy for his legs. His Era's ankles buckled in 1929, gave out altogether in 1932; his own were gone by 1934."

The defense rests.

GEORGE HERMAN (BABE) RUTH

Born February 6, 1895, Baltimore, Md. Died August 16, 1948, New York, N. Y.
Height 6' 2". Weight 215. Batted and threw left-handed.

YEAR	CLUB	LEAGUE	POS	G	AB	R	H	HR	2B	BA
1914	Baltimore-Providence	Int.	P-OF	46	121	22	28	1	4	.231
1914	Boston	Amer.	P	5	10	1	2	0	0	.200
1915	Boston	Amer.	P-OF	42	92	16	29	4	0	.315
1916	Boston	Amer.	P-OF	67	136	18	37	3	0	.272
1917	Boston	Amer.	P-OF	52	123	14	40	2	0	.325
1918	Boston	Amer.	P-1B-OF	95	317	50	95	x11	6	.300
1919	Boston (A)	Amer.	P-OF	130	432	*103	139	*29	7	.322
1920	New York	Amer.	1B-OF	142	458	*158	172	*54	14	.376
1921	New York	Amer.	OF-1B	152	540	*177	204	*59	17	.378
1922	New York	Amer.	OF	110	403	94	128	35	2	.315
1923	New York	Amer.	OF	152	522	*151	205	*41	17	.393
1924	New York	Amer.	OF	153	529	*143	200	*46	9	*.378
1925	New York	Amer.	OF	98	359	61	104	25	2	.290
1926	New York	Amer.	OF	152	495	x139	184	*47	11	.372
1927	New York	Amer.	OF	151	540	x158	192	*60	7	.356
1928	New York	Amer.	OF	154	536	163	173	*54	4	.323
1929	New York	Amer.	OF	135	499	121	172	*46	5	.345
1930	New York	Amer.	OF	145	518	150	186	*49	10	.359
1931	New York	Amer.	OF	145	534	149	199	x46	5	.373
1932	New York	Amer.	OF-1B	133	457	120	156	41	2	.341
1933	New York	Amer.	OF	137	459	97	138	34	4	.301
1934	New York	Amer.	OF	125	365	78	105	22	1	.288
1935	Boston	Nat.	OF	28	72	13	13	6	0	.181
	Major League Totals			2503	8396	2174	2873	714	123	.342

WORLD SERIES RECORD

YEAR	CLUB	LEAGUE	POS	G	AB	R	H	HR	2B	BA
1915	Boston	Amer.	PH	1	1	0	0	0	0	.300
1916	Boston	Amer.	P	1	5	0	0	0	0	.200
1918	Boston	Amer.	P-OF	3	5	0	1	0	0	.200
1921	New York	Amer.	OF	6	16	3	5	1	2	.313
1922	New York	Amer.	OF	5	17	1	2	0	0	.118
1923	New York	Amer.	OF-1B	6	19	8	7	3	0	.368
1926	New York	Amer.	OF	7	20	6	6	4	1	.300
1927	New York	Amer.	OF	4	15	4	6	2	1	.400
1928	New York	Amer.	OF	4	16	9	10	3	0	.625
1932	New York	Amer.	OF	4	15	6	5	2	0	.333
	World Series Totals			41	129	37	42	15	4	.325

(A) Sold to New York A.L. for $125,000, January 1920
* Led league
x Tied for lead
Released Boston Braves, June 2, 1935
Coach Brooklyn Dodgers, June 18, 1938 to end of season
Elected to Hall of Fame, 1936

ALL-STAR GAME RECORD

YEAR	LEAGUE	POS	AB	R	H	2B	3B	HR	RBI	BA
1933	American	OF	4	1	2	0	0	1	2	.500
1934	American	OF	2	1	0	0	0	0	0	.000
	All-Star Game Totals		6	2	2	0	0	1	2	.333

PITCHING RECORD

YEAR	CLUB	LEAGUE	G	IP	W	L	PCT	H	R	ER	BB	SO	ERA
1914	Baltimore-Providence	Int.	35	245	22	9	.709	210	88	...	101	139	...
1914	Boston	Amer.	4	22	2	1	.667	21	12	10	7	2	3.91
1915	Boston	Amer.	32	218	18	6	.750	166	80	59	85	112	2.44
1916	Boston	Amer.	44	324	23	12	.657	230	83	63	118	170	1.75
1917	Boston	Amer.	41	326	23	13	.639	244	93	73	108	128	2.02
1918	Boston	Amer.	20	166	13	7	.650	125	51	41	49	40	2.22
1919	Boston	Amer.	17	133	8	5	.615	148	59	44	58	30	2.97
1920	New York	Amer.	1	4	1	0	1.000	3	4	2	2	0	4.50
1921	New York	Amer.	2	9	2	0	1.000	14	10	4	10	2	4.00
1930	New York	Amer.	1	9	1	0	1.000	11	3	3	3	2	3.00
1933	New York	Amer.	1	9	1	0	1.000	12	5	5	3	0	5.00
	Major League Totals		163	1220	92	44	.667	974	400	307	443	486	2.24

WORLD SERIES PITCHING RECORD

YEAR	CLUB	LEAGUE	G	IP	W	L	PCT	H	R	ER	BB	SO	ERA
1916	Boston	Amer.	1	14	1	0	1.000	6	1	1	3	4	0.64
1918	Boston	Amer.	2	17	2	0	1.000	13	2	2	7	4	1.06
	World Series Totals		3	31	3	0	1.000	19	3	3	10	8	0.87

CHAPTER XIX

THE PICTURE PLAYER

George Harold Sisler

GEORGE SISLER when a student at Central High in Akron, Ohio upheld a tradition which is as old as baseball itself by becoming a pitcher. Almost invariably you'll find that in kid baseball, the best ballplayer on the block is the pitcher. It is probable that 80 per cent of the professional ballplayers in America today were pitchers when they first played on an organized team, even if the team hadn't been organized to the point of wearing uniforms.

Another tradition of young ballplayers which Sisler preserved in 1910 was that of selecting a major leaguer as a model and an idol. He picked Walter Johnson, who was just then coming into greatness with the Washington Senators, which was more than might be said for the Senators. Young George read every line he could find about Johnson, saved every picture of the Big Train he could get.

Sisler kept on as a pitcher after leaving Central High. He had signed a contract to play with his home town team of Akron, then in the Ohio State League, but he paid little attention to it, since he had never reported to the club, or indeed told anybody about it. He went on to the University of Michigan and finally was signed, after graduation by the St. Louis Browns.

There was a terrific furor over this, which will be related in detail later on. At the moment our concern is with Sisler and his pitching idol, the great Johnson. For George, though he later was to go into Cooperstown's Hall of Fame acclaimed as one of the two greatest fielding first basemen of all time and to hold the record for the most number of hits ever made by any major leaguer in any one season, 257, still thinks that his greatest thrill in baseball came as a pitcher, came when he pitched and defeated his idol, Walter Johnson.

In *My Greatest Day in Baseball* (A. S. Barnes & Co., New York) Sisler told Lyall Smith of the Detroit *Free Press* that he remembers his game against Johnson over and above all of the two thousand he played in the majors. And this was when George was only two months out of the University of Michigan, on August 29, 1915.

After the game ended the day before, Branch Rickey, then managing the Browns, told Sisler that he would face Johnson the next day. It was like telling an earthling that he was going to wrestle a god.

"I couldn't sleep that night," confided Sisler to Smith. "I kept tossing and finally, at about four, I gave it up altogether. I just sat on the edge of the bed and waited for the day to break. I managed to get some breakfast in me and was at Sportsman's Park before they opened the gates.

"Even while I was warming up, I sneaked a look at Johnson and tried to do everything he did, making allowances for the fact that he was right-handed and I was a southpaw. Even when I went to the dugout before the game started, I kept watching Johnson."

Sisler calmed down sufficiently to strike out the first Washington batter, Moeller, on three pitches but Foster and Milan singled. Howie Shanks flied deep to center and Foster tried for third after the catch. The throw from the outfield was fumbled and the runner kept on to score. It looked rough for young George but it was the last run the Senators scored. In the second inning, also aided by an error, the Browns scored twice against Johnson and those were the only runs of the game. Johnson allowed one earned run and Sisler none.

"When I got the last man out in the ninth," said Sisler, "I looked over to the Washington bench for Johnson but Walter already had ducked.

"I don't know what I expected to do if I had seen him. For a minute I thought maybe I'd go over and shake his hand and tell him that I was sorry I beat him but I guess that was just the silly idea of a young kid who had just come face to face with his idol and beaten him."

Sisler, whose fielding grace at first base later was to make many call him "The Picture Player," apparently had equal grace in his manners, even as a rookie.

The first time Branch Rickey saw George Sisler was in the winter of 1912. It was in the field house at Ann Arbor and Sisler was a candidate for the freshman team at Michigan. A skinny kid weighing less than 140 pounds, Sisler wasn't an impressive sight. But Rickey, the Michigan baseball coach, had heard about this kid pitcher from Akron, Ohio and he wanted to get a good look at him. But neither he nor the skinny kid from Ohio had any idea of how much dramatic baseball lore was being born that wintry afternoon at Ann Arbor. Neither could even dream that their baseball careers would be so intertwined.

"I'll never forget that first time I saw him," said Rickey one afternoon almost forty years later in his sumptuous Brooklyn office. "He was wearing a blue sweater. It's funny but that was the first thing I noticed about him. I'd heard about him and now I wanted to watch him pitch. It didn't take me more than a few minutes to realize that he could pitch, too, even though he wasn't too big. He had a dandy fast ball and a three-fingered curve that was a honey. I told him to stick around and gave him permission to work out with the varsity even though freshmen weren't eligible to play.

"I didn't see too much of him that winter. I was too busy picking a varsity squad that would go South on a ten-game tour during the spring vacation. But when we came back from the South and were able to get outdoors, I really began to notice him. For it was then that I saw him pick up a bat and hit for the first time. I saw him run and I knew just like that that here was a remarkable athlete, one of those young men you don't find but once in a generation. Because he instinctively knew how to handle a bat and he could run as fast as any ballplayer I'd ever seen."

Sisler could run and there are those like Billy Evans who insist that no other hitter in baseball history with the possible exception of Ty Cobb ever put that speed to better use. But beyond his speed, Sisler had a great deal else, including as fine and sharp a mind as baseball has known. Almost from the first he seemed to know all the answers. He was and is a perfectionist.

Of course when Rickey first saw him Sisler wasn't exactly a raw unknown. Though he was only nineteen at the time, he had two years before signed a contract to play professional baseball. It was that contract that was to fan the flames of one of the bitterest feuds baseball has ever known and one that was eventually to lead to the naming of Judge Kenesaw Mountain Landis as high commissioner of baseball. As a kid fresh out of high school, Sisler had signed a contract to play ball for the Akron club of the old Ohio-Pennsylvania League. Though he never played an inning for Akron, that contract was to prove one of the hottest potatoes baseball has ever had to handle.

Sisler went to Michigan because his high school catcher, a young man named Russell Baer, convinced him that it was the finest college in the land. "I knew nothing about it," Sisler recalls, "but Russ talked so long and so persuasively that I couldn't have gone anywhere else even if I'd had any inclination to, which I didn't." And thus it was that fate began weaving the wonderful tapestry that is the baseball story of George Sisler and Branch Rickey. For strange as it may seem, baseball might never have known Rickey if Sisler hadn't chosen to follow his high school battery mate to Ann Arbor. Or at least it might only have remembered him as a mediocre catcher who couldn't hit and whose most memorable contribution to the game had been a monstrous afternoon under the bat for the St. Louis Browns when he had allowed the New York Yankees to steal 15 bases on him.

Rickey, you see, had dropped out of baseball in 1908 to enter the Michigan law school, a three-year course that he completed in two. After a year of semi-starvation as a lawyer in Boise, Idaho, he had returned to Michigan as baseball coach and it was there, as recorded, that Rickey and Sisler came face to face.

Once Rickey had seen Sisler hit and run, he knew that he was headed for the big leagues and he determined that it would be for the Browns, his old team. "The first thing I did after watching Sisler that first day outdoors," Rickey recalls, "was to approach Fielding Yost, Michigan's great football coach, and tell him that Sisler would play no football for him. Yost was disappointed and he needed a little persuasion, but it didn't take long to convince him that it would be the sheerest sort of folly to let George risk a brilliant baseball career for a few mediocre minutes on the football field. He was a good football player, of course, but he was too light to ever be great. And in those days there was no future in professional football."

Sisler proceeded on his brilliant baseball way as a pitcher and part-time outfielder for the Wolverines. By the time he had graduated, Rickey had moved on to St. Louis. Taking shrewd note that Sisler had signed that Akron pact when he was seventeen and a minor, Rickey had quietly signed him for the Browns, making Colonel Robert Hedges, owner of the St. Louis American League club forever grateful. But while Sisler had been starring for Michigan, his contract with Akron had taken on additional baseball value. In 1912, Akron had sold it to the Columbus club in the American Association and a year later Columbus in turn had sold it to the Pirates.

Naturally when Sisler graduated from Michigan he was ordered to report to the Pirates. But Sisler had already signed his new contract with the Browns and, ignoring the Pirate edict, he joined the Browns in Comiskey Park in Chicago one June day in 1915. That was Rickey's last year as manager of the Browns and, as they have been most of the time during their baseball life, the Browns were deep in the second division and Ricky was desperately seeking means to lift them out of their doldrums.

"I had been thinking about Sisler for a long time before he arrived. It was obvious to me that he was far too good a ballplayer to waste his time pitching. He had never played first base at Michigan and though he wasn't as tall as the average first baseman I had a hunch that this might be the spot for him. So the first thing I did when he reported was to hand him a first baseman's mitt and tell him to work out there. Two days later, he started his first game at first and it was easy to see from the start that he was going to be a natural there."

Sisler did some good pitching that first season with the Browns. He beat Walter Johnson, as related, 2–1, and he lost a couple of tough 1–0 decisions. His final pitching record that year was four and five. He didn't break any windows with his bat but he hit .285 in 81 games that first year.

"Yes it was obvious that he was a natural hitter. He was young and inexperienced and he went after bad balls just as young Duke

Snider did in Brooklyn many years later," recalls Rickey, "but you could see he wasn't going to miss. His pitching days were over."

Sisler played 151 games for the 1916 Browns and hit .305 in his first full season as a first baseman. Phil Ball had bought the Browns from Colonel Hedges the previous winter and Rickey had been moved into the front office as vice president and general manager. After that 1916 season, the trails of Rickey and Sisler parted but twenty-six years later they were to come together again in Brooklyn and Pittsburgh.

Barney Dreyfuss, the Pirate owner, was still giving off cries of a wounded bull moose as a result of the awarding of Sisler in 1915 permanently to the Browns by the three-man Commission that had ruled baseball since 1903 and the better Sisler got the angrier Dreyfuss became. The Commission, you see, had been composed of Governor John K. Tener, president of the National League, Ban Johnson, stormy and colorful boss of the American League, and Garry Herrmann, owner of the Cincinnati Reds. On a 2–1 vote—Johnson and Hermann, ruling for the Browns, had outvoted Governor Tener—Sisler's original contract had been ruled illegal because he had signed while still a minor. Dreyfuss never forgave Hermann and Johnson and he never forgot, either. All through the years he waged relentless war on the Commission until finally the White Sox scandal brought about the demise of the three-man Commission and the naming of Judge Landis as the supreme boss of the game. It was a long and stormy fight but it was to prove one of the greatest things that has ever happened to baseball and it all started when Sisler was awarded to the Browns.

It was in 1917 that Sisler suddenly emerged as a full-blown star. He hit a walloping .353 that wartime season and from then until his eyes went bad at the end of the 1922 season he hit under .350 only once. To Sisler anything under that figure represented a bad season and it is significant that in his greatest years he usually hit far above it. He hit .341 in 1918 and a lusty .352 a year later. In addition he was fielding brilliantly around first base and running wild on the bases. There wasn't apparently anything he couldn't do but the baseball world still hadn't seen anything yet.

It was in 1920 that he embarked on a three-year splurge that remains the greatest three-year stretch that any player has ever had. In those three years—1920–21–22—he unloaded 719 hits, scored 396 runs and stole 128 bases. His batting averages for the three successive years were .407, .371 and .420. Though 1922 is generally remembered as his peak year, Sisler himself thinks that 1920 was his greatest and he has sound reasons for so thinking.

He was twenty-seven that season and at his physical zenith. He played every minute of every game and he collected a total of 257 base hits, a figure which has never been equaled by any player before or since. But Sisler's greatest pride that season was that he hit 19 home runs. That was more than any man had ever hit in a single season with the exception of Babe Ruth who had stunned the baseball world by hitting 29 for the Red Sox in his final season at Fenway Park the year before. Nineteen homers doesn't seem like many in these days of the juiced-up ball and the long distance belts but it was a tremendous total then, especially for a young man who never was known for his ability to belt the ball out of the park.

Sisler, you know, was essentially a spray hitter built much in the mold of Willie Keeler, the little guy who used to "hit 'em where they ain't." He could and did hit to all fields and he hit searing line drives that rocketed off his bat with explosive regularity. "He was the nearest thing to Keeler of all the modern hitters. He used his speed to more advantage than any man save Cobb. He used his head every minute of the time, too. He was always watching the rival infield. If they crept in to avoid a bunt, he would poke the ball over their heads. If they dropped back he would lay down a deft bunt and beat the play to first—sometimes without even drawing a throw." That is the picture of him as portrayed by Billy Evans, who was an American League umpire when Sisler was rolling high and wide around the American League.

"I'd say," adjudges Rickey, "that he was the smartest hitter that ever lived. He was a professional with that bat in his hand. He never stopped thinking. Like Stan Musial today, he was a menace every time he stepped to the plate. You could feel the ripple of anticipation in the crowd as he moved up there. And he seldom failed to provide the excitement they expected. On the bases he ran with the judgment of a Pee Wee Reese and with vastly greater speed. In the field, he was the picture player, the acme of grace and fluency."

If 1920 was Sisler's greatest year in his own estimation, the season of 1922 was the one for which he will always be remembered. That was the year he hit .420 and led the Browns on a vain but valiant pursuit of their first pennant. He was the American League's most valuable player that year even though the Yankees sneaked off with the pennant and he was undoubtedly the greatest player in the game. But for a tragic injury on the very eve of the most important series the Browns had ever played up to that time, the Brownie boosters would not have had to wait another twenty-two years and the coming of a second World War for that first and only pennant. There was dancing in the streets that October Sunday in 1944 when a journeyman house painter, rescued from obscurity by the manpower shortage brought on by the war, pitched the Browns to a fourth straight victory over the Yankees and that lone flag. Sig Jakucki and Chet Laabs, who made Jakucki's victory possible with two two-run homers against Mel Queen, were the toast of St. Louis that day but no more so than Sisler and Hub Pruett were on Sunday, September 17, 1922. The only difference was that the celebration in 1922 was just a bit premature.

When Labor Day rolled around, it was evident that the race would be decided by a three-game series scheduled for mid-September in St. Louis. And as it turned out it was. As luck would have it, Sisler fell on his right shoulder while stretching for a ball against Detroit in the series before the Yanks came to town. He pulled a muscle so badly that his right arm was virtually useless for the series.

"Actually I should never have played," recalls Sisler. "The arm was so badly crippled that I had to lift my gloved hand with my left hand in order to catch balls at first base. I told the guys to be sure and throw the ball low and I couldn't possibly catch a ball over my head. At bat, I was practically one-handed. It was ridiculous for me to even try to play but I was young then and you couldn't have kept me out of there with a gun."

Actually nobody, least of all Lee Fohl who piloted the Browns through that tension-filled campaign, wanted to keep him out of there. Sisler with one arm was still better than anybody else with two. This series was for all the money and for the three games Sportsman's Park was crowded. In addition, Sisler was riding the crest of a hitting streak that was the focus of the whole baseball world. As the series opened, Sisler had hit in 39 straight games and was only one short of the American League record held by Ty Cobb. In the first game, Bob Shawkey beat the Brownie ace, Urban Shocker, in a tense 2–1 pitching duel. That was the game in which Whitey Witt, the towheaded little Yankee who roamed the picket patrol in center field, was skulled by a flying bottle in the outfield and had to be carted from the premises. Sisler got one hit off Shawkey that day to tie Cobb's record but in the ninth with the tying and winning runs on base he banged into the double play that ended the last St. Louis hopes.

The Browns bounced back behind little Pruett the next day, though, to beat Waite Hoyt, 5–1, with Ken Williams hitting his 38th home run to put him in front of Babe Ruth in the home run derby that he eventually won. Sisler got a hit in that game, too, to break Cobb's record and set a mark of 41 games that was to live for nineteen years until a guy named Joe DiMaggio came along in 1941 to set a mark of 56 straight games.

The St. Louis fans swarmed down on the field in the dusk that Sunday afternoon in 1922 to carry Pruett and Sisler and Williams off the field in triumph. Now, they seemed to think, they couldn't miss. But disillusion wasn't far behind those jubilant moments. In the rubber game on Monday the Browns went into the ninth leading 2–1 behind Dixie Davis who had held the Yankee sluggers to just four infield singles over the first eight frames. Sisler's hitting skein had been stopped by Sad Sam Jones and Bullet Joe Bush but nobody in the stands cared as the Yanks came to bat for their last licks. Their beloved Brownies were only three outs away from victory and a tie for first place. To their utter dismay, though, the Browns couldn't get even one of those outs before the tide had turned tragically against them.

"I'll never forget that last inning," murmured Sisler nostalgically many years later. "We just couldn't get a break and they couldn't get the ball out of the infield until that last fatal hit by Witt."

Wally Schang, the Yankee catcher, started things off with a smash to the box that ricocheted off Davis' glove for an infield single. Elmer Smith came up to hit for Everett Scott, the durable but light-hitting Yankee shortstop, and Davis uncorked a wild pitch that sent Schang rumbling down to second. Fohl in desperation yanked Davis and brought in Pruett to pitch to the left-handed long ball-hitting Smith. Huggins in turn sent the right-handed Mike McNally up to swing for Smith. McNally, trying to get the tying run around to third from whence it could be delivered by a fly ball, bunted just in front of the plate.

It was a bad bunt but Hank Severeid, the Brown catcher, slipped on the plate while in pursuit of the ball and his hurried throw to third was high and late. Pruett then walked the next hitter to fill the bases with still nobody out. That finished Pruett and in from the bull pen trudged Shocker, the ace. But Whitey Witt, his gashed head swathed in bandages, greeted him with a two-run single and the game and the visions of the only World Series George Sisler ever had a chance to play in were gone.

George Sisler couldn't know it then but it was to be all downhill from there on. He never again was to know the greatness that he achieved that tremendous season of 1922 and the Browns themselves weren't ever to come that close again in the years that Sisler was to stay with them.

In the winter of 1922–23, the sinus trouble that had plagued him off and on for several seasons was to take a serious turn and for a while it looked as though tragedy had curtailed a meteoric career. The poisonous sinusitis affected his optic nerve and for a long spell his eyesight was despaired of by the best oculists in the country. He had to sit out the entire 1923 season and there were dreary days when he doubted that he would ever play again.

In the winter of 1923–4 his eyesight began to clear up and Phil Ball named him to replace Lee Fohl as manager. He reported for spring training still far from sure that he would be able to hit as he once did. For the first few weeks he began to have doubts whether he would even be able to play at all. His vision, once the sharpest in baseball, was still a bit blurry. But it got better as he went along and in the final exhibition series with the Cardinals he got two hits off Willie Sherdel, the little left-hander, and that convinced him he was on his way back.

"I never was a real good hitter again," he insists. "Oh, I know

I hit .345 and got 228 hits in 1925 but that never gave me much satisfaction. That isn't what I call real good hitting."

Sisler's three-year tenure at the helm of the Browns was unmarked by any of the spectacular heroics of his earlier years. He was on the seamy side of thirty now and his future was pretty much behind him. He brought the Browns home fourth in 1924 and drove them up to third in 1925. That was the last year incidentally that the Yankees failed to finish in the first division. Sisler had his last really good year that season and the Browns even made some menacing gestures at the pennant that was won for the second straight year by Bucky Harris' Washington Senators.

"In 1926, though," says Sisler, "we really came apart at the seams. Everything went wrong and the club wound deep in the second division in seventh place. I guess I let the way the club was going affect my hitting because for the first and only time since my rookie year I fell under the .300 mark."

Sisler dropped all the way down to .289 that year and even now he still shudders at the thought of it. Over the winter he was relieved of his managerial duties. In 1927—his final year with the Browns—he bounced back at the plate, hitting .327 and collecting more than 200 hits for the fifth time in his career. But he was thirty-four now and by the next season he would be thirty-five and at the winter meetings that December he was sold to Washington for $25,000. With the Senators he never could get going and he played only 20 games for Bucky Harris before he was waived out of the American League and shipped to Braves Field where Judge Emil Fuchs was employing all sorts of fanciful and futile schemes to lift the Braves out of the doldrums.

"The big thing at Washington was that I found my speed had vanished overnight. I'd spent the winter out at Laguna Beach in California and I'd done a lot of mountain-climbing, hunting mountain quail. I think now that was the craziest stunt I ever pulled because when I reported to the Senators I found that my legs just weren't what they used to be. I hit .245 in those 20 games for Washington and what hurt most was the fact that I couldn't steal a single base. I couldn't blame them for getting rid of me as fast as they could."

It was Rogers Hornsby, another of Rickey's products, who urged Judge Fuchs to give Sisler a new shot in Boston. The Rajah had a contract for $40,000 and was named captain of the 1928 Braves. Jack Slattery had been named manager of the Braves, succeeding Dave Bancroft. But all the play that spring went to Hornsby who only two years before had piloted the cards to a world championship. Like the Braves of 1949, the spring training session that year was filled with dissension and rumors of trouble. Six weeks after the season started Hornsby was named manager and the first move he made was to get Sisler.

The aging star hit .340 that season in 118 games for the Braves and Hornsby hit .387 but the club finished in seventh place and lost 103 games. Between September 4 and 15, the Braves played nine consecutive double-headers which was pretty tough going for an old guy whose legs were moaning. It is in the books that they lost five of these double-headers in a row.

Hornsby talked Judge Fuchs into dealing him to Chicago that fall and he helped Joe McCarthy pilot the Cubs to a pennant. But Sisler, thirty-six now and aging with almost every pitch, lingered on to hit .326 for the Braves. That was the year that Fuchs got the startling idea of managing the club himself and Sisler says he'll never forget it. "We can't do any worse than we have the last few years," said Fuchs when he decided to take a fling at managing. But he was wrong. The Braves finished last, 43 games back of the champion Cubs. Sisler led the club in hitting with a .326 mark but he had slowed down to a walk in the field.

The next year found the Braves with their fifth manager in four years—Deacon Bill McKechnie who had been fired by Sam Breadon in 1928 for winning a pennant but losing the World Series in four straight games to the Yankees. They didn't think old George could make it that spring and they drafted Johnny Neun from Baltimore as insurance. But Sisler stuck it out gamely and hit .309 in 107 games. But that was the end of the big league trail for the once great star. The next season found him back under Branch Rickey with the Cardinal farm club at Rochester and he hit .303 in 159 games. The great irony of that season was that after sixteen years in the majors without playing on a pennant-winner his first season in the minors was with a team that won the International League pennant and then went on to beat St. Paul in the little World Series.

The last line in George Sisler's lustrous record finds him managing and playing a part-time first base at Shreveport-Tyler in the Texas League in 1932. There at the age of thirty-nine he hit only .287 in 70 games and he knew it was finally time to call it quits. This he did and baseball heard little of him—save for his election to the Hall of Fame in 1938—until Branch Rickey moved his base of operations from St. Louis to Brooklyn in the winter of 1942–43. One of his first moves was to name Sisler as a scout and George accompanied him to Pittsburgh in December, 1950.

GEORGE HAROLD SISLER

Born March 24, 1893, Manchester, Ohio.
Height 6' 1½". Weight 170. Batted and threw left-handed.

YEAR	CLUB	LEAGUE	G	AB	R	H	HR	SB	BA
1915	St. Louis	Amer.	81	274	28	78	3	10	.285
1916	St. Louis	Amer.	151	580	83	177	3	34	.305
1917	St. Louis	Amer.	135	539	60	190	2	37	.353
1918	St. Louis	Amer.	114	452	69	154	2	45	.341
1919	St. Louis	Amer.	132	511	96	180	10	28	.352
1920	St. Louis	Amer.	154	631	137	*257	19	42	*.407
1921	St. Louis	Amer.	138	582	125	216	11	35	.371
1922	St. Louis	Amer.	142	586	134	246	8	51	*.420
1923	St. Louis	Amer.			Out with eye trouble				
1924	St. Louis	Amer.	151	636	94	194	9	19	.305
1925	St. Louis	Amer.	150	649	100	224	12	11	.345
1926	St. Louis	Amer.	150	613	78	178	7	12	.289
1927	St. Louis (A)	Amer.	149	614	87	201	5	27	.327
1928	Washington †	Amer.	20	49	1	12	0	0	.245
1928	Boston	Nat.	118	491	71	167	4	11	.340
1929	Boston	Nat.	154	629	67	205	1	6	.326
1930	Boston	Nat.	116	431	54	133	3	7	.309
1931	Rochester	Int.	159	613	86	186	3	7	.303
1932	Shreveport-Tyler	Texas	70	258	28	74	1	0	.287
	Major League Totals		2055	8267	1284	2812	99	375	.341

(A) Sold to Washington for $25,000 December 14, 1927
† Purchased by Boston N.L. for $7,500 May 27, 1928
* Led league
Managed St. Louis Browns, 1924–25–26
Manager, Shreveport-Tyler, Texas League part of 1932
Elected to Hall of Fame, 1938

Sisler's greatest asset is as a teacher of hitters in spring training. It wasn't any mere coincidence that the Dodgers slugged their way to a pennant in 1949—the first year that Sisler was put in full charge of the varsity hitters at spring training—and that young guys like Jackie Robinson, Carl Furillo, Gil Hodges and Duke Snider overnight became awesome hitters.

"He's an even more remarkable teacher of hitters," says Rickey of his prize product, "than he was a hitter himself. He has the greatest eye for detail and he's the most meticulous person in correcting mistakes I've ever seen. He has a wonderful knack of making his pupils do what he wants them to do and conning them into thinking that it was their idea all along."

CHAPTER XX

THE GRAY EAGLE

Tristram E. Speaker

NOWHERE in baseball's Hall of Fame at Cooperstown, New York will you find any reference to Mickey Finn. In fact, you hear little about Mickey Finn in baseball save in jest. Some old-timers may remember that an infielder named Neal Finn, who was called Mickey, was briefly with the Dodgers and Phillies back in the early thirties. The Mickey Finn of this particular tale, however, probably changed the entire history of baseball by the simple fact that he kept his word.

Mickey Finn owned the Little Rock franchise, lock, stock and barrel, in the Southern Association in 1908. The Boston Red Sox trained in the Arkansas capital in the spring of that year and when they were ready to pull up stakes and head North they discovered themselves short in the pocket, a condition which was chronic with the ball clubs of that era. There was the little matter of rent for the ball park, due Mr. Finn. The Red Sox had some cash and a couple of ballplayers they were prepared to leave behind. Since it was obvious that the hotel wouldn't be interested in ballplayers to square the tab, the Red Sox wondered if Mr. Finn would mind taking the playing talent and allowing the hotel to take the cash? Mr. Finn said it was all right by him and the Red Sox turned over to him a young Texan who claimed to be an outfielder. The name was Tristram E. Speaker.

It turned out that the claims of the Texan were no idle boasts. He was the sensation of the Southern Association before the season was half over and scouts from several clubs approached Mr. Finn with an eye to taking Speaker off his hands, leaving in exchange bundles of the cash that Mickey had failed to get in the spring. The Giants, Pirates and Senators all sent representatives.

Finn remembered, however, that he had promised Boston first call on Speaker's services if the boy showed anything. And Speaker's .350 batting average indicated that he was indeed showing something. Finn got in touch with the Red Sox president, John I. Taylor, and allowed him to buy back Speaker for $500.

Had Finn reneged on his promise and yielded to the blandishments of the Giants or Pirates, Speaker would have wound up a National Leaguer. In that circuit, not having to play second fiddle to Ty Cobb, Speaker probably would have won several batting titles with his extraordinary high batting averages. As it was, the Texan was able to break Ty's service only once in his thirteen peak years.

If Speaker had been sold to Washington, he still would have been fated to follow in Cobb's shadow but then what would have happened to the American League's first great outfielding triumvirate of Speaker, Duffy Lewis and Harry Hooper?

It does seem as if fate and the forthrightness of the unsung Mr. Finn had Speaker ticketed for the Red Sox all along. Boston was remarkably careless in its contractual negotiations, even for a period when baseball was a haphazard, shirt-sleeved business. The year before, Speaker had been purchased from the Houston Club of the Texas League for $750. He had played a few games with Boston in the tag-end of the 1907 season and hadn't been particularly eye-catching.

No contract for 1908 ever was forwarded to Speaker, which automatically made him a free agent. He went over to Marlin in his native Texas and tried to insinuate himself into the Giant training camp. John McGraw told Spoke he was filled up with talent, which, indeed, he was and advised the boy to try elsewhere. Speaker shopped around, found no takers and eventually showed up at the Red Sox camp in Little Rock.

Jim McGuire, who was the third person to manage the Sox the season before, apparently had other problems besides giving a thorough examination to a youngster who had hit only .158 in the scattered games he had played in Boston at the end of the previous season. When the Red Sox eventually headed North, Speaker was left behind with Finn in lieu of ground rent.

As the summer went on, Tris, who had tried his hand at being a left-handed pitcher and had been literally batted into the outfield, found outfielding was his special dish. His great speed enabled him to cover more ground than anybody in the Southern League thought possible and he hit harder than anybody ever had in that loop before. Spoke's average of .350 was the highest ever attained in the league and it was then the other clubs closed in. It was then, too, that Mickey Finn remembered his word was as good as his bond.

Although Speaker was one of the select few in major league history ever to bat out more than 3000 base hits, it is ironical that he should be remembered chiefly for a defensive idiosyncrasy which contributed greatly to his superb outfielding. Spoke played an extremely short center field—"shallow," as the ballplayers call it. This enabled him to catch line singles hit over second base and saved the shortstop and second baseman the trouble of worrying over those looping flies which are called Texas Leaguers when they fall safely. Few Texas Leaguers ever fell safely when this Texas League alumnus was in center.

So shallow did Speaker play that twice in the month of April, 1918, he was able to make unassisted double plays. That meant he was able to catch the batted ball and beat the runner who had been on second base back to the bag. Remarkable as are the sheer mechanics of the play, the true testimonial to Speaker is that the runner would not have left second base if he thought there was even a possibility of the ball being caught.

At the plate, Speaker batted from a semi-crouch, standing deep in the batter's box with his right foot about five inches in front of his left, or rear, foot. The right foot also was some two to four inches nearer the plate. He took a full stride and held his bat rather low, almost seeming to rest his hands on his left hip. Tris also was a bat-waggler, moving the bat up and down slowly, like the lazy twitching of a cat's tail.

After Speaker had been traded from Boston to Cleveland, he altered his stance slightly, so as to be able to pull for the short fence at League Park, or Dunn Field, as it was then known. While not a home run hitter of distinction—his home run production went into double figures only three times and never reached 20—Speaker hit more than his share of two-baggers. As a matter of fact, Spoke hit more doubles than any man who ever played ball, a grand total of 793, more than one hundred above the National League record of Honus Wagner. On eight different times, Tris led the American League in two-baggers, four seasons in succession. And he was hitting against men like Cobb, Sisler, Ruth, Heilmann, etc.

Just as Lou Gehrig spent almost a lifetime playing in the shadow of Babe Ruth, so was it Speaker's misfortune to be an American League star when Ty Cobb was its entire solar system. In 1916, Speaker batted .386 to lead the American League in batting, the only season between 1907 and 1919 when anybody except Cobb held the batting crown. Spoke hit over .350 on several occasions and went over .380 four times but 1916 was his only batting championship.

It may have been because of Speaker's vastly superior fielding that his boosters stressed that point in their arguments about the relative values of the Gray Eagle and Cobb. As the years go by, there is tendency to remember Speaker only for his great outfielding to forget that he was one of the mightiest batters of a league which was known for its lusty hitting.

Like Cobb, Speaker was a man who knew what he wanted. And who, most of the time, got what he wanted. In the spring of 1916, Joe Lannin, his bank balance bearing the scars of the Federal League war even though his Red Sox had beaten the Phillies in the World Series the fall before, sent to Hubbard, Texas, Spoke's home, a contract calling for $9,000. That was almost twice what a teammate, Babe Ruth, signed for that year but it was precisely half of what Speaker had received in 1914 and 1915. Tris was being set back to his 1913 salary. Or at least, Lannin thought he was.

Speaker declared that he would not play for less than $15,000. That he was willing to take a $3,000 cut was due to the fact World War I already was in full swing in France and that the depredations of the Federal League had made grievous inroads into major league receipts.

Lannin was as adamant as his great outfielder. Rough Carrigan, the manager, was caught in the switches. He didn't think he could repeat as the pennant winner without Speaker and he knew that he couldn't high-pressure Lannin into budging.

Rough figured that if he could get Spoke to the Hot Springs camp he might be able to work out a compromise.

Actually, it was only an expediency that Carrigan was able to manipulate. He arranged for Speaker to train with the Sox and come North in the exhibition games at a per diem rate, probably the first time in history a ballplayer was paid for spring training. Tris was ready and he played in a manner in the exhibition games which should have convinced Lannin that he was a bargain at $15,000 a season. It was Carrigan's hope that Lannin and Speaker would sit down in Boston at the end of the exhibition trip and settle their differences.

Speaker, however, was not destined to reach Boston. The Red Sox wound up their exhibition tour with a Saturday game in Brooklyn. Tris won the game by breaking a ninth-inning tie with a home run against Rube Marquard, the ball clearing the right field wall at Ebbets Field. Owner Lannin met him after the game and congratulated him on his homer. Joe did more than that. He told Spoke everything would be all right when they reached Boston.

When an owner tells a ballplayer everything is going to be all right, the player assumes that his terms have been met. To a ballplayer, it doesn't mean a compromise. Therefore, Speaker was well pleased with himself that Saturday evening. Well pleased for just so long as it took the phone in his hotel room to ring. His caller was Rob McRoy, the Cleveland general manager, who previously had held a similar position with the Red Sox until the club was sold to Lannin.

McRoy asked Speaker how he would like to play in Cleveland and it was all Spoke could do to keep a straight face. He explained that he thought the Red Sox had an excellent chance for the pennant, while the Indians were strictly second division—and likely to stay there, too.

"That's too bad, Tris," said McRoy, "because we just bought you from the Red Sox."

When Speaker got his breath, he said what ballplayers before him and since have said upon being informed that they have been traded: "I won't play. I'll quit baseball first." So far, for the record, nobody ever has quit.

It was then Speaker learned the details of the deal. Lannin had received $55,000 and two players, Sam Jones, a pitcher who was to develop into an American League winner, and Freddie Thomas, a rookie infielder.

Now Spoke really saw red. He reached Lannin by phone and informed the Boston owner that he would not go to Cleveland unless he received $10,000 of the purchase money. Joe wasn't keen about giving in to Tris but Spoke said he would take the next train for Texas unless he received what he wanted. Cleveland, of course, agreed to pay him the $15,000 he sought for salary from the Red Sox.

When Lannin gave in, and only then, Speaker left to join his new club which had finished seventh in the American League the previous year. Tris arrived in Cleveland the morning of the opening game. The first order of the day's business was a phone call to Jim Dunn, the Cleveland owner. Spoke explained that he hadn't yet received the $10,000 of the purchase money from Lannin and wouldn't play until he received it. By way of making the point clear, he told Dunn that he had a train reservation for Hubbard, Texas, in the event the money was not forthcoming.

Dunn, who had engineered what was at that time the biggest trade in the history of baseball, was frantic at the thought of his star being absent on a day when thousands of Clevelanders who otherwise would not be near the ball park were laying it on the line to see Speaker in an Indian uniform. He phoned Lannin in Boston but couldn't locate him. Spoke refused Dunn's suggestion that Cleveland advance the money.

Then Dunn called his pal, Ban Johnson, president of the American League, and asked him to get Lannin. Ban, who in many quarters was accused of having put over the deal to strengthen Cleveland where he was supposed to have a financial interest, got Lannin on the phone and ordered him to mail the check to Speaker.

Even that didn't budge Tris. Whether he lacked faith in Lannin or in the United States mails, he didn't say but it wasn't until President Johnson got Spoke on the phone and told him that he had ordered Lannin to send him the $10,000 and would guarantee its delivery, that Speaker agreed to put on a Cleveland uniform. He didn't take it off for eleven seasons.

One of the many rumors of the American League in the days

immediately preceding and following the first World War was that there was a feud between Speaker and Babe Ruth. Some said it had its origin because Ruth was a fresh rookie when he came to Boston and Speaker resented his efforts to move in with the regulars when it came time to take batting practice. Others said the Texan made slurring references to Babe's career at St. Mary's Institute for Boys in Baltimore. The cause was a mystery but it was evident to even a casual observer that the big fellow and the Gray Eagle weren't exactly buddies.

Baseball in those days ran more to cliques among the players than it does today. Speaker and Smokey Joe Wood were bosom pals and the brash Ruth had a run-in with Wood one afternoon, an exchange of words over a trifling incident on the ball field. After a while, however, the words were no longer trifling. The challenge was flung and accepted. Wood and Ruth didn't come to blows but neither spoke to the other after, except when it was strictly necessary. Speaker, being Wood's roommate, also gave the Babe the silent treatment.

It was many years later, when Ruth and Speaker were at the initial Hall of Fame ceremonies in Cooperstown, New York, that they became chummy. And this despite the fact that there was no real feud between them, only a tiff between Ruth and Speaker's crony, Wood.

Few people know that there was a half-season feud between Duffy Lewis, left fielder of the great Red Sox outfield, and Speaker, the center fielder. Like the Ruth-Wood fight, it had its inception in a trivial bit of by-play before a Red Sox game.

On one Western trip, several of the Red Sox had their hair clipped to the bone, if you'll pardon the expression. The idea was to alleviate the intense heat of midsummer but the comforts of the close crop were outweighed by its social handicaps. Nobody wanted to go around with a person showing a shaved pate in that period, although now the scalpee might get by socially by claiming to be a member of the Harvard crew.

When the Sox returned to Boston, Spoke thought it was a great joke to sneak up behind Lewis and snatch the cap from his head while Duffy was awaiting his turn at the batting cage. The sensitive Lewis didn't like it and told Speaker he didn't like it. To be precise, what Duffy said was:

"If you ever do that again, Spoke, I'll kill you."

Spoke did it again, a few days later, and while Lewis didn't kill him he had a good try at it. He flung his bat with as much force as he could against his tormentor and, while no bones were broken, Speaker had to be carried from the field.

"For the next three months, we never spoke to each other," recalled Duffy, now the dignified road secretary of the Boston Braves. "If a fly was hit to left center, between us, one of us would say 'I got it' and the other would answer 'Take it.' Outside of that, we said nothing."

It was probable that Speaker from time to time thought of the exhibition game home run he hit against Rube Marquard in Brooklyn the Saturday before the 1916 season opened, the home run he thought solidified him in Boston but which, instead, sent him all the way to Cleveland.

There was another home run which marked a turning point in the career of the Gray Eagle, too, but this wasn't a home run hit by him but by Babe Ruth. It happened in Cleveland in 1919, on July 19. Lee Fohl was the Indian manager when Babe hit this homer but within a few hours Speaker had succeeded him as manager.

Boston had lost nine straight to Cleveland and, although Ruth had hit a homer earlier against Hy Jasper, the Indian pitcher, the Tribe held a 7–3 lead going into the top half of the ninth. Jasper was replaced by Elmer Myers but Boston had one run in, the bases filled and two out. The batter was Ruth.

Fohl halted the game and signalled to the Indian bull pen where a couple of pitchers were warming up. Lee wanted Fritz Coumbe, a left-hander, to pitch to Ruth. This was the proper percentage, if there was any such thing as percentage when it involved pitching to Ruth. Some say Speaker, in center field, disagreed violently with Fohl. Spoke was a sort of assistant-manager, without portfolio, and Fohl often took his advice on pitcher-switches.

Coumbe got a slow curve by the Babe for a strike but the mighty whiffy Ruth took was an omen of what to come. Fritz tried another curve and Ruth hit it out of sight for a grand-slam home run. It won the game for Boston, 8–7, and it elevated Speaker to the managership that night.

Speaker brought the Indians home second that season, which is where the club was when he took charge. Nobody could catch the still untainted White Sox who marched to the American League pennant but Tris caught them the next season to win for Cleveland its first American League pennant in twenty years.

As a manager, Speaker must be termed successful, even though he had only one pennant to show for seven and a half seasons at the helm. There is no telling what successes he might have achieved except that it was his misfortune to be managing in the American League when the Yankees were siphoning away all of the great talent of the Red Sox. He had only two second division finishes as Tribal leader and had the club in second place in 1926, his final year as manager. The Indians didn't finish that high again for fourteen years.

Playing in a World Series was no new experience for the Gray Eagle. He had been one of the Red Sox stars in the feverish 1912 Series with the Giants and it was Speaker who delivered the hit which tied the final game in the tenth and put the winning Boston run on third, whence it scored on a fly ball.

In 1915, the Red Sox played the first Philadelphia team ever to win a National League pennant. After losing the opener to Grover Cleveland Alexander, Boston took the next four straight. It wasn't that easy, however, for the first three Sox wins were by 2 to 1 margins. And, if it hadn't been for a great catch by Speaker, the Phils might have won the second game as well as the opener and changed the entire complexion of the Series. The Phils might have taken it all if they had been able to win the second game.

After Alexander won the opener in Baker Bowl, Philadelphia, the teams met there for the second game. Among the spectators was President Woodrow Wilson and his fiancée, Mrs. Edith Galt. The Sox held a 2–1 lead in the last half of the ninth and Dode Paskert made a desperate bid to tie up the game with a long shot toward the center field seats. Despite a stiff wind, which made judging fly balls difficult, the fleet Speaker caught up with the ball just as it was about to descend among the customers, lunged into the stands and made the catch.

Having added to World Series history with both his batting and his fielding skill, Speaker received the chance to do it with his brains when he brought Cleveland against Brooklyn in 1920. Again he was with a team which made a run of four straight, for this was a five-out-of-nine Series. The Dodgers took two of the first three at Ebbets Field but lost four in a row when the side-show moved to Cleveland.

Speaker had brought the Indians into this Series through all sorts of terrific excitement, including the fatal beaning of his star shortstop, Ray Chapman, in a game at the Polo Grounds on August 16. And the pennant was won in the final week of the season while the discredited stars of the White Sox were suspended for their actions in conspiring to throw the 1919 World Series to Cincinnati.

Cleveland, which had lost its previous series to the White Sox, two games out of three, was in first place by half a game when the indictments were returned against the Black Sox. They won by two games, as they swept a series from Detroit while the patched-up Sox lost two out of three to the St. Louis Browns.

The season ended in turmoil, with the Cleveland papers vehemently asserting that the Indians had won the pennant on their merits. In this opinion, Steve O'Neill, Speaker's doughty catcher concurred, although years later, when Stout Steve was managing the Indians, he didn't always see eye-to-eye with the Cleveland newspapers. Nor they with him.

"We stayed ahead of them all year, even when they were at full strength," declared O'Neill.

If it was a madcap season, it was an ever more febrile World Series. In one game alone, there was an unassisted triple play by Bill Wambsganss, Cleveland second baseman, the only triple play, unassisted or otherwise, in World Series history, and a home run with the bases filled by Elmer Smith, Cleveland outfielder, the first grand slam in Series history and only two have been hit since.

When it was all over, and Cleveland had won five games to two, the ball with which the final putout was made was handed to Speaker as he trotted in from center field. Spoke forced his way across the field to where his mother was sitting and presented the baseball to her. It was the happiest moment he ever had known in baseball. And the happiest he ever was to know.

TRISTRAM E. (TRIS) SPEAKER

Born April 4, 1888, Hubbard City, Tex.
Height 5' 11½". Weight 193. Batted and threw left-handed.

YEAR	CLUB	LEAGUE	POS	G	AB	R	H	SB	AVG
1905	Fort Worth	Polytechnic Institute		...	...	...	...	..	...
1906	Cleburne a	North Tex.	OF	84	287	35	77	33	.260
1907	Houston b	Tex.	OF	118	468	70	147	36	.314
1907	Boston	Amer.	OF	7	18	...	3	..	.167
1908	Little Rock c	So. L	OF	127	471	81	165	28	.350
1908	Boston	Amer.	OF	31	118	12	26	2	.220
1909	Boston	Amer.	OF	143	544	73	168	35	.309
1910	Boston	Amer.	OF	141	538	92	183	35	.340
1911	Boston	Amer.	OF	141	510	88	167	25	.327
1912	Boston	Amer.	OF	153	580	136	222	52	.383
1913	Boston	Amer.	OF	141	520	94	190	46	.365
1914	Boston	Amer.	OF	158	571	100	193	42	.338
1915	Boston	Amer.	OF	150	547	108	196	29	.322
1916	Cleveland d	Amer.	OF	151	546	102	211	35	*.386
1917	Cleveland	Amer.	OF	142	523	90	184	30	.352
1918	Cleveland	Amer.	OF	127	471	73	150	27	.319
1919	Cleveland	Amer.	OF	134	494	83	146	15	.296
1920	Cleveland	Amer.	OF	150	552	137	214	10	.388
1921	Cleveland	Amer.	OF	132	506	107	183	2	.362
1922	Cleveland	Amer.	OF	131	426	85	161	8	.378
1923	Cleveland	Amer.	OF	150	574	133	218	10	.380
1924	Cleveland	Amer.	OF	135	486	94	167	5	.344
1925	Cleveland	Amer.	OF	117	429	79	167	5	.389
1926	Cleveland	Amer.	OF	150	540	96	164	6	.304
1927	Washington g	Amer.	1B-OF	141	523	71	171	9	.327
1928	Philadelphia	Amer.	OF	64	191	28	51	5	.267
	Complete Major League Totals			2789	10207	1181	3515	433	.344

WORLD SERIES RECORDS

YEAR	CLUB	LEAGUE	POS	G	AB	R	H	SB	AVG
1912	Boston	Amer.	OF	8	30	4	9	1	.300
1915	Boston	Amer.	OF	5	17	2	5	0	.294
1920	Cleveland	Amer.	OF	7	25	6	8	0	.320
	World Series Totals			20	72	12	22	1	.306

* Led league
a Transferred to Houston, consideration of Texas Leagues
b Purchased September 2 for $400
c Loaned to Little Rock, February 5; repurchased for $500
d Traded April 12 to Cleveland for Thomas and Jones and cash. Released valued at $55,000

Manager Cleveland Indians, July 20, 1919; December 2, 1926
Manager Newark Bears, November 11, 1928; June 26, 1930
Elected to Hall of Fame, 1937

CHAPTER XXI

THE RUBE

George Edward Waddell

ONE of the great fictions of baseball is the oft-told tale of Rube Waddell, the delightfully eccentric southpaw, holding a one-run lead in the ninth inning and calling in his infielders and his outfielders to sit around him on the grass while he struck out the side, usually on nine pitched balls. This entertaining bit of folklore has been in existence for over forty years and it wasn't so long ago that there were dozens of people who were willing, nay, eager, to swear that they were there and saw it happen.

It never happened, of course. Certainly not in a major league game, for which we have the authority of Connie Mack, who probably had more pleasure and more pain from the unique personality of George Edward Waddell than any other man who ever lived, excepting possibly George Edward himself.

Waddell, who was one of baseball's greatest drawing cards in the pre-Cobb, pre-Ruth era, pitched a tremendous number of exhibition games, as many as Bob Feller or Satchel Paige did in later years. Undoubtedly this stunt was employed on some of Rube's barnstorming tours but, despite the fans who insist they were there when it happened, Waddell never used this dodge in a regular game.

Mack told his biographer, Fred Lieb, that it never happened in American League competition. Ban Johnson, who had just sired the American League and was fighting the strongly entrenched National League, would never have permitted his umpires to countenance such clowning.

"Waddell used to do it quite often in exhibition games," explained Connie, "and it worked—most of the time.

"I remember one game in Memphis when for some reason

244

Mike Powers caught Rube instead of Ossie Schreckengost, his regular catcher. Harry Davis was managing the club for me that day and we had a 6–0 lead in the ninth when Rube called in his infielders and outfielders. He fanned the first two batters and struck out the third, too, but Powers dropped the ball on the third strike and the batter reached first.

"The next two batters hit little pop flies behind Rube and his tongue was hanging out chasing them. He wanted the players to return but Davis insisted that Waddell work it out the best he could. He finally struck out the last batter with the bases filled, and this time Powers held the ball. Rube was just about exhausted by then."

Mack's clarification of this particular Waddell legend is indicative of the snarls facing anyone trying to record the antics of the Rube. He did a great many bizarre things, perhaps more than any other ballplayer, including Babe Ruth, but helpful historians added to the confusion by inventing a great many fanciful feats that the Rube did not perform.

It is unfortunate that fact and fable are intermingled in the story of Waddell and even more regrettable that early baseball chroniclers devoted so much more space to Rube's deeds off the diamond than to his truly remarkable achievements on the pitching mound. The left-hander was one of the greatest pitchers of all time. Cy Young goes so far as to call him the greatest southpaw of all time. Ed Barrow, founder of the Yankee baseball empire and discoverer of Hans Wagner, picked Waddell as his left-handed pitcher on his all-time team.

Not only have the historians betrayed Waddell but even the statisticians have muddied up his record. Box scores now are checked and cross-checked with the meticulousness of the Federal Reserve records, but in Rube's day the auditors were not so careful. Even *The Sporting News,* aptly called "baseball's bible," finds itself unable to account for some dozen games in which Rube appeared. His total strikeouts have been variously listed as 2,375 and 2,369.

Rube had exceptional control for a left-hander. He walked only 81 men in 1904, in which year he started 46 games for Connie and finished 39 of them. He won 25 and lost 19, which was the least impressive part of his record. This was the year in which

Waddell fanned 343, which stood as the major league strikeout record until Feller's great postwar season of 1946. In 1902, Rube walked only 67 while fanning 248. He consistently bagged about four strikeouts for each pass he gave up.

If Waddell was a hard man to hit he was even more difficult to manage. No less a disciplinarian than Fred Clarke, the game-cock outfielder and pilot of the Pittsburgh Pirates, gave up on him, even though he instantly saw that Rube had pitching greatness. Fred had him at both Louisville and Pittsburgh and found the southpaw too much for him.

"I could have stood his drinking, maybe," related Clarke nearly a half-century later, "but I couldn't forgive the fact that he wouldn't get serious."

It wasn't until Connie Mack caught up with him that Waddell came even close to cashing in on the pitching genius that was his. And Rube cashed in only on the record books, for it is doubtful if his top salary ever went as high as $3,000 a year. Connie did make a winning pitcher of Waddell for a six-year period, in which the Rube averaged 22 victories a season and never had fewer than 200 strikeouts in any of those seasons between 1902 and 1907.

Mack caught up with Waddell in the little town of Punxsutawney, Pennsylvania, whither the Rube had drifted after he decided that he could stand no more of Clarke's iron hand. Punxsutawney was about midway between Bradford, where Waddell had been born 24 years before, and Pittsburgh, which he had fled.

Punxsutawney seemed ideal to Rube. He hunted and fished and pitched when he jolly well felt like it. He had no worries, unless you want to count a flock of small tabs about town, which Rube never did. He was getting by, which was all he ever asked.

Mack was managing Milwaukee at the time and he remembered Waddell's pitching from two years before when the course of the southpaw's peregrinations had carried him to Grand Rapids, Michigan. Rube had thrown a two-hit shutout at Milwaukee and fanned thirteen. Connie knew that Waddell had jumped the Pirates and asked permission to talk to him, which was given forthwith by Barney Dreyfuss, the Pittsburgh owner.

Waddell had no desire to leave hospitable Punxsutawney as

long as his credit held out. Eventually Mack had to go and get him, pay off the various bills he had run up with the local merchants and personally shepherd him aboard the train to Milwaukee. Connie swears that a group of citizens met him on the station platform as he was leaving, shook his hand and said, "You are doing us a great favor. We feel that Waddell is a great pitcher but we feel that Punxsutawney will be better off without him."

Mack gave Waddell his head and the Rube thrived, both on and off the field. In fact, he did so well that Dreyfuss demanded his return and Connie had to give him up. It probably was the only time in history that a manager reluctantly parted with the left-hander. It was 1902 before their paths crossed again and this time Mack acquired him from Los Angeles. The Rube was on his way to fame, glory and Ossis Schreckengost.

Born Ossee Freeman Schreckengost at New Bethlehem, Pennsylvania, in 1875, this amiable athlete spent several years discovering whether he was a first baseman, outfielder or catcher, finally settling for the latter position. He was the first of the one-handed catchers. Ossie would rearrange the padding in his glove until it was as limber a that of an infielder. He caught everything in his gloved hand.

Schreck—the name was abbreviated to that by the good-natured catcher at the behest of the writers—had just about made up his mind to settle down to the trade of catching when Waddell joined the Athletics in 1902, which also was Schreck's first year with the club.

Ossie and Rube were battery mates on and off the field. It was Schreck who pulled Waddell out of the harbor at Jacksonville, Florida, when Rube decided to commit suicide because of unrequited love; Schreck who demanded Mack insert a clause in Waddell's contract forbidding him to eat animal crackers in bed, this being at a period when ballplayers slept two in a bed to cut down expenses.

It was under Schreckengost that Waddell had most of his great seasons. Rube, who pitched almost full overhand, was a rubber-armed pitcher, even in an era when one pitcher did almost as much work as two moderns. He was strong and he was big, six feet, two inches, 200 pounds.

Rube was proud of his strength and bear-wrestled anybody he could con into a match. In fact, one spring when the A's were training at Jacksonville, a man visited Mack with the complaint that Waddell was wrestling his alligators in a side show, spoiling the guy's act and passing the hat among the spectators!

Before a game with the Red Sox one day, Waddell wrestled George (Candy) La Chance, the big Boston first baseman, for nearly a half hour before pinning him. Chance was unable to play for the Red Sox that afternoon but Waddell went out and blanked the opposition.

It was Rube's love of horseplay which deprived him of his only chance to pitch in a World Series. Through the years the story has become distorted that Waddell's shoulder was injured as the result of a friendly wrestling match with a fellow pitcher, Andy Coakley. Coakley, who had been an outstanding college pitcher at Holy Cross, and was for many years head baseball coach at Columbia University, gave an authentic account of the incident in a letter to J. G. Taylor Spink, publisher of *The Sporting News,* in 1943.

Coakley explained that he had rejoined the Athletics after visiting his folks in Providence, Rhode Island, as their train came through that city, after the conclusion of a series with the Red Sox on September 1, 1905.

"When the train stopped, Gene Mack, Connie's brother, told me to watch my straw hat, as Rube was breaking every one in sight," wrote Coakley. "I had a suitcase in one hand and a canvas bag in the other. I put my straw hat under my coat, in the back, and walked up to our car.

"Rube came after me, and as I backed away I swung the bag lightly and hit Rube, who slipped and fell on his left shoulder. I have always believed that it was more because Rube was overheated rather than the force of the fall that caused the subsequent troubles; that Rube caught cold in his slightly bruised shoulder."

The Pullman conductor arranged for Waddell and Coakley to shake hands immediately after the scuffle, which they did. There never was any animosity between Rube and Andy, but the left-hander could pitch no more that year and was sidelined throughout the World Series with the Giants, which the National Leaguers won four games to one, with all five games ending in shutouts.

There is no question that Waddell's injury cost him a chance for his greatest season. He won 27 games and lost ten and missed the last five weeks of the schedule. This also was the season in which the Rube defeated the great Cy Young in a twenty-inning game, 4 to 2.

Waddell made a good comeback from his shoulder injury in 1906, turning in a 16–16 record and pitching eight shutouts, but Connie still had his troubles with him and the fun-loving Schreck. Rube was beaten up and robbed in a back alley in Montgomery, Alabama, where the team trained; and Schreck had the ball club evicted, en masse, from a hotel in New Orleans because he showed what he thought of a tough steak by sending the waiter for a hammer and nailing the steak on the wall of the dining room.

As good a tribute to Waddell's physical prowess as any is that Mack employed him as a professional football player in the off-season of 1902! This is one of the darker chapters in Connie's life, but he managed a pro football team which claimed the championship of the United States. They played at Shibe Park and even played under lights, more than thirty years before Larry MacPhail brought the arcs to the major leagues in Cincinnati.

Waddell wasn't a skillful player but football then wasn't the intricate game it was to become later. It required principally a strong back and Rube had that to offer. He finally quit the team after an incident at the Monongahela House in Pittsburgh, where he returned somewhat the worse for wear after explaining to Mack that he had been to see a billiard match between Willie Hoppe and Alfredo DeOro.

One look at Rube in the lobby convinced Mack that nobody could get into that condition watching a billiard match, not even if the contestants had paused between shots to belabor him with their cues. Connie curtly told him to go upstairs to bed. As Rube approached the desk for his key he pulled his handkerchief from his pocket to mop his fevered brow. As he did so a loaded revolver fell from his pocket and discharged itself, the bullet imbedding itself in the office wall. Rube quietly went upstairs to bed.

"That man is unpredictable," said Mack to the clerk in what must be ranked as one of the great understatements of all time.

It wasn't anything as complicated as a loaded revolver which caused Mack finally to get rid of Waddell after six years. Connie had all sorts of troubles with Rube financially. It wasn't that the southpaw was looking for big salaries but simply that he never had any money.

Waddell resorted to all sorts of dodges to get his "walking-around" money. One of his tricks was to "lose" his watch charm, which he received as a member of the 1905 American League champions. He would then offer a "reward," which Connie would pay for the return of the emblem. Invariably, the finder turned out to be a bartender friend of Rube's.

One of Waddell's pet deals was to offer a saloonkeeper a baseball in exchange for bar credit, the baseball being the one he had pitched in his memorable twenty-inning victory over Cy Young and the Red Sox. There must have been dozens of them scattered throughout the country.

Yet it was none of these things which ultimately led to Mack sending Waddell to the Browns. The truth was that baseball was growing up, edging toward being a business and no longer could be conducted as informally as the Rube would like. There couldn't be time off for chasing fire engines or for fishing or benders. Especially not for benders.

In late September, 1907, the Athletics led Detroit by three percentage points as the Tigers came to Columbia Park to open a three-game series. If the Mackmen could take two out of three, the flag was in, but the visitors won the first game when George Mullin edged Eddie Plank by 5 to 4. And, though there never was any decision in the other two games, that victory by Mullin won the pennant.

The game of September 28, a Saturday, was rained out, and with no Sunday ball a double-header was scheduled for Monday before the largest baseball crowd Philadelphia had ever seen. It also saw more baseball history than any one crowd has a right to expect, including the swan song of Waddell in an Athletic uniform.

It was Mack's original plan to start Jimmy Dygert in the opener and come back with Plank, Friday's victim, in the second game. Waddell had been what Connie chose to call "unreliable" in the stretch and was pretty much shelved.

The A's gave Dygert a three-run lead against Wild Bill Donovan in the first inning, but Mack lifted Dygert when the Tigers scored in the second because he thought Jimmy, who made two errors, seemed nervous. In came Waddell. If ever a game should have been a cinch for a pitcher of Rube's talents, this was it.

Waddell was leading Donovan 7 to 1 going into the seventh. Two errors and a pass by Rube filled the bases with Tigers with none out. Wahoo Sam Crawford doubled home two runs. Infield outs by Ty Cobb and Claude Rossman scored two more and Detroit was only two behind.

The A's scored another run against Donovan in their half but Waddell also yielded a run in the eighth and carried an 8–6 lead into the ninth. Crawford singled and Cobb, who had hit only five home runs all season, picked this moment to hit his fifth, a line drive which whistled over the fence in right, tying the score and virtually blowing Waddell out of Philadelphia.

With Plank replacing Waddell in the tenth, the teams battled all the way to the seventeenth, when the game was called because of darkness with the score still tied and the Tigers, by virtue of their one victory in the series opener, still leading the league.

Rube made one more start after his thumping by the Tigers, against Washington, and was taken out in the first inning after giving up three walks. Detroit won the pennant and Waddell was on his way to the Browns.

Waddell wasn't the same pitcher once he got away from Mack and his buddy, Schreck. He had spots of effectiveness, to be sure, such as the game against Philadelphia in which he struck out sixteen of his former teammates for what was then a record, although it since has been surpassed. He won nineteen games for the Browns in 1908 but began to fade from there on.

If Waddell seemed lost without Schreck it was mutual and Mack couldn't get much catching out of big Ossie. Schreck didn't even last a full season after the Rube left, and was released to the White Sox near the end of 1908. There was no fun for Ossie without Waddell.

It was ironic that Schreck and Waddell both died in the same year, 1914, and at approximately the same age, 38, and of the same dread disease, tuberculosis. The catcher died in Philadelphia, Rube in San Antonio, Texas.

Pongo Joe Cantillon, himself one of the colorful figures of that period, salvaged Waddell from Newark and had him pitching at Minneapolis for him. Rube came back to win twenty for Joe in 1911, but in the spring of the following year he contracted the illness which led to his death.

Cantillon took Waddell to his home in Hickman, Kentucky, to spend the winter. The town, situated on the east bank of the Mississippi just south of its confluence with the Ohio, was threatened with inundation early in 1912 when the Mississippi rose. Waddell joined with the volunteer workers, heroically standing above his waist in the chilly February waters as he passed sandbags up to those who were stacking them on the levee. Out of these round-the-clock labors came a cold and a racking cough which never left Waddell.

He still tried to pitch but it was too much of a physical strain. He quit a little more than a year later and Cantillon paid his way into the San Antonio sanitarium.

Waddell, shrunken now to a little more than 100 pounds, died on April 1, 1914, preceding Schreckengost to the grave by about three months. There is a stone tablet over his grave, erected almost ten years later by John McGraw when the Giants did their spring training at San Antonio. Learning that Rube's grave was virtually unmarked, McGraw got in touch with Connie Mack and, with the co-operation of H. J. Benson, owner of the San Antonio Club, a fund of $500 was raised for a six-foot shaft of granite, topped with a baseball. The inscription reads simply: "George Edward Waddell—1876–1914"

He never did like strangers to call him "Rube."

GEORGE EDWARD WADDELL

Born October 13, 1876 at Bradford, Pa.
Height, 6' 2". Weight, 205. Threw and batted left-handed.

YEAR	CLUB	LEAGUE	G	W	L	AVE	H	BB	SO
1897	Louisville	Nat.	2	0	1	.000	13	6	5
1898	Detroit	W. L.	9	4	4	.500	61	30	31
1899	Columbus-Grand Rap.	W. L.	40	26	8	.764	249	97	200
1899	Louisville	Nat.	10	7	2	.778	71	16	41
1900	Pittsburgh	Nat.	29	9	11	.450	186	53	133
1900	Milwaukee	Amer.	15	10	3	.769	90	20	75
1901	Pittsburgh-Chicago	Nat.	31	13	16	.448	248	67	168
1902	Los Angeles	P. C.	19	12	7	.621	...	...	...
1902	Philadelphia	Amer.	33	23	7	.766	224	67	210
1903	Philadelphia	Amer.	39	21	16	.568	265	74	301
1904	Philadelphia	Amer.	46	25	19	.568	302	81	343
1905	Philadelphia	Amer.	45	27	10	.730	229	91	286
1906	Philadelphia	Amer.	43	16	16	.500	219	89	203
1907	Philadelphia	Amer.	44	19	13	.594	247	71	226
1908	St. Louis	Amer.	43	19	14	.576	223	90	232
1909	St. Louis	Amer.	31	11	14	.440	204	57	141
1910	St. Louis	Amer.	10	3	1	.750	31	9	11
1910	Newark	E. L.	15	5	3	.625	73	41	53
1911	Minneapolis	A. A.	54	20	17	.541	262	96	185
1912	Minneapolis	A. A.	33	12	6	.667	138	59	113
1913	Virginia	No. L.	15	3	9	.250	86	20	82
	Major League Totals		421	203	143	.587	2552	791	2375

CHAPTER XXII

THE FLYING DUTCHMAN

John Peter Wagner

BACK IN 1897, the National League was a sprawling, twelve-club organization. There wasn't much national interest in baseball and there weren't too many rules, although there may have been too many clubs. In addition to the eight clubs now comprising the senior circuit, Louisville, Baltimore, Cleveland and Washington also held franchises. Few clubs were making any money, none was making much.

Interest in the National League was sporadic. Certainly there was no sign of fever-pitch excitement on July 19, 1887, when Baltimore's rugged Orioles came in to play Fred Clarke's Louisville Club. There were a couple of hundred fans about, mostly for the purpose of hurling abuse at the visitors. The home club, eleventh in the league, was beneath abuse.

Considering the historical importance that many of the players on the field that day were to acquire later in life, it is a pity that there wasn't a larger crowd. John Joseph McGraw, the truculent bantam was in the Oriole lineup and so were Uncle Wilbert Robinson, Hughey Jennings, Jack Doyle, Wee Willie Keeler, Joe Kelley among others. And Clarke put a player into the Louisville lineup that afternoon who was to last longer than all of the others and to outshine all of them, John Peter Wagner, better known as Honus or Hans.

Wagner received a baptism of fire in the National League. On his first time at bat, he rifled a single, the first of 3430 hits he was to make in his career. On his second trip, he blasted what should have been a triple.

"It wasn't, though," smiled Honus as he described the play years later. "Jack Doyle, feller who became a big-shot scout with

254

and, as a consequence, made up one of the four one-hitters Alexander pitched that season to set a National League mark which has never been surpassed. Yet, oddly enough, Alexander in his great career, which embraced 373 National League victories, never pitched a no-hit game!

Defensively, Wagner was one of the great shortstops of all time. And his contemporaries insist he would have been equally sensational had he remained in the outfield, the position he played when he broke into the National League. Literally, the Flying Dutchman was such a natural ballplayer that he didn't know where he belonged. He was a big league regular for five years before he settled on shortstop as his regular position.

It was Clarke who made Wagner a permanent shortstop, shifting him to that position in 1902 against the expressed wishes and opinions of the Pittsburgh press and fans. The Pirate incumbent, one Bones Ely, was a smooth fielder, slender and graceful, the antithesis of Wagner in appearance. It seemed impossible that the lumbering, bow-legged Honus could make an adequate replacement for him. But Hans, wherever he played, always was more than adequate. The great throwing arm he employed in the outfield was even more valuable when he roamed from second to third making impossible stops and rifle-like pegs.

Until the day he died, John McGraw always maintained that Hans Wagner was the greatest ballplayer who ever lived. The fact that the Dutchman was a National Leaguer may have influenced Mac's opinion but it is more likely that the leader of the Giants rated Honus over Ty Cobb and Babe Ruth because Wagner wound up as an infielder. All other things being equal, an infielder always is more valuable to a club than an outfielder because he has so many more opportunities to help on the defense.

At the close of the nineteenth century, the National League was reduced from its unwieldy twelve clubs to eight. Fourteen of the Louisville players were transferred to Pittsburgh, among them such illustrious baseball names as Wagner, Clarke, Deacon Phillippe, Tommy Leach, Rube Waddell and Chief Zimmer. It was in Pittsburgh, hard by his native Carnegie, that Wagner was to spend the rest of his baseball days and achieve his greatest glory.

Honus by this time was twenty-six, or twenty-eight, depending upon which version of his age you accepted. He had put in three National League seasons at Louisville and had revealed himself as a formidable hitter, even though it hadn't yet been decided whether his talents were best employed in the outfield or at first or third bases.

It was just as well that Wagner came into the compact National League in his maturity, for it was no place for a callow youth. At the beginning of this century, there was almost a league within a a league in the National—the Giants, the Cubs and the Pirates. And it was to remain that way for more than a decade. In the thirteen seasons between 1901 and 1913, New York won five pennants and Pittsburgh and Chicago four each. None of the three ever finished out of the first division in that stretch.

As the star of the Pirates and, usually, the league's leading batsman, Wagner was a target for both Giants and Cubs. Under the stinging lash of Clarke's tongue Wagner learned to retaliate and his rivals learned to give him racing room. Honus didn't deal out much rough stuff but he didn't take much, either. Baseball still was fun to him. He played it to the hilt but he played it without rancor. As a result, he was allowed to go on his Olympian way, aloof from the brawling of lesser mortals.

No better example of the spirit of the baseball of those times can be presented than the 1909 World Series, in which Wagner, as the National League's leading hitter, outshone Ty Cobb, the American League's leading batter. It was the year Forbes Field opened and the Pirates made it a memorable one for Pittsburgh fans by winning the World Series, four games to three.

Manager Clarke, in the Series opener in Pittsburgh, nicked George Mullin for a home run. Wagner, who followed Fred in the Pirate batting order, knew what was coming. Honus always stood deep in the box and away from the plate but it didn't matter, for Mullin plunked a fast ball against his ribs.

Later Cobb, on first base, yelled to Wagner, "Hey, Krauthead! I'm coming down." Wagner's reply, "I'll be here," was so softly spoken that it was heard only by Dots Miller, the Pirate second baseman. True to his word, the Georgia Peach did go down, sliding into second with his spikes gleaming. George Gibson, the Pirate catcher, made an accurate throw and Wagner gloved the ball and laid it against Cobb's face so purposefully that Ty got up spitting blood and teeth.

The 1909 Series was a great one for Wagner and for the National League. Honus had had a poor Series against the Red Sox in 1903 but in this one he batted .333, outhitting Cobb by more than a hundred points and he stole six bases. No player ever displayed a greater aptitude for larceny in a World Series, although Jake Slagle of the Cubs also stole six bases successfully in the 1907 World Series.

Wagner's base-running skill, like his adroitness in the field, is forgotten because of his great hitting, yet the bow-legged Honus was one of the all-time greats on the bases. Only three players in the history of baseball stole more bases than Wagner—Cobb, Billy Hamilton and Max Carey. Honus stole 720 bases in his career and, in one five-year stretch from 1904 through 1908, he snagged a total of 277 bases, an average of slightly better than 55 per season!

Horatio Alger sagas to the contrary, the work Wagner had done as a child in the mines was not the reason for his rugged constitution. The dampness of the pits left Honus susceptible to rheumatism and, after the great triumphs of 1909, he announced he was through with baseball. Barney Dreyfuss, the Pirate owner, who also had been president in Louisville when Hans broke in, personally waited on the Flying Dutchman, along with Manager Clarke. They persuaded Wagner that the Pirates needed him and Honus came back to play seven more seasons as a regular, four of them as a .300 hitter.

Honus was well over forty when he finally insisted he had had enough. Fred Clarke quit after the 1915 season and the old Pirate gang didn't seem the same to Honus without "ole Cap," as he called his leader. Wagner worked under Jimmy Callahan in 1916 and through part of 1917 when Callahan was let out and Honus himself installed in his place. Hans took the job distrustfully and with foreboding.

As a manager Wagner lasted exactly three days. He took the job on July 1 and resigned on July 4, when Dreyfuss appointed Hugo Bezdek to replace him.

"It ain't for me," said old Honus simply as he handed over the managerial portfolio.

Wagner still retained his great love for baseball, even after he quit the Pirates in 1917. He essayed many business ventures, including the inevitable sporting goods store, but none of them enriched him. A decade after he had quit, he still picked up a few bucks playing first base for the Green Cab Co. of Pittsburgh. I saw him in a twilight game at Forbes Field one evening against the Homestead Grays, a powerful Negro team, and on his first trip to the plate, Honus lashed a triple off the top of the exit gate in right center.

After the death of Dreyfuss, his son-in-law, Bill Benswanger took over the presidency of the club and in 1933 appointed Wagner as coach, a job he has held ever since despite changes of both managership and ownership.

The job opened new vistas to the sixty-year-old veteran. First, it gave him an income and security, and second, it returned him to baseball. His first visit to Brooklyn, of all places, was celebrated with a parade around the town and a civic banquet. And Honus, shy and retiring in private life when he was a player, suddenly found himself much in demand as a speaker around the rubber-chicken circuit in the winter.

Thus, it was late in life that Wagner developed a Munchausen complex as remarkable as his hitting skill had been. With a merry twinkle, Honus told the most outrageous stories from the dais, apparently determined to seek the breaking point of the credulity of his audience.

"Ever hear about the time I was at bat with the bases filled and none out and never got a chance to swing at the ball?" Wagner is likely to ask an interviewer. "We wuz playin' the Cubs and Tinker and Evers and Chance, them slick guys, they picked all our runners off base, clean as a whistle, without a ball ever being thrown to the plate!"

On an opening day a few years ago, Wagner was dreamily listening to the band recruited for Forbes Field for the occasion, a band of some twenty tootlers, dressed in uniforms somewhat the worse for wear. Suddenly he turned to a rookie alongside him on the Pirate bench.

JOHN PETER (HANS) WAGNER

Born February 24, 1874, Mansfield (now Carnegie), Pa.
Height 5' 11". Weight 200. Batted and threw right-handed.

YEAR	CLUB	LEAGUE	POS	G	AB	R	H	2B	3B	HR	RBI	BA
1895	Adrian	Mich. St.	SS	20	...	...	...	..	..	..	...	.365
1895	Steubenville	Tri. St.	SS-OF	44	...	44	...	..	..	..	...	.402
1895	Warren	Iron-Oil	SS	65	...	...	...	..	..	..	...	.369
1896	Paterson	Atl.	1B-3B-OF	109	416	106	145	..	..	..	...	.348
1897	Paterson	Atl.	3B	74	301	61	114	..	..	..	...	.379
1897	Louisville	Nat.	OF	61	241	38	83	17	4	2	...	.344
1898	Louisville	Nat.	1B-3B	148	591	80	180	31	4	10	...	.305
1899	Louisville *	Nat.	3B-OF	144	549	102	197	47	13	7	...	*.380
1900	Pittsburgh	Nat.	OF	134	528	107	201	*45	*22	4	...	.352
1901	Pittsburgh	Nat.	IF-OF	141	556	100	196	x39	10	6	...	*.329
1902	Pittsburgh	Nat.	IF-OF	137	538	*105	177	*33	16	3	...	.355
1903	Pittsburgh	Nat.	SS	129	512	97	182	30	*19	5	...	*.349
1904	Pittsburgh	Nat.	SS	132	490	97	171	*44	14	4	...	.363
1905	Pittsburgh	Nat.	SS	147	548	114	199	32	14	6	...	*.339
1906	Pittsburgh	Nat.	SS	140	516	x103	175	*38	9	2	...	.350
1907	Pittsburgh	Nat.	SS	142	515	98	180	*38	14	6	*91	*.354
1908	Pittsburgh	Nat.	SS	151	568	100	*201	*39	*19	10	*106	*.339
1909	Pittsburgh	Nat.	SS	137	495	92	168	*39	10	5	102	.320
1910	Pittsburgh	Nat.	SS	150	556	90	*178	*34	8	4	84	*.334
1911	Pittsburgh	Nat.	SS-1B	130	473	87	158	23	16	9	108	.324
1912	Pittsburgh	Nat.	SS	145	558	91	181	35	20	7	94	.300
1913	Pittsburgh	Nat.	SS	114	413	41	124	18	4	3	55	.252
1914	Pittsburgh	Nat.	3B-SS	150	552	60	139	15	9	1	46	.274
1915	Pittsburgh	Nat.	SS	156	566	68	155	32	17	6	78	.287
1916	Pittsburgh	Nat.	1B-SS	123	432	45	124	15	9	1	38	.265
1917	Pittsburgh	Nat.	1B-3B-SS	74	230	15	61	7	1	0	22	.265

Major League Totals   2785   10427   1740   3430   651   252   101   824   .329

WORLD SERIES RECORD

YEAR	CLUB	LEAGUE	POS	G	AB	R	H	2B	3B	HR	RBI	BA
1903	Pittsburgh	Nat.	SS	8	28	2	6	1	0	0	4	.214
1909	Pittsburgh	Nat.	SS	7	24	4	8	2	1	0	5	.333

World Series Totals   15   52   6   14   3   1   0   9   .269

* Led League
x Tied for lead
Coach, Pittsburgh Pirates, February 1933
Elected to Hall of Fame, 1936

"Same band they had here when they opened the park thirty-five years ago," Wagner informed the bug-eyed rookie. "Had about a hunnert pieces in the band then. 'Course, a lot of 'em has died off during the years."

Wagner's tall yarns were well received by the Pirate players, regular and rookie alike. They did much to relieve pre-game tensions. As a coach, Wagner was frankly a pensioner.

Most ball players and managers would have resented the presence of Wagner. The streak of sentiment among baseball people is neither as wide as a barn door nor as deep as a well. Yet such was the pleasant disposition of Honus that he was respected by all, which perhaps is the greatest tribute to his position in baseball, an honor greater by far than his installation in the Hall of Fame at Cooperstown, since that was coming to him through his skills. This comes to him from his personality.

Frankie Gustine, who put in several years with the Pirates without making any appreciable headway toward a niche in Cooperstown, summed it up pretty aptly.

"He must have been one of the truly great ball players," said Gustine sincerely. "I wasn't even alive when he was playing but if you hang around him very long, you sort of sense that he must have been great."

He was, too.

CHAPTER XXIII

THE WORKHORSE

Edward Arthur Walsh

STAID old permanent guests of the Broadway Central Hotel were a little startled by the proceedings that crisp afternoon of February 2, 1951. It took a certain tuning up of hearing aids for them to understand that the National League had been founded in that very same hostelry just three quarters of a century before and that this was the jubilee celebration.

Ford C. Frick, National League president, had invited all living members of the Hall of Fame and those who could make the trip were there. It was an impressive turnout and sports writers, young and old, goggled at not only the stars of yesterday but the stars of the day before yesterday, for they were all there—Ty Cobb and Tris Speaker, Eddie Collins and George Sisler, Cy Young and Kid Nichols, Carl Hubbell and Mel Ott, Mickey Cochrane and Charley Gehringer, Hugh Duffy, Ed Walsh, Jimmy Foxx, Pie Traynor and Rogers Hornsby.

Not only were the Hall of Famers present but Frick had invited all the ball players who lived within a reasonable distance of New York. There was Jack Warhop, victim of the first home run Babe Ruth had ever hit; Jimmy Ring and Lew Wendell, an old Philadelphia battery; Dut Chalmers, who pitched for the 1915 Phils; Otto Miller, the battery mate of Brooklyn's fabulous Nap Rucker; John Arnold Heydler, the retired president of the National League; Edward Grant Barrow, the Yankee brain; Al Moore, former Giant and Cardinal outfielder; Fresco Thompson, who had made the climb from a Philly infielder to a Dodger vice president; Moe Berg, the linguistic catcher and literally dozens of others. It was possibly the greatest concentration of baseball names ever assembled at any one spot, not even excepting the initial Hall of Fame Day at Cooperstown in 1939.

First there was a sidewalk broadcast to open the ceremonies— there really were no ceremonies, just an open house. Which explains how a reporter happened to ease up to a table where Berg was in conversation with a tall, husky black-haired chap, who obviously had the stamp of athlete on him.

Moe, ever the gentleman, turned to his reporter friend and introduced his acquaintance. "I'd like you to meet Big Ed Walsh," he said.

The reporter gaped, thinking Berg was up to one of his practical jokes. "Come off it, Moe," said the writer. "Why, Big Ed Walsh must be seventy if he's a day."

"No," said the stranger, "only sixty-nine."

It was not only to the reporter but to most of those present one of the biggest surprises of the afternoon. Walsh, who had pitched and won two World Series games for the Chicago White Sox, the famous Hitless Wonders of 1906, didn't look to be fifty. He looked, in fact, younger than some of the ball players who had quit within the last decade.

Walsh was one of the old-timers who stayed young. A handsome man, his six feet unstooped, his weight about the 190 pounds of his playing days, his hair luxuriant and still jet black, Ed looked as if he still might go out and work a few innings. It was difficult to believe that Walsh had set a record some 43 years before for pitching durability which still stands.

Walsh had two sons who became professional pitchers, although with nothing like their dad's success. One, Big Ed Junior, had pitched for the White Sox the same as his dad had and died before he was forty of rheumatic fever. The other, Bob, had had a tryout with the Yankees but wasn't quite a big leaguer.

Walsh was a spitballer and one of the best. Although the pitch was outlawed in 1920, there seemed to be something about the delivery which kept those who used it active long beyond their years. Red Faber, for instance, was winning for the White Sox when he was 45; Burleigh Grimes was pitching in the majors at forty; so were Clarence Mitchell and Bill Doak. And John Picus Quinn pitched in a World Series when he was 44, by his own admission.

Branch Rickey once declared that if the spitball were again legalized it would add to the pitching longevity of many who were fading from baseball. He also said it could be taught to a player in a couple of weeks. The last seems dubious, for the spitball isn't something you can pick up like the common cold.

The moisture of a spitball is applied to the tips of the first two fingers of the throwing hand. These fingers are placed on the top side of the ball, the thumb underneath. The ball is held firmly, but not tightly, and is delivered with a wrist snap that makes it come off the thumb and slip from under the moistened finger tips. The ball rotates with a forward spin and sinks as it nears the plate. While the pitch may be easily taught, since the wrist snap is the most important part, controlling it is not so easy.

The spitter, in the days when it was legal, usually was picked up by rookies from veterans on the club. Walsh was taught the spitter when he was breaking in with the White Sox at their spring camp at Marlin, Texas, by Elmer Stricklett. There is some mystery as to where Stricklett, who also was in his first year with the Sox, learned the delivery. One source said it was George Hildebrand, who later became an American League umpire. Others claimed he learned it from a minor leaguer at Newark named Joe Corridon.

Wherever Stricklett picked up the delivery, he never mastered it with the skill of his pupil. Elmer went on from the White Sox to Brooklyn, where he lingered a few years without doing anything sensational, but Walsh was to be a White Sox hero for a decade with the pitch.

There are many stories of Walsh but the best insight into Big Ed is the story of the 1908 season. This was the year in which he set most of his records, but the story itself ties around the unusual American League pennant race of that season. It was the first of four times in American League history when the pennant was decided on the last day of the season, and it didn't happen again until 1944, when the Browns won their only American League pennant. The other last-day winners were the Tigers in 1945 and the Yankees in 1949. Cleveland, of course, won in a postseason play-off in 1948.

The American League race of 1908 was unusual, to say the least. On the final Saturday of the season, the Tigers and Sox had two games left against each other, and the Indians had three with the Browns. Because of rain, only Cleveland was to play the regular 154-game schedule. Detroit was playing 153 games, the White Sox 152.

On the penultimate day, Walsh stepped out and beat the Tigers 6 to 1, while the Indians split a double-header with the Browns. Cleveland could have won the pennant had it swept all three games with the Browns, regardless of what the Tigers and Sox did, but the one defeat in the Saturday double-header knocked out the Indians. Thus, due to Walsh's victory over the Tigers, the pennant was up for grabs at the old South Side Park in Chicago on the last day of the season. And Detroit grabbed it when Wild Bill Donovan pitched a two-hit shutout to beat Doc White, 7 to 0.

It was entirely due to Walsh's durability that Fielder Jones was able to keep his club in the race. This was the year that Big Ed really was a workhorse in the stretch. The victory he scored over Detroit on the next-to-last day of the season was his fortieth! It also was his 65th appearance of the season and he told Manager Jones he was ready to start the next day. He didn't start but he did relieve, the 66th game in which he pitched that season. The 464 innings he pitched that season is a still-standing record and one which is likely to stand for some time, if not forever.

In the last eight days of that feverish race, Walsh appeared in no fewer than six games. On September 29, he pitched both games of a double-header against Boston and won both, allowing three hits in the first game and only four in the nightcap.

Then, with a rest of only two days between starts, Big Ed became involved in what still remains one of the most fantastic games of all time. Facing the Indians—or Naps as they then were known in honor of their manager. Napoleon Lajoie—in Cleveland, Walsh fanned fifteen, walked only one, allowed four singles and was beaten 1 to 0! The lone Cleveland run was scored under circumstances which would drive strong men to drink and kill weak men.

Joe Birmingham opened the Cleveland third with a short fly to center which Eddie Hahn couldn't quite reach. It was the first hit of the game and Walsh almost erased it by picking Birmingham off first with a snap throw to Frank Isbell. Joe, with no chance to get back, lit out for second and Isbell's throw hit him on the head and caromed into the outfield, Birmingham reaching third. George Perring hit an easy infield grounder on which Bimingham had to hold third and Walsh then fanned his pitching opponent, Addie Joss.

The leadoff batter, Wilbur Goode, had two strikes on him, and the next pitch got away from Ossie Schreckengost for a passed ball, Birmingham scoring. Then Walsh whipped a third strike past Goode, whom he was to fan four times in the course of the afternoon.

While it was admittedly a tough way to lose a ball game, it also must be admitted that Walsh was pitted against a pretty good pitcher. In fact, Joss pitched a perfect game, not a Chicago player reaching base. There have been only a half-dozen perfect games in baseball history, none since Charley Robertson in 1922 and Joss's game was the only perfect game pitched in the heat of a pennant race. All the others have been in the spring.

Thus Walsh, who had pitched and won a double-header on Sunday, ran into a perfect game on Wednesday and his fifteen strikeouts went for naught. Far from being upset, Big Ed was back in the lists on Thursday to relieve Frank Smith in the seventh.

Of all the fine pitching Walsh did in his career, he considers his relief job against Cleveland that day his outstanding achievement. The Sox had a 3–1 lead and Cleveland had filled the bases with one out when Ed rushed in from the bull pen.

Relating the story many years later to Francis J. Powers, then a Chicago sports columnist, Walsh recalled the details with the clarity which always amazes one in ball players.

"Bill Hinchman, their left fielder, was the first man to face me," related Ed, "and I fed him my spitter. He got a piece of the ball and hit it to Lee Tannehill, our third baseman, who made a one-handed stop and forced a runner at the plate. That made two out but left the bases still filled and brought up Lajoie himself.

"Lajoie fouled off the first two spitters I threw him, one a 'screamer' to left field and the other back into the stands. Billy Sullivan signaled for another spitter but I just stared at him. I never shook him off with a nod or anything like that. He signed for the spitter twice more but still I just looked at him. Then

Sully walked out to the box. 'What's the matter?' Bill asked me. 'I'll give him a fast one,' I said, but Billy was dubious. Finally, he agreed. I threw Larry an overhand fast ball that raised and he watched it come over without even an offer. 'Strike three!' roared Umpire Silk O'Loughlin. Lajoie sort of grinned, tossed his bat to the bench without ever a word. That was the high spot of my baseball career, fanning Larry in the clutch and without him swinging."

Walsh finished out that Thursday game, protecting Smith's lead, rested on Friday and on Saturday beat the Tigers, 6 to 1, with a four-hitter. And then pitched three and two-thirds innings relief in the final game of the year as Detroit won the pennant.

There are, incidentally, a couple of asides to that hectic 1908 season. One was that the passed ball by Schreckengost which gave Cleveland its only run in Joss's perfect game might not have been committed had Walsh the services of his regular catcher, Sullivan. The other is that years later the battery of Walsh and Sullivan again was in White Sox uniform when Big Ed's son pitched to Billy, Jr., in 1932.

Although Walsh picked up the spitter from Stricklett in the spring of 1904, he was a couple of seasons mastering it. It was not until the latter part of 1906 that he stepped with a rush into the White Sox pitching picture. He was 6–3 his freshman year and 8–3 the next, but he came roaring down the stretch in 1906 to wind up with a 17–13 record. In the six following seasons he was to win 151 games for Chicago, an average of 25 a season.

Contrary to popular belief, the 464-inning season in 1908 did not ruin Walsh's arm. He tapered off somewhat the following season, when he won only fifteen games, but he won eighteen in 1910 and 27 in each of the two seasons following. It wasn't until 1913, five years later, that his arm gave out.

In addition to the double victory he scored over the Red Sox in 1908, Walsh also is in the record books for another iron-man stunt in 1905 and for a no-hitter against Boston in 1911. Big Ed and Grover Alexander are the only pitchers with two iron-man victories to their credit, taking a back seat, of course, to the original Iron Man, Joe McGinnity, who not only pitched and won three double-headers but pitched in two more in which he split the decisions.

Walsh was in only one World Series but, although only the third Series in history and the second under the so-called Brush rules, it still stands as one of the most remarkable. Big Ed's team was not called the Hitless Wonders for nothing. The leading batter, Isbell, batted .279. Not one of the outfielders hit over .230, and Jiggs Donohue, the fine-fielding first baseman, batted .257 and Tannehill the third baseman, batted a microscopic .175. Sullivan, Walsh's battery mate, had an average of .214.

It was the late Ring W. Lardner who commented on "the prescience of Manager Jones's parents in christening him Fielder Alliston Jones." Never was a manager more aptly named, for obviously this was a club which had to win the pennant through fielding and pitching. As its foe, it drew its West Side rivals, the Cubs of Frank Chance, the Peerless Leader, who had set a record which still stands of 116 victories in winning the National League pennant.

Just before the Series opened, Davis, the Sox shortstop, was injured, but what seemed to be a bad break for the American Leaguers turned out to be the deciding factor for their victory. It forced Jones to play George Rohe at third and shift Tannehill to short. Rohe was the batting star of the Series, delivering clutch blows throughout.

Nick Altrock won the first game for the lightly regarded Sox when he defeated Mordecai Brown, 2 to 1, but Ed Reulbach evened things the next day when he tossed a one-hitter at the Sox, beating Doc White by 7 to 1.

Walsh faced Jack Pfeister in the third game and gave a masterful performance, holding the Cubs to two hits and fanning a dozen, a Series mark which lasted almost a quarter of a century until Howard Ehmke, Connie Mack's surprise starter for the A's in the opener of the 1929 Series, fanned thirteen Cubs. In the sixth, Rohe tripled against Pfeister with the bases filled and that was enough for Big Ed, who won by a 3–0 score. Chance and the other cagey Cub hitters couldn't even bunt his spitter.

In the fourth game, Brown gave the Sox only two hits in twelve innings to beat Altrock by 1 to 0 and even the Series.

Walsh came back in the fifth game to beat Reulbach but neither was as good as in his previous appearance. The Cub's Ed was chased after three innings and Walsh couldn't get past the seventh. Big Ed's control was off. He had the Cubs 8 to 4 going into the bottom of the sixth and the Nationals picked up two more runs. When Ed still was unsteady in the seventh he was lifted with one out, and White, the lean left-hander, protected his lead for him.

In the sixth game, the Sox romped home 8 to 3, as White easily had the best of Brown. The winning of the Series was a big thing

EDWARD ARTHUR WALSH

Born May 19, 1882 at Plains, Pa.
Height, 6' 1''. Weight, 196. Threw and batted right-handed.

YEAR	CLUB	LEAGUE	G	IP	W	L	PCT	SO	BB	H	ERA
1902	Wilkes-Barre	Pa. St.	4	36	1	2	.333	20	8	31	...
1902	Meriden	Conn.	21	182	15	5	.750	98	48	125	...
1903	Meriden	Conn.	23	182	11	10	.524	176	46	135	...
1903	Newark	Eas.	19	117	9	5	.643	77	28	70	...
1904	Chicago	A. L.	18	97	6	3	.667	52	34	89	...
1905	Chicago	A. L.	22	138	8	3	.727	71	35	128	...
1906	Chicago	A. L.	41	275	17	13	.567	171	58	216	...
1907	Chicago	A. L.	56	405	24	18	.571	213	87	341	...
1908	Chicago	A. L.	66	464*	40	15*	.727	269	56	343	...
1909	Chicago	A. L.	31	230	15	11	.577	127	50	166	...
1910	Chicago	A. L.	45	370	18	20	.474	258	61	242	...
1911	Chicago	A. L.	55	369	27	18	.600	255	72	327	...
1912	Chicago	A. L.	62	393	27	17	.614	254	94	332	...
1913	Chicago	A. L.	16	98	8	3	.727	34	37	91	...
1914	Chicago	A. L.	9	46	2	3	.400	14	26	34	...
1917	Boston	N. L.	4	18	0	1	.000	4	9	22	...
1919	Milwaukee	A. A.	4	21	2	2	.500	6	8	22	...
1920	Bridgeport	Eas.	3	22	1	1	.500	6	6	22	...
	Major League Totals		431	2868	195	126	.607	1728	613	2331	...

* Led league.

WORLD SERIES RECORD

YEAR	CLUB	LEAGUE	G	IP	W	L	PCT	SO	BB	H	ERA
1906	Chicago	A. L.	2	15⅓	2	0	1.000	17	6	7	3.52
	World Series Totals		2	15⅓	2	0	1.000	17	6	7	3.52

to Walsh and the other White Sox, for their shares amounted to $1,874 each as President Charles Comiskey threw in the club's share of the receipts to the winning players' pool. The Cubs received less than $500.

You had to enjoy baseball in those days, for the monetary rewards were small, even if you were a star. The largest salary Walsh ever received was $3,500 and Comiskey once matched that for him with a bonus, which gave Big Ed a total of $7,000 for his most rewarding year in baseball. You couldn't get a batting practice pitcher for that kind of money today.

Walsh has one final comment on his teammates, the Hitless Wonders, as he looks back on the past. "There was one season," says Big Ed, "1908, the year I won forty games when our whole club hit exactly three home runs in the entire year. Jones, the manager, hit one, Isbell hit another and I got the third."

CHAPTER XXIV

HITTING, UNLIMITED

Theodore Samuel Williams

KIRBY HIGBE, the uninhibited knuckle baller, was seated in the club car, doing what comes naturally—talking—surrounded by four or five baseball writers who were on their way from Boston to Chicago after leaving behind them the wreck of the 1946 All-Star game in Fenway Park. The topic of conversation was Ted Williams, since the 1946 All-Star game was one it was impossible to discuss without Williams, who had made a one-man show of it.

Higbe had had quite a time of it in the All-Star game. He had pitched an inning and one-third, during which brief period the game had degenerated from a respectable 2–0 lead held by the Americans to a complete and utter rout of the National League. A lesser man might have brooded but not ol' Hig.

"That Williams, tch!" spat Kirby. "Everybody thinks he's a great hitter. We got dozens better in our league."

When one of the audience suggested that Higbe name one, he changed the subject.

"That home run he hit against me today," continued the pitcher. "First, I thought I might catch it myself in the pitcher's box. Then I thought maybe Marty Marion might catch it at shortstop. Next I thought maybe Johnny Hopp might catch it in center. And what happened? It landed it in the bleachers. Shucks, 'twarn't nothin' but a wind-blown pop fly!"

Again one of Higbe's auditors was unkind enough to point out that the so-called "wind-blown pop fly" had landed eight rows deep in the bleachers in the farthermost reaches of Fenway's center field, a drive that carried 400 feet-plus on a rising trajectory, possibly as hard a blow as mortal man ever struck.

Williams was the first batter Higbe faced when he took over

the National League pitching in the fourth and the count was two balls and one strike when Ted unloaded. Williams was the tenth and last batter Higbe faced in the fifth, when he lashed a terrific single to left to give Kirby the rest of the afternoon off. As a consequence, Higbe's belittling of the Red Sox slugger was rather difficult to fathom.

"I still say he ain't a great hitter," stoutly maintained Hig. "I just wish he wuz in our league. I'd like to pitch against him all year."

"I imagine Williams would like it, too," said one of the writers, ending the discussion.

As befits a hitter of his stature, Williams had many days of glory but it is improbable that Ted, or anybody else, ever gave a batting exhibition such as the one he presented before 34,906 fans on July 9, 1946, in Fenway Park. He hit two home runs, getting one off Rip Sewell in the eighth which was one of the most remarkable of all time. He also drew a pass and hit two singles, having a perfect four-for-four day, scoring four runs for the American Leaguers and batting in five. His amazing performance glossed over the fact that the Nationals suffered a disgraceful 12–0 defeat.

Sewell developed what he called the "ephus" pitch, a delivery which was more spectacular than effective. It was an extraordinarily slow pitch which resembled a pitch shot in golf, since the apex of its arch toward the plate was a good 30 feet from the ground. You could have driven a load of hay under it.

There didn't seem to be much rhyme or reason to the pitch, there being some who were unkind enough to insinuate that Rip used it only to take the minds of the fans off his pitching. It was a diversion, no more, no less. He frequently got it over the plate for a called strike but rarely was anybody foolish enough to swing at it.

Williams, however, decided to have a swing at it. He timed it perfectly, ran up on it and smashed it into the right field bull pen, where it was caught on the fly by one of the reservists after it had crossed the screen barrier for a home run. It was over 390 feet, a startling distance when you consider that on a slow-motion, looping pitch such as this the batter has to supply all the power.

Let us leave Higbe and his conversation in the club car that July evening and advance some four months to an evening in October. The sixth game of the World Series has just been won by the Cardinals to pull them even with the Red Sox. Rogers Hornsby and a couple of writers are jolting through the streets of St. Louis from Sportsman's Park to press headquarters at the Hotel Jefferson.

"What ever has come over that Williams?" rasped Hornsby.

"He's not hitting," replied a writer, happy to have the correct answer, Ted's batting average of the moment being a neat, though not gaudy, .238. "That shift has got him all fouled up."

"It isn't just the shift," rasped Rog. "He just doesn't look like he's ever gonna hit. He's fiddlin' around up at the plate, jerkin' his bat one way and then the other as if he didn't know what town he was in. I never saw a good hitter look so bad in my life."

When the seventh game was played, Williams went four-for-oh, as the phrase has it, and wound up with five singles to show for 25 times at bat in the Series, an average of .200 and precisely one run batted in. It was one of the biggest flops of all time by a star player in World Series competition.

Somehow those two conversations, the one in the club car in July and the one in the cab in October, are illustrative of Williams. There was no middle ground for Ted. He was either a hero or a goat. Indisputably, the figures show Williams to be one of the greatest hitters of his time. Nobody can be part-hero and part-goat and maintain such an average, but with Ted the goat roles are remembered long after the hero roles are forgotten, maybe because there are so many of the latter.

Lou Boudreau, the quondam boy manager of Cleveland, probably did as much to cause Williams mental anguish and heartache as all the hooting of the fans and the barbs of the sports writers put together. With Lou, however, it was not deliberate, but a matter of self-preservation. For it was Boudreau who decided that supermethods would have to be taken to check a superhitter. And even Lou didn't realize the full effect his over-shifted defense was going to have upon Williams.

It was in July of 1946, only five days after the All-Star game in which Williams clouted his two home runs. Ted was still riding on the momentum of those homers and in the first game of a Sunday double-header, he whacked three against an assortment of Cleveland pitchers. In the clubhouse between games, Boudreau devised the shift which was to cause Williams so much trouble.

Boudreau lined up the Indians on the right side of the diamond and dared Williams to pull the ball. The right fielder played on the foul line and so did the first baseman, who played deep. The second baseman was back on the grass and closer to first base than he was to second. The shortstop (Boudreau) was on the right side of second base, near the normal second baseman's position. The third baseman played directly behind second base. The center fielder moved over to the right fielder's regular position, while the left fielder moved in to a position just behind shortstop.

This unorthodox alignment left only the pitcher or catcher to field bunts and nobody at all to field anything hit to left field, save the left fielder who was playing in a deep shortstop position. Ted, of course, didn't try to bunt nor did he try to hit to left. He accepted Boudreau's challenge and that very afternoon whacked out two hits. In view of what has happened since, it might have been better if he had been horse-collared the first time he faced the shift.

Fenway Park has an unusual construction, with a short left field fence and a deep stretch in right. Boudreau first said that the purpose of the shift was to limit Williams to singles, but since has confessed in his biography that he regarded the efficacy of the shift as a psychological, rather than a tactical, victory. Ted, of course, could have defeated the purpose of the shift at any time by bunting or placing his hits to left. And since has, forcing teams who over-shift against him to employ a much more modified version of the original Boudreau shift.

Eddie Dyer, who managed the Cardinals against Joe Cronin's Red Sox in the 1946 World Series, guessed that Williams would accept the challenge again, particularly since it was a World Series and the eyes of all baseball were upon him. Eddie guessed correctly. The Dyer shift was an offspring of the one devised by Boudreau, with the difference that the shortstop, Marty Marion, remained on the left side of second base, but close to the bag and Whitey Kurowski, the third baseman, played on the right side of second. The outfield swung around, but Eddie didn't bring his left fielder in as close as Boudreau had.

Williams succeeded in pulling a ball through this defense in the opener but was blanked in the second game. When the Series moved to Boston, Williams dropped a bunt down the third base-line and, thereafter, Dyer played Kurowski in the corner but some 20 feet off the base to protect against bunts. Ted never tried another bunt in the Series.

Considering all the trouble, mental and physical, which the Boudreau shift piled up for Williams in that year of 1946, there is an ironic twist to it. The Red Sox, who won 40 of their first 50 games that year and tow-roped the American League field, had difficulty in clinching the pennant, the first Red Sox flag in twenty-eight years. They finally made the grade in Cleveland on Sept. 13 on a home run by Williams, hit into left field over the head of Pat Seerey, the Cleveland left fielder, who was playing in close in accordance with his position in the Boudreau shift!

The shift, of course, was a compliment to the great batting ability of Williams. Ted's stubborn refusal to accommodate himself to its vagaries and take advantage of the wide, open spaces in left is a revealing insight into the young man's personality. He took the challenge when he could have circumvented it by judicious application of his unrivaled batting skills. Nobody was going to show him up, by golly. Nobody did, save Ted himself.

John Chamberlain, writing in *Life* about Williams, declared that Ted was almost "monomaniacal" in his efforts to make himself baseball's most perfect hitter. That, John, is putting it mildly. Williams lived to hit. No other hitter—Ty Cobb, Rogers Hornsby, George Sisler—ever studied the art as much as Ted, asked so many questions of so many people or practiced as assiduously as Williams.

Because of Williams' well-known and oft-demonstrated eagerness to hit, many pitchers formed the hasty opinion that so impulsive a batter might be lured into hitting at bad pitches as Babe Ruth was. Nothing was farther from the case. Williams would not offer at a ball if it was a fraction of an inch out of the strike zone. Umpires had such respect for Ted's keen eye that he rarely was called out on strikes. As a result of pitchers trying to entice him into biting at bad pitches, pitching carefully to him because of the damage he could do and of giving him intentional passes, Williams drew more walks than any living player. He always got more than 100 bases on balls in a season and usually led the American League in that statistic.

Loose is the word for Williams at the plate. He looked like a marionette with the puppeteer's strings relaxed. Tall and gangly, he dipped his knees slightly, took a few nervous swishes with the bat, wrapped his fingers around the handle as though he were going to wring sawdust from it and then became immobile as the pitcher prepared to deliver. Ted stood fairly deep in the box, right foot somewhat closer to the plate than his left, which was about 15 inches behind the right. He used to bat with his feet somewhat closer together and take a longer stride but later he widened his stance somewhat and shortened his stride.

When Williams swung, it was a marvelously rhythmic and coordinated swing, with his strong wrists snapping into the swing at the moment of impact. Admitting that Ted had the fine sense of timing and the whiplash swing so vital to a good hitter, the two characteristics which made him a super-hitter were his exceptional eyesight and his great wrist action.

Considering how many raps Williams took for his fielding it was ironical that it was a rap sustained *because* of his fielding that should give him the first major injury of his career. It happened in the 1950 All-Star game in Chicago's Comiskey Park when Ted gamely crashed into the left field scoreboard after catching a drive hit by Ralph Kiner, the Pirates' home run king.

Williams continued to play for a couple of innings after the collision but the pain became too severe and Casey Stengel, managing the All-Stars for the first time, relieved him. It was only after the game that it was discovered that he had sustained a fracture in his left forearm.

The slugger was out for several weeks, but strangely enough the Red Sox made quite a run at the Yankees without him. By now Steve O'Neill had succeeded Joe McCarthy as the Bosox manager and he was criticized when he returned Williams to the lineup and the Red Sox tailed off.

"Good Lord," said Steve in quiet exasperation at his second

guessers, "they didn't expect me to win the pennant *without* the best hitter in baseball, did they?"

Although he played in only 89 games that year, a couple of them as a pinch-hitter, Williams managed to hit 28 home runs and knock in 97 runs. His average was only .317 and in 1951 Ted had what was for him an ordinary year. He played almost the entire season but he knocked in only 29 more runs than he had the year before and hit only two more homers.

It was in 1952 that Williams made his peace with the fans of Fenway—or vice versa. In April of that year he was summoned to appear before a Marine Corps agency in Jacksonville, Florida, to take his physical. Like Jerry Coleman of the Yankees, Ted had maintained a reserve commission after World War II, and the Marines, who were left desperately short of fliers after the emergence of the Army Air Forces as a separate fighting group, commenced the recalling of former pilots.

Williams passed and was given the customary 30 days to "get his affairs in order" as the phrase so baldly puts it. He played only a half-dozen games, hitting one home run to raise his lifetime total to 324, but the Red Sox fans gave him a day before he reported back to service and showered him with gifts. And Ted responded by tipping his cap!

Williams himself had little hope of returning to baseball. He figured when the Marines released him he would be past 35 and that his reflexes, rusted by inactivity, would be of no use for baseball. He left behind him a lifetime batting average of .346 and the record of never having hit under .300 while wearing the uniform of the Red Sox.

The greatest of all Williams batting accomplishments, of course, is the .406 average he achieved in 1941. Bill Terry, who hit .401 in 1930, was the last major leaguer to hit .400 before Ted and nobody has hit that high since. Only eight men have broken .400 since the turn of the century, only two in the last quarter-century. It takes, as you will note, a bit of doing.

Williams was hitting over .400 when the schedule had a week to go and Manager Cronin told Ted he could take the rest of the season off and protect his average if he wished. Ted refused on the grounds that if he was to be a .400 hitter, he'd be a legitimate one. The Yanks already had clinched the pennant and the remaining games were meaningless but Williams, to his everlasting credit, insisted on playing out the string.

On the final day of the season, with a Sunday double-header coming up in Philadelphia, it looked as though Williams had made a poor guess. His average had dipped to .399 and he would need at least four hits in the double-header to put him over the top. Ted did a little better than that—he belted four out of five in the opener, two out of three in the nightcap to wind up with a resplendent .406, highest American League average since George Sisler batted .420 in 1922. One of his hits was a home run and another would have been had it not hit the horn atop the scoreboard at Shibe Park and rebounded back to the playing field for a two-bagger.

Williams' batting average, particularly his home run production, was remarkable when you consider that he played 77 games each season in Fenway Park, the layout of which was diametrically and geometrically inimical to his hitting talent. Ted pulled to right field, the longest stretch in the Fenway, where the average home run to right field must travel 382 feet. Left field, which Ted avoided as though it were a leper colony, is a cozy 315 feet.

Williams led the American League four times in batting and in 1949 he lost out by a fraction of a percentage point to George Kell of Detroit. Because of the number of bases on balls he received, Ted invariably led the league in runs scored.

It is doubtful if Williams ever found a park more suited to his hitting talents than Nicollet Park in Minneapolis, where the Red Sox sent him in 1938. It was here for the first time that the long drink of water began to display the attributes which were to make him the scourge of rival pitchers. And traits which often drove his own manager to the aspirin bottle.

Billy Evans, general manager of the Red Sox, and Vice-president Eddie Collins had plucked Williams from San Diego before he was ripe. And with good reason. Ted went right from Herbert Hoover High School in his native San Diego to the local club in the Pacific Coast League in midsummer of 1936. He finished out the season without doing anything spectacular, or even anything temperamental. The Red Sox had a working agreement with the Padres and the fine, level swing of the kid rookie was dutifully reported back to the home office. Williams didn't hit .300 in that first half-season with San Diego, nor did he hit it in his next year, either, but he already was showing signs of greatness. Before he took on too much glamor, the Red Sox closed the deal for him, getting him for something like $25,000 and five minor league players. And they got him just before some really big offers were in the making.

Williams aroused some little interest at Sarasota, mainly because he refused to wear a necktie and again because he missed a bus which was to take him for an exhibition game. Cronin decided that a year at Minneapolis would do Williams no harm and himself a lot of good.

Minneapolis then was owned by Mike Kelley, the last of the truly great "independent" owners, who stood off the chain-store system as long as he could. The manager of the Millers was Donie Bush, a mild-mannered little fellow who had played with Detroit's ferocious Tigers back in the century's first decade, a major and minor league manager of note with the reputation of being able to handle men.

That Donie could handle men there was no doubt. Apparently his special skills didn't extend to boys. Ted found American Association pitching inviting and the short fences of Nicollet Park even more so. He promptly proceeded to tear the league apart, eventually leading it in batting, in home runs, in runs batted in, in total bases, in runs scored and in bases on balls.

One morning Bush walked into President Kelley's office, where Mike sat, guarded by his faithful and fierce Dalmatian, Jitterbug.

"Mike," said Donie, skillfully avoiding an attempted nip by Jitterbug, "either that kid takes off his uniform or I do."

"I've known you a long time now, Donie, haven't I?" began Kelley placatingly.

"Better than thirty years," moodily agreed Bush.

"How many years has it been," asked Mike, "since you saw a kid who could hit like that one? You certainly don't think that after all the years I've known you I'd ask you to turn in your uniform, do you? And, after all the years we've both known each other, you don't think I'm crazy enough to ask a hitter like that to take off his uniform, do you?"

Bush wasn't the first manager who felt that even Ted's great batting didn't compensate for other things, nor was he the last. Cronin on at least three occasions took Williams out of a ball game for loafing. Or, to put it more aptly, sulking.

When Joe McCarthy succeeded Cronin as manager of the Red Sox, the Hot Stove simmered and bubbled all winter with speculation as to how McCarthy, a strict disciplinarian, would handle Williams. Joe, for instance, had an aversion to sports shirts. He wanted his players to look and act like champions, in the dining room as well as on the ball field.

One fact nobody bothered to take into consideration was that McCarthy was a great handler of men only because he was a great handler of individuals. He solved the tieless problem, for instance, by wearing a sports shirt himself the first few days around the Sarasota training camp. The issue of neckties never came up because McCarthy buried it beforehand.

As to how McCarthy "handled" Williams, there is only this to report. Ted had two of the greatest seasons of his life under Joe and the Red Sox narrowly missed two straight pennants in the first two years of their association, losing one in a playoff and the other in the final game of the season.

Probably Williams irritated as many baseball fans as irritated him, which is saying a great deal. Ted, even when he made a great play in the outfield, gave the impression that he was only half-trying. His nonchalance at the plate, so amazing when he hit safely, became annoying when he popped up.

Actually, the gangling appearance of Williams, the long, loping stride created the impression of nonchalance. That, added to the fact that there were occasions when he indubitably didn't feel like trying, made him fair game for the customers. When Ted first came up, he couldn't stand the riding of the bleacherites, particularly the patrons in Fenway Park's left field stand. No ball player, save a Cobb or a McGraw, enjoys having the fans "on" him but most of them get used to it. Ted never tried to get used to it.

A couple of Williams' mannerisms which irritated the fans were his refusal to tip his hat after hitting a home run. Another was the fact that when he was on base and Vernon (Junior) Stephens followed him with a home run, Ted never waited at home plate to shake Junior's hand. The rumor was printed that Ted was jealous of the newcomer to the Red Sox.

There is much evidence at hand to indicate that Williams was not the self-centered athlete he so often was depicted as being. During the great batting streak of Joe DiMaggio in 1941, when Joe hit in 56 straight games, Ted, from his left field position in front of the scoreboard at Fenway Park, always had Bill Daley, the operator, let him know the progress of Joe's streak and he then shouted the information across to Dom DiMaggio in center. Hardly jealous that, considering that the rivalry between Williams and the older DiMaggio has practically split Boston and New York into armed camps.

Williams was close with Johnny Orlando, manager of the Red Sox clubhouse and considered the rotund Johnny one of his best friends. After the 1946 season, Ted gave Johnny a check which was bigger than the losers' share of the World Series that fall. Certainly Johnny hardy would classify his favorite slugger as inconsiderate or self-centered.

It is unfortunate for Ted that his kindly acts, his thoughtful deeds never received the publicity accorded his sulks. He never tried to grasp the fact that the public always is searching for traces of clay in its idols. His run-in with the Boston newspapermen when his baby was born is typical of the poor press Williams received for incidents which weren't the public's business. Or which he thought weren't the public's business.

One of Williams' truly big days among his fellow American Leaguers was his performance in the All-Star game in Boston in 1946, related at the outset of this chapter. It is possible he enjoyed an even greater one in Detroit five years earlier when his ninth-inning home run smash against the roof of Briggs Stadium broke up the game.

The Americans went into the ninth trailing, 5–3. With one out and the bases filled, Claude Passeau was in a tough spot but he pitched craftily to Joe DiMaggio and the Yankee Clipper hit a perfect double play ball to Eddie Miller at short. It should have ended the game but Billy Herman, taking the relay at second, pivoted and threw wide to first base. One run scored.

Herman, one of the best pivot men in the game, claimed he

THEODORE SAMUEL (TED) WILLIAMS

Born Oct. 30, 1918, San Diego, Calif.
Height 6' 3''. Weight 190. Bats left, throws right.

YEAR	CLUB	LEAGUE	POS	G	AB	R	H	2B	3B	HR	RBI	BA
1936	San Diego	P.C.	OF	42	107	18	29	8	2	0	11	.271
1937	San Diego	P.C.	OF	138	454	66	132	24	2	23	98	.291
1938	Minneapolis	A.A.	OF	148	528	130	193	30	9	43	142	.366
1939	Boston	Amer.	OF	149	565	131	185	44	11	31	145	.327
1940	Boston	Amer.	OF	144	561	*134	193	43	14	23	113	.344
1941	Boston	Amer.	OF	143	456	*135	185	33	3	*37	120	*.406
1942	Boston	Amer.	OF	150	522	x141	186	34	5	*36	*137	*.356
1943–44–45	Boston	Amer.					(In military service)					
1946	Boston	Amer.	OF	150	514	*142	176	37	8	38	123	.342
1947	Boston	Amer.	OF	156	528	*125	181	40	9	*32	*114	*.343
1948	Boston	Amer.	OF	137	509	124	188	*44	3	25	127	*.369
1949	Boston	Amer.	OF	155	566	*150	194	*39	3	*43	x159	.342
1950	Boston	Amer.	OF	89	334	82	106	24	1	28	97	.317
1951	Boston	Amer.	OF	148	531	109	169	28	4	30	126	.318
1952	Boston (a)	Amer.	OF	6	10	2	4	0	1	1	3	.400
	Major League Totals			1427	5096	1275	1767	366	62	324	1264	.346

WORLD SERIES RECORD

YEAR	CLUB	LEAGUE	POS	G	AB	R	H	2B	3B	HR	RBI	BA
1946	Boston	Amer.	OF	7	25	2	5	0	0	0	1	.200

ALL-STAR GAME RECORD

YEAR	LEAGUE	POS	AB	R	H	2B	3B	HR	RBI	BA
1940	American	OF	2	0	0	0	0	0	0	.000
1941	American	OF	4	1	2	1	0	1	4	.500
1942	American	OF	4	0	1	0	0	0	0	.250
1946	American	OF	4	4	4	0	0	2	5	1.000
1947	American	OF	4	0	2	1	0	0	0	.500
1948	American	PH	0	0	0	0	0	0	0	.000
1949	American	OF	2	1	0	0	0	0	0	.000
1950	American	OF	4	0	1	0	0	0	1	.250
1951	American	OF	3	0	1	0	1	0	0	.333
	All-Star Totals		27	6	10	2	1	3	10	.370

* Led League
x Tied for lead
(a) Rejoined U. S. Marines, May 1, 1952

was confused by the collection of uniforms at first base, understandable enough since each player wears the uniform of his own team. Whatever the reason, the failure to make the double play was costly, since it brought Williams to bat.

Passeau had one strike and two balls on Ted when the kid's bat lashed out. The ball crashed against the façade atop the third tier of the stadium, fair by a comfortable margin. Joe Gordon and DiMaggio scored ahead of Williams, waited for him at home plate and smothered him with hugs. And so did as many of the other American League as could reach him. For one day at least, the lonesome Williams was one of the boys.

CHAPTER XXV

THE OLD MASTER

Denton True Young

BACK IN 1938, Bill Terry, manager of the Giants, signed a two-year contract to train his club on the grounds of Louisiana State University in Baton Rouge. Not quite certain as to how the weather would be—it turned out to be ideal—Terry took his pitchers and catchers to Hot Springs, Arkansas, for a two-week "boiling-out" period at the baths there, coupled with mild workouts at the local ball park.

A husky gentleman, somewhat portly, who seemed to be in his late fifty's but actually was past seventy, turned up at the field one day. It was Denton True Young, the fabulous Cy Young who had pitched from baseball's neolithic age right into modern baseball.

The writers clustered around Young, for anything he had to say would be obviously more interesting than a report on the Giant batterymen taking part in an informal ball game. In addition to the New York scribes, there also was a young boy from the local paper, a teen-ager who seemed somewhat puzzled by the questions which were being put to the elderly gentleman. Finally the kid ventured a question on his own.

"Mr. Young," asked the cub, "did you ever pitch in the major leagues?"

"Son," replied Cy, not at all unkindly, "I *won* more big league games than you'll ever see!"

It wasn't nearly as rash a statement as it appears on the surface. Cy Young won 511 games in the major leagues. The average fan sees no more than a dozen games a season. Even a fan who attends as often as twenty times a season would have to keep up that mark for better than a quarter of a century to *see* as many major league games as Young *won!*

287

The total of Young's victories, which were distributed between the American and National Leagues—291 in the National, 220 in the American—is so fabulous that it is difficult to grasp its greatness. In all baseball history, going back to the horse-and-buggy days, only 55 pitchers have won better than 200 games. Young won better than 200 in each of the major leagues!

There are several phases of Young's career almost as fabulous as his total of 511 victories, such as his winning more than 200 games in each of the major leagues. And he was in his mid-thirties when he came into the infant American League. He played for all sorts of managers, such as the violent Patsy Tebeau of the Cleveland Spiders, kindly managers, bench-managers, playing-managers, a manager who committed suicide in spring training camp, a manager who came from a college athletic director's desk and lasted exactly thirteen days! Cy won for all of 'em.

Young actually began his pitching career when the distance from the pitching slab to home plate was fifty feet, instead of the current distance of 60 feet, six inches, which was adopted in 1893. In two full seasons of pitching at fifty feet, Cy won a total of 63 games, and in the two full seasons immediately following the increased distance, he won a total of 57 games, so the altered pitching distance meant little to him.

When Young broke into professional baseball in 1890 with Canton, Ohio, in the old Tri-State League, the game wasn't covered as completely in the newspapers as it was to be later. The result is that Cy's beginnings are hazy with shadows, there are conflicting stories about his start. At no time, however, were there any doubts about his pitching skill. The big fellow had it from the first time he ever threw a baseball. In fact, just before Cleveland called him up from the Tri-State League, the only minor league ball Cy ever pitched, by the way, he pitched a no-hit no-run game against McKeesport, Pennsylvania, in which he fanned eighteen batters. That game is on record as being played July 25, 1890. Twelve days later Young was pitching in the major leagues. And he was to stick around for 22 years!

George Moreland, one of baseball's early historians and the manager of the Canton Club, is as much Young's discoverer as anybody, although with the talents Cy had he eventually would have been discovered if he had been in the deepest recesses of Mammoth Cave, instead of pitching for the Tuscarawas County team some eighty miles south of Cleveland. It was Moreland, incidentally, who almost landed Walter Johnson for Pittsburgh some years later. Had George been the discoverer of both Young and Johnson it would have been the greatest one-two in history, for this pair won nearly 1,000 games between them!

Young already had been scouted and passed by as a third baseman in 1889, but Moreland visited the Young farm in the spring of the following year and talked business with the boy's father, McKenzie Young. He offered $40 a month for young Dent, who was then 22 years old. His dad at first demurred on the grounds that his son was needed to help on the farm, but Dent finally persuaded him that he had a future in baseball.

At the start, Young had nothing but blinding speed. He had difficulty controlling the ball and difficulty getting catchers who could hold him. Cap Anson personally scouted him at Canton and decided that he wouldn't do, a decision Anson was to regret before the year was out. Gradually control came to Young and Davis Hawley of Cleveland weighed in with an offer of $250 after the pitcher had won five straight and pitched a no-hitter. The bid was accepted and Young was through with the minor leagues forever.

Legend and fact grow confused on Young's reporting to Cleveland. One report has him showing up dressed like a Dutch comic of the Weber & Fields era, another that he had worked out several days around the ball park because the Spiders, as Cleveland was then known, were on a road trip.

There are no disputes about Young's first start. It was in Cleveland against Anson's Chicago Colts and the farmer boy pitched a three-hitter, winning 3 to 1. Among Young's strikeout victims was Anson himself. It was the first of his 511 victories and he was getting $75 a month from Cleveland at the time!

Young was known as Dent Young at this time, but the nickname Cy was soon tagged on him and he rarely was called anything else after that. Some insist that Cy was short for "Cyclone" and that he gained the appellation because of his great speed, but the most commonly accepted version is that he was called Cy because that was the popular name for the stage rube of that period. And Young never was, nor ever pretended to be, anything but a farmer boy.

On February 2, 1951, Young was among the several members of the Hall of Fame invited to New York by Ford C. Frick, president of the National League, when that circuit celebrated its 75th birthday at the Broadway Central Hotel, the hostelry in which it had been founded. Now 84, Young was but a shadow of the pitching giant he had been, but even though the flesh had fallen away from his frame it was easy to see that he had been a big man.

After the ceremonies Young had difficulty in gripping a baseball to autograph for a grandson of Ed Barrow, the former Yankee boss. Barrow, only a year younger than Cy, recalled that in the pitcher's heyday he could grip a ball in his hand and defy any player to pry his fingers loose from it.

Young pitched at 210 pounds and stood six feet, two inches. He was broad-shouldered, thick-chested and stout-legged. Possibly he was the most durable pitcher who ever lived, as the records attest. He not only won more games than any other pitcher, he also lost more and pitched more!

One of the most remarkable facts about Young was that Cy was still a strong pitcher in his mid-forties. Young was 36 when he pitched in his first World Series, for the Red Sox against the Pirates. In this, the first World Series ever played between representatives of the American and National League, Young won two games, lost one and relieved in another. His two victories against Pittsburgh were scored with only two days between starts.

Earlier, back in the Temple Cup days, Young defeated the legendary Baltimore Orioles three times for Cleveland in 1895, but in the following year the Orioles knocked him off in the opener by a 7–1 score and then belted Cleveland there straight to take the Cup without ever getting another shot at Cy.

Rube Waddell pitched a one-hitter against Boston on May 1, 1904, defeating Jesse Tannehill by a score of 3 to 0. Rube was a left-hander with plenty of what later came to be known as color, and he crowed mightily about his pitching masterpiece, even challenging Young to face him.

Cy faced Rube four days later in the last game of the series and he showed what he could do when he bore down. He retired every batter who faced him, sending down 27 Athletics in a row for the second no-hitter of his career and one of the few perfect games in history.

When Young joined the Boston club of the newly formed American League, the team wasn't yet known as the Red Sox. They were called the Pilgrims or the Puritans, but it must be admitted that Young was neither a pilgrim nor a puritan.

Cy was no roisterer but Ed Barrow recalls that it was Young's custom to belt over a couple of fast ones in the privacy of the clubhouse before stepping out on the pitcher's mound to take charge. He was a pleasant, natural companion, fond of hunting and fond of conversation and not averse to standing up to the bar with his pals.

In 1905, when Young had passed his 38th birthday, he tangled with his old pal, Rube Waddell. Facing the Athletics in the afternoon game of a holiday bill on July 4, Young battled with the left-hander for twenty innings before losing 4 to 2, after an error had opened the gates. And in the twenty innings, Cy didn't walk a batter!

Young won 22 games when he was forty years old for the seventh-place Red Sox, more than one third of his club's total victories. He made 37 starts that year and pitched 35 complete games! By this time, the once-husky Young could be described only as portly. He had a bay window which made fielding his position difficult, particularly when the opposition bunted, but he was still a winner with a tail-end club.

Young's career was dotted with unusual incidents. Certainly he is the only major leaguer who ever was offered a manager's job because the incumbent had just committed suicide. Chick Stahl, who was appointed manager of the Red Sox for the 1907 season —the year the club officially adopted that nickname, incidentally—drank carbolic acid on March 28 when the team stopped off at West Baden Springs, Indiana.

John I. Taylor, owner of the Red Sox, wired Young to take charge as manager but Cy couldn't see it. He agreed to handle the club until Taylor selected a manager but made it clear that he didn't regard the position as permanent. Indeed, Young's temporary elevation to the pilot's seat resulted in Cy making one of his few public statements, and a rather remarkable one, all things considered.

"Judging by the way I have been going this spring," declared Cy, "I believe I will have one of my best seasons this year and I would not have anything worry me. I also believe I do not have the ability to manage the team. I feel highly honored by Mr. Taylor's offer, but I know that I could not do justice to both positions."

Some believed that Young wanted the manager's job for his battery mate, Lou Criger, a man, incidentally, who should be mentioned more frequently because of the help he was to Cy through the years. The truth was, however, that Young had no candidate. He just didn't want to manage. And he wasn't kidding about having a better year, either. In 1906, Young fell below .500, winning thirteen and losing 21, but in 1907 he bounced back to win 22 while losing fifteen.

Fred Lieb, the baseball author who is gifted with one of the most retentive memories in the game, recalls seeing one of Young's pitching efforts in 1903. As a kid in the two-bit bleachers at old Columbia Park in his native Philadelphia, Fred saw Cy lose a thirteen-inning heartbreaker to Eddie Plank and the A's by a 1-0 score.

In one of the late innings, Danny Murphy opened fire for the Athletics with a triple and Young fanned the next three hitters, Monte Cross, Mike Powers and Plank, on nine pitched balls. There were no called strikes, no foul strikes. All three batters took their three swings and hit exactly nothing. "In the some five thousand big league games I attended as a baseball writer," wrote Mr. Lieb, "I never again saw a pitcher retire the side in exactly that manner."

A run-of-the-mine pitcher can, on a good day, come up with a no-hitter. When a hurler turns in a couple of no-hitters, you know he has something special, like Bob Feller, Johnny Vander Meer, Christy Mathewson or Addie Joss. When a pitcher comes up with a no-hitter three times, then you have the genuine bottled-in-bond article. Cy Young was the only modern pitcher with three no-hitters to his credit, until Feller scored his third in 1951.

Larry Corcoran, pitching in the long-forgotten days of the 'eighties, had three no-hitters to his credit, but baseball wasn't quite the same game then. Young pitched his no-hitters in 1897, 1904 and 1908, the last when he was 41 years old!

Young's last victims were the Yankees in New York and he won rather easily, 8 to 0. Almost as remarkable as his achievement was the fact that in recognition of his great pitching through the years, he received an award from the players of the American League. Throughout the circuit, players made donations to purchase a loving cup for Cy. It was inscribed: "From the ball players of the American League to show their appreciation of Cy Young, as a man and as a ball player. August 13, 1908."

There is no other such award in baseball. A player's teammates often have chipped in to give him a present and leagues have made awards to players but the gift to Young was the only one in which players of the entire league chipped in to give a spontaneous gift to another player. The cup was donated to the baseball museum at Cooperstown by Young.

Another of the unusual incidents marking Young's career is that he was pitching at the time of the first unassisted triple play in the history of baseball. There have been only a half-dozen in regular season play and one (by Bill Wambsganss) in World Series play. Young, sold back to Cleveland by the Red Sox, was pitching against Boston in the first game of a double-header at League Park, Cleveland, July 19, 1909, when the first unassisted triple play was executed by Neal Ball, the Cleveland shortstop.

The first two Sox to face Young on this particular afternoon, Heinie Wagner and Jake Stahl, beat out infield hits. Ambie McConnell, the next hitter, worked the count to three-and-two, which meant the runners were moving when Young pitched. McConnell lined the ball through the box and Ball, moving to his left from his shortstop position, grabbed the ball a few feet from second. He stepped on the bag to double up Wagner and then stepped off the bag and toward first to put the ball on Stahl for the third out.

Young went on to win the game from his former teammates by a score of 6 to 1, and it was one of nineteen he was to win for the sixth-place Cleveland team that season, victories which would have been appreciated by Boston, which was a contender and wound up third.

Nineteen victories by a man who had passed his 42nd birthday was excellent work but it was the last time old Cy's victories went into double figures. The man who fifteen times won twenty or more games in a season and five times won over thirty was at the end of the road. He won only seven games for Cleveland in 1910 and midway through the next season went to the Boston Braves, where he finished his career with a record of four wins and five losses.

When Young quit before the 1912 season opened he was a fairly prosperous man. Born in Gilmore, Ohio, Cy went back to his farm after 22 years in the major leagues, happy and with no regrets. Until he reached eighty, he remained a fine figure of a man, with evident traces of his athletic background.

During the 1940 World Series, Young visited Cincinnati to take in a couple of the games. Grantland Rice, the veteran sports authority, had quite a chat with Cy, in the course of which the great pitcher revealed that Wee Willie Keeler, the hit-'em-where-they-ain't kid, had given him more trouble than Ty Cobb or any of the other hitters he faced.

Rice asked Young how he would pitch to the batters of today, including Joe DiMaggio.

"I couldn't tell you unless I stood out there on the mound and saw him standing up there at the plate," replied Cy simply. And you could tell that Young saw himself in his mind's eye on the mound and facing DiMaggio.

Rice brought Young into press headquarters to a table where a group of writers were chewing the fat about this and that.

"Gentlemen," said Rice impressively, "I want you to meet the greatest pitcher that ever lived—Cy Young. He won five hundred and eleven ball games!"

"Five hundred and twelve, Granny," insisted Cy. "I won one that they never gave me credit for!"

DENTON TRUE YOUNG

Born March 28, 1867 at Gilmore, Ohio.
Height, 6' 2". Weight, 210. Threw and batted right-handed.
Elected to Hall of Fame in 1937.

YEAR	CLUB	LEAGUE	G	W	L	PCT	SO	BB
1890	Canton	Tri-State	27	14	13	.519	178	...
1890	Cleveland	Nat.	17	9	7	.563	36	32
1891	Cleveland	Nat.	54	27	20	.574	146	132
1892	Cleveland	Nat.	53	36	11	.766	167	114
1893	Cleveland	Nat.	53	32	16	.667	102	104
1894	Cleveland	Nat.	52	25	22	.532	101	101
1895	Cleveland	Nat.	47	35	10	.778	120	77
1896	Cleveland	Nat.	51	29	16	.644	137	64
1897	Cleveland	Nat.	47	21	18	.538	87	50
1898	Cleveland *	Nat.	46	25	14	.641	107	40
1899	St. Louis	Nat.	44	26	15	.634	112	43
1900	St. Louis	Nat.	41	19	18	.514	119	38
1901	Boston	Amer.	43	33	10	.767	159	38
1902	Boston	Amer.	45	32	10	.762	166	51
1903	Boston	Amer.	40	28	10	.737	183	37
1904	Boston	Amer.	43	26	16	.619	203	28
1905	Boston	Amer.	38	18	19	.487	208	30
1906	Boston	Amer.	39	13	21	.382	146	27
1907	Boston	Amer.	43	22	15	.595	148	52
1908	Boston †	Amer.	36	21	11	.656	150	37
1909	Cleveland	Amer.	35	19	15	.559	109	59
1910	Cleveland	Amer.	21	7	10	.412	58	27
1911	Cleveland ‡	Amer.	7	3	4	.429	20	13
1911	Boston	Nat.	11	4	5	.444	35	15
	Major League Totals		906	510	313	.620	2819	1209

TEMPLE CUP RECORD

YEAR	CLUB	LEAGUE	G	IP	W	L	AVE	BB	SO	H
1895	Cleveland	Nat.	3	27	3	0	1.000	4	2	27
1896	Cleveland	Nat.	1	9	0	1	.000	1	0	13
	Temple Cup Totals		4	36	3	1	.750	5	2	40

WORLD SERIES RECORD

YEAR	CLUB	LEAGUE	G	IP	W	L	AVE	BB	SO	H
1903	Boston	Amer.	4	33	2	1	.667	4	17	31

* Transferred with pick of team to St. Louis by Frank DeHaas Robison, owner of both clubs, 1898.

† Sold to Cleveland for $12,500, 1908.

‡ Released, August, 1911, and signed with Boston N. L.